The Reminiscences of

REAR ADMIRAL CHARLES J. WHEELER

U. S. Navy, Retired

U. S. Naval Institute
Annapolis, Maryland
1970

Preface

This manuscript is the result of a series of tape-recorded interviews with Rear Admiral Charles J. Wheeler, USN (Ret.) at his home in Menlo Park, California during the year 1969. These interviews were conducted by Commander Etta-Belle Kitchen, USN (Ret.) for the Oral History Office in the U. S. Naval Institute.

Only minor emendations and corrections have been made by Admiral Wheeler. Therefore the reader is asked to bear in mind that he is reading a transcript of the spoken word rather than the written one.

Copies of several articles written by Admiral Wheeler are appended to the manuscript.

DECLARATION OF TRUST

The undersigned does hereby appoint and designate as his (her) Trustee herein, the Secretary-Treasurer and Publisher of the United States Naval Institute to perform and discharge the following duties, powers, and privileges in connection with the possession and use of a certain taped interview between the undersigned and the Oral History Department of the United States Naval Institute.

1. Classification of Transcript.

    ( )a. If classified OPEN, the transcript(s) may be read or the recording(s) audited by the qualified personnel upon presentation of proper credentials, as determined by the Secretary-Treasurer of the U. S. Naval Institute.

    (✓)b. If classified PERMISSION REQUIRED TO CITE OR QUOTE, the user will be required to obtain permission in writing from the interviewee prior to quoting or citing from either the transcript(s) or the recording(s).

    ( )c. If classified PERMISSION REQUIRED, permission must be obtained in writing from the interviewee before the transcribed interview(s) can be examined or the tape recording(s) audited.

    ( )d. If classified CLOSED, the transcribed interview(s) and the tape recording(s) will be sealed until a time specified by the interviewee. This may be until the death of the interviewee or for any specified number of years.

2. It is expressly understood that in giving this authorization, I am in no way precluded from placing such restrictions as I may desire upon use of the interview at any time during my lifetime, nor does this authorization in any way affect my rights to the copyright of my literary expressions that may be contained in the interview.

Witness my hand and seal this 10th day of July 1970

C. Julian Wheeler
Rear Adm. USN (Ret.)

I hereby accept and consent to the foregoing Declaration of Trust and the powers therein conferred upon me as Trustee:

R. E. Bowler Jr.

REAR ADMIRAL CHARLES JULIAN WHEELER
UNITED STATES NAVY, RETIRED.

Rear Admiral Wheeler was born in Mobile, Alabama on July 27, 1895, a son of Mr. Charles James Wheeler and Mrs. Julia Malone Wheeler. He attended the University Military School in Mobile prior to his appointment to the U.S. Naval Academy from the first Congressional District of Alabama in July, 1912. Graduated and commissioned Ensign in June, 1916, he progressed in grade until promoted to rank of Captain, effective January 1, 1942. He was transferred to the Retired List of the Navy on April 1, 1948 and advanced in rank to Rear Admiral.

His first assignment after graduation was in the USS BENHAM, employed during the World War in escort duty from bases on Queenstown Ireland, later on Brest, France. In June, 1919 he joined the USS SOUTH DAKOTA, renamed the HURON, and cruised in her to the Far East, where she became flagship of the Commander in Chief, Asiatic Fleet. Detached from the HURON in October, 1920, he reported to the USS PAL operating on the Yangtze Patrol as a unit of the Asiatic Fleet.

In November, 1921 Rear Admiral Wheeler reported for duty as Flag Lieutenant to the Commander U.S. Naval Detachment in Turkish waters and U.S. High Commissioner to Turkey. While in that assignment, he served as a member of the American delegation to the Lausanne Peace Conference in 1922. Upon returning to the United States, he joined the USS NEVADA in January, 1925, and from May, 1926 until September 1927 he was District Communication Officer, Twelfth Naval District. In September, 1927 he returned to the Asiatic Station to serve again as Aide and Flag Lieutenant to the Commander in Chief, Asiatic Fleet in the USS PITTSBURGH, flagship. During this period he attended the Imperial Japanese Coronation Naval Review.

Returning to the United States in November, 1929, Rear Admiral Wheeler served in the Division of Naval Communications, Navy Department for two years. He returned to sea duty in command of the USS WATERS in October, 1931, and in June, 1934 he again reported to the Office of Naval Communications, Navy Department to serve for two years. In July, 1936 he joined the USS WEST VIRGINIA and had duty as her First Lieutenant until January, 1938 when he reported as Aide and Flag Secretary to the Commander in Chief, U.S. Fleet, USS PENNSYLVANIA, flagship, and served in that capacity until December, 193

Rear Admiral Wheeler was Executive Officer of the cruiser ASTORIA for one year from March, 1940. From March until July, 1941 he was Commanding Officer of the USS RELIEF, hospital ship. Relieved of that command, he served as Professor of Naval Science and Tactics College of the Holy Cross, Worcester, Massachusetts until December, 1942.

In January, 1943 he reported to the Newport News Shipbuilding and Dry Dock Company, Newport News, Virginia, where the USS MOBILE was building. He fitted her out, commissioned her on March 24, 19 and assumed command. Proceeding to the Pacific. Arriving Honolulu late in July, the MOBILE participated in the bombardment of Wake Island, October 5 and 6, 1943. She was in the task force involved in the occupation of the Tarawa Atoll in the Gilbert Islands,

Rear Admiral C.J. Wheeler, USN Ret.

November 20 and 21, and on December 4 and 5 again steamed into enemy waters as part of the task force of carriers, cruisers and destroyers that conducted an air attack on Kwajalein and Wotje in the Marshall Islands. On January 31, 1941, the MOBILE went back to Kwajalein as part of our occupation force.

Rear Admiral Wheeler was awarded the Legion of Merit for his services in the USS MOBILE, and was cited as follows:

LEGION OF MERIT

"For exceptionally meritorious conduct in the performance of outstanding services to the Government of the United States as Commanding Officer of the USS MOBILE, operating against enemy Japanese forces in the Central and South Pacific Area from September 1, 1943 to June 23, 1944. Displaying brilliant leadership and distinctive professional ability, Captain Wheeler maintained his ship at the highest point of efficiency at all times, thereby contributing to the combat readiness of his gallant command during numerous engagements and campaigns throughout this important period. His superb seamanship and aggressive fighting spirit were vital factors in the success of his vessel as an extremely effective unit of our fleet."

Detached from the command of the USS MOBILE, Rear Admiral Wheeler served as senior Naval Liaison Officer with the British Pacific Fleet from October, 1944, and for his wartime services in this connection he was awarded the Bronze Star Medal and cited as follows:

BRONZE STAR MEDAL

"For meritorious achievement as Senior United States Naval Liaison Officer serving with the British Pacific Fleet from October 1944, to September 1945. Maintaining contact with the Commander in Chief, United States Pacific Fleet and Pacific Ocean Areas, Captain Wheeler assisted and advised the Commander-in-Chief, British Pacific Fleet, in all matters pertaining to the United States Pacific Fleet, insuring the coordination of joint operations and procedures in order to bring maximum power to bear against the Japanese. His devotion to duty was in keeping with the highest traditions of the United States Naval Service."

Upon his return to the United States, Rear Admiral Wheeler was ordered in January 1946 to the Naval War College, Newport, Rhode Island. In February 1947 he was designated Member of the U.S. Naval Mission to Brazil, Rio de Janeiro, Brazil. Upon completion of his duty in Brazil, he returned to the Office of the Chief of Naval Operations, Navy Department, where he had had brief temporary duty prior to leaving with the Mission. He served there until relieved of all active duty pending his retirement on April 1, 1948.

In addition to the Legion of Merit and Bronze Star Medal, Rear Admiral Wheeler has a Letter of Commendation (with Ribbon) from the

Commander in Chief, Pacific Fleet; the Victory Medal, Destroyer Clasp (USS BENHAM); the Ynagtze Service Medal (USS PITTSBURGH); the American Defense Service Medal, Fleet Clasp (USS RELIEF); the Asiatic-Pacific Campaign Medal; the European-African-Middle Eastern Campaign Medal; the Asiatic-Pacific Campaign Medal; and the World War II Victory Medal.

Rear Admiral Wheeler was married in 1929 to the former Miss Doanda Risley Putman of New York, New York, at Amoy, China, while he was on duty with the Asiatic Fleet. They have two daughters, Doanda Risley Wheeler and Jacqueline Putnam Wheeler.

Rear Admiral Wheeler's present address is 73 Sagamore Road, Worcester, Massachusetts.

* * *

21 October 1949

Interview with Rear Admiral Charles J. Wheeler
at his home at 1850 Oak Dell Drive, Menlo Park, California
Date: 22 June 1969
By: Etta Belle Kitchen

Q: I notice that although Navy records always have your name as Charles J. Wheeler, your friends call you Julian. So, I'm happy to be here and to be able to start this biographical history of your illustrious and distinguished career, Admiral, and appreciate your giving us the time, and Good Morning.

Adm. W.: Thank you very much, Commander. I first learned of the Navy in my home at Mobile, Alabama, which is a port visited several times a year by naval ships, generally at Mardi Gras and the 4th of July. I was immediately interested in visiting these ships and, later, learned of the Naval Academy from a friend of mine who lived across the street, who went to Annapolis to take the examinations and failed and came home and was quite bitter about it, but the more he talked about it, the more I was intrigued. So about that time my father took me with him to Europe on a business trip. We were all sitting in the Pullman and my father was talking with Congressman Taylor - George Washington Taylor - in the seat in front of me, and I heard Mr. Taylor say, "Charlie, what are you going to do with that boy when he grows up?" My father said, "Oh, I don't know. I don't think he's much count, anyhow." I heard Mr. Taylor say, "Well, if he wants

Wheeler - 2

to go to Annapolis or West Point, I'll give him an appointment." So in a few years I recalled that and decided I wanted to go to Annapolis. I spoke about it to my father, and he said, well, you'd better see your mother about that, so I mentioned it to mother and she burst into tears and said, "But I'll never see you again." So I said, "Well, mother, I'm afraid you're not going to see very much of me anyhow, because I'm not going to live in Mobile, it's too hot." Therefore, she gave her consent and, at the age of 16...

Q: What year was that, Admiral?

Adm. W.: 1912. I left Mobile after one and a half years of high school and went to New York, first, to a school specially designed for training applicants for Annapolis. I was there a month and discovered that it was not the kind of place that I wanted to be, so I asked my father to let me go to Annapolis, where I went to one of the two preparatory schools - this one was run by the man that we called Johnny Chew. Of course, I was very badly unprepared and I remember just before the examination, I said to Mr. Chew, "What do you think of my chances?" and he said, "You have a fighting chance." Actually, when I went in to the examinations, I found that mathematics, which had been my weakest subject, was my easiest test, and that grammar, which had been my best subject, which I had neglected to study, was my toughest test. When the tumult and the shouting was all over, we went down to the Naval Academy gate, which is where they posted the names of the people who passed, and there was my name as a successful candidate for midshipman.

Q: What building did you take the test? On the grounds of the Academy?

Adm. W.: Now, you've got me. I can't remember. It seems strange, but I can't remember. It seems to me it was a post office in Annapolis, or some place like that.

Q: I see. It was not on the grounds of the Academy.

Adm. W.: I don't think it was on the grounds of the Academy. The strange thing was that when I first applied for the appointment, Mr. Taylor said that, at that time, he could only give me a second alternate because of having promised some other boys also, and Senator Johnson also gave me a second alternate - but when the smoke all cleared away, why, both principals and both first alternates had failed, so when I went for swearing in, the officer who swore me in asked me which appointment I wanted to go in on. I don't remember which one, but nevertheless I was sworn in, and I had a pretty tough time in my first year at the Naval Academy, as you can well imagine, because a lot of these things were completely over my head. But after I crossed that Rubicon, why, I had no trouble from there on out, and graduated when I was 20.

Q: Excuse me, do you remember where you stood in your class?

Adm. W.: I stood about the middle of the class.

Q: How many midshipmen were at the Academy in those days?

Adm. W.: In those days, there were about 800.

Q: The total?

Adm. W.: The total was about 800, and my class had 187. We graduated about 167, as I remember.

Q: Did you feel that the education at the Academy fitted you for the life of a naval officer?

Adm. W.: I thought it was the best education that could have possibly been devised for the life of a naval officer. There were no elective courses. The whole curriculum was set out and everybody had to take exactly the same subjects. We had monthly examinations, and the last month of each semester was review month. Then we had a semi-annual examination in January and again in May, and those were really very tough. Of course, they counted a great deal on your past marks. I understand that the curriculum has now been changed and that a good many courses are elective, and they've introduced a good many academic courses into the curriculum, which may be all right, but it's always been my thought that the Naval Academy was, and I think should be, primarily designed to train naval officers. Anyone can get a course in academic subjects at any college or university in the United States but, as I say, it's my belief that there must be a certain background of technical information which is necessary to turn out a good naval officer, army officer, or air force officer.

Wheeler - 5

Q: What about the professors, were they...?

Adm. W.: Most of the professors were naval officers. There were a good many in the English department who were civilians and, of course, also in the modern languages department, and some in the physics and chemistry department. But the discipline was strict. We had a month's leave after being there the first year, and the second, and the third, of course, but with the exception of those vacations, there were no other leaves until Christmas of our first class year, and I believe that we were the first class at the Naval Academy to get any Christmas leave.

Q: Is that right? Did you feel the discipline good, harsh?

Adm. W.: The discipline, according to present standards, would be considered very, very harsh. I recall that while a plebe, that is the first year I was there, I - no one - was allowed to leave the academic limits any time, except when invited by a relative or close friend. We were all required to remain within the academic limits for the first year, and, as far as I'm concerned, I think that although it was sort of hard to take at the time, I think that the discipline there was very, very helpful to everyone in after life. I deplore the fact that this discipline has been relaxed, I understand, at the Naval Academy and I feel that the relaxing of the discipline, not so much at the Naval Academy, but in other places is the real basis for the difficulty that we're having throughout the country today.

Q: Do you have any recollection of any interesting or amusing anecdotes that happened to you while you were at the Academy?

Adm. W.: I don't recall any now. It was a pretty serious time for me. My one object was to be successful. I had determined that no power on earth was going to get me out of that Naval Academy until I graduated, and I had a great desire to be a naval officer. So I devoted most of my time to that. I was not an athlete. I did get my numerals in soccer and I played tennis a good deal, but I was not a star in any of those activities. Whereas I enjoyed my life at the Naval Academy, I was glad when it was over.

Q: Well, I'm sure the character which you indicate at the Academy and your determination are the same characteristics that made you successful throughout your career. People, I don't think, change.

Adm. W.: Thank you, very much. There was one interesting event that happened at the inauguration of President Wilson in 1913. Both the Naval Academy midshipmen and, of course, the West Point cadets participated in that inauguration, and after that was over all of the midshipmen were invited to the home of, I think, the McLeans and, there, we had the great privilege and honor of meeting Admiral Dewey.

Q: Oh, how interesting. How old would he have been then?

Adm. W.: Well, let's see, it was 1912. He was in command, of course, at the Battle of Manila Bay during the Spanish-

Wheeler - 7

American War. I would say he was in his late 70s or 80.

Q: Wasn't that an exciting experience?

Adm. W.: Yes, it really was.

Q: I always enjoyed the observation of a men who went to Annapolis in the early days, because it's really the basis for your career. Admiral, did you have any interesting trips as a midshipman?

Adm. W.: We went through the Panama Canal in the summer of 1915, that is in the midshipmen's cruise. There were three battleships. I was aboard the first one, which was the old Missouri, and we anchored in San Francisco, off of what is now the Marina, where the San Francisco-Panama Exposition was located.

Q: Did you say this was the first time the fleet had gone through the canal?

Adm. W.: The first time any battleship had gone through the canal, because it was just opened before we made that trip. As a matter of fact, there was a good deal of discussion about whether we'd be able to get back through the canal because there had been a number of slides and we, as midshipmen, kind of hoped that there would be a slide so we wouldn't get back to the Naval Academy as soon as planned.

Q: Was this your last year?

Adm. W.: This was my last year, beginning of the last year.

Wheeler - 8

The summer before it. Just before our graduation in June of 1916, one of our newest destroyers, the USS Benham, came in to Annapolis and made fast to a wharf near the old USS Santee. I expect every midshipman at the Academy went on board that destroyer at some time or other and, of course, everyone hoped - in my class, at least - hoped that he would be assigned to that ship after he graduated. I had already put in for a battleship, but when my orders came through they were to join the USS Benham, which I considered very fortunate, especially in view of the fact that up to that time, practically all midshipmen had been ordered to larger ships, where it was felt that they would have better training.

Q: I enjoyed seeing the picture you have here of the Benham and it looks antiquated now with its four stacks, but it was the first of its class then?

Adm. W.: Not the first of its class. It was one of the - I can't just recall now which one, I think the first one was the Cassin, which was No. 43. But she had only been commissioned a short time before and was the pride of the destroyer flotilla.

Q: You were lucky to get that duty.

Adm. W.: Yes, I was.

Q: Then, where was your first duty aboard the Benham?

Adm. W.: I joined the Benham in Portland Harbor on 17 June 1916, and we spent the summer investogating all of the harbors large enough for a destroyer to enter on the Maine coast, with the idea of locating any harbors which might be useful for a German submarine to enter and refuel. We took part, of course, in some exercises, but our main duty was searching out these possible submarine refueling bases.

Q: War was already going on in Europe, wasn't it?

Adm. W.: War was already going on but we were not yet in it, of course. In the fall of that year, we went to Norfolk, our regular Navy yard, and among other things had the first twin mount 4-inch gun in the Navy mounted on the bow of our ship. Then we went to participate in the usual winter fleet exercises in Guantanamo Bay. After they were over, we returned to Hampton Roads and, although we were not yet in the war, the fleet was completely darkened in view of the fact that no one knew what the Germans might do and there was always the possibility of a submarine attack.

Q: Did everyone get home safely?

Adm. W.: Everyone got home safely, and the fleet anchored off Yorktown, north of Old Point Comfort, and it was while there that we saw the signal from the flagship, in flags, that the United States had declared war on Germany. Three weeks later, we were ordered to proceed to Queenstown, Ireland, to join the British escort vessels there, who would go out several hundred miles to meet incoming transports and cargo vessels and escort them in to St. Nazaire or Brest, France.

Q: Where were they coming from?

Adm. W.: From the United States. The previous plan followed by the British had been that they had divided the whole area west of England and Ireland into squares, and they had attempted to place an escort vessel in each square, with the idea that whenever an American vessel bearing troops or cargo entered that square, it would be met by one of these escort vessels and escorted through that particular square. Unfortunately, the British didn't have enough escort vessels to fill all these squares and there were a tremendous number of ships that were being sunk because of lack of escorts. Soon after we declared war on Germany, the British prime minister made a secret trip to Washington and explained to President Wilson that their greatest need was for escort ships. Therefore, as quickly as American destroyers could be made ready, they were ordered to Queenstown, where they based, and served under the command of Vice Admiral Sir Lewis Bailey, Royal Navy. This was a very unusual procedure, of course, because, as far as I know, it was the first time that any American ships had ever served under any foreign admiral. Technically, of course, Admiral Simms was in command of the destroyers, but he was in London in contact with the British Admiralty.

Q: Do you have any idea how many American destroyers there were?

Adm. W.: At that time, there must have been about 50 that eventually arrived in Queenstown.

Q: Do you remember the name of the prime minister who came to

Washington?

Adm. W.: I can't recall his name. I thought of it the other day, but it escapes my mind now. In any case, we remained in Queenstown until the President Lincoln was sunk by German submarines off the coast of France in the spring of the following year, after which we were transferred, that is to say, my division of destroyers, was transferred to Brest. This transfer caused a good deal of discomfort because it took place while we were at sea and no one on the ship ever got back to Queenstown to pick up his laundry or any possessions - golf clubs or anything that he may have left ashore. One of the amusing things was that when we first arrived in Queenstown we had been loaded down with spare parts and food and every possible thing that we could carry on the destroyer and, of course, after we arrived all the spare parts were taken off and put in the British dockyard called Haulbowline in little cages each labeled with the name of the ship. After some months at Brest we received the signal that a barge would come alongside bringing with it all the spare parts which had been left in Queenstown. Unfortunately when the barge arrived alongside the Benham there was only one windscoop left on it, everybody else having helped themselves before it reached us. I was quite worried about this because I had been assigned as the accounting officer for the ship inasmuch as in those days there were no paymasters on destroyers, and I wondered how I was going to account for these $30,000 worth of supplies. So I went over to the destroyer tender and poured out my woes to the supply officer there, and he said, "Well don't worry about it.

Wheeler - 12

Everybody knows you couldn't make good the $30,000. It will all be straightened out. If it was $300 you'd probably have to pay it."

Q: I don't understand your job on the ship. I know you said you had to account for this particular amount, but otherwise what was your assignment?

Adm. W.: I was executive officer, by that time.

Q: Still an ensign?

Adm. W.: No, I had been promoted by that time to lieutenant. In fact, in those days, we used to say if you didn't get a commission every six months you were being badly treated. So I went up from ensign to lieutenant in less than two years.

Q: How many officers were on the ship?

Adm. W.: We had, at that time, about ten officers. The ship, which had been built for five, had been converted to accommodate ten by doubling the bunks, putting in overhead bunks.

Q: Wasn't that escort duty awfully dangerous?

Adm. W.: It was dangerous, not especially from submarines, because they didn't appear to use destroyers as targets because destroyers have such light draft that the torpedoes are apt to run underneath them. Our greatest danger was from collision because, of course, in order to avoid the submarines all of the convoy ships were zigzaging and all of the escort ships, including destroyers were zigzaging, and the problem was to avoid running into each other.

Q: And of course they were all dark at night.

Adm. W.: They were all dark at night.

Q: How far out did you go?

Adm. W.: We'd go out about 200 miles, west of Ireland.

Q: And did you go over the same distance when you were at Brest?

Adm. W.: Yes, it would have been farther from Brest, it would have been about 250 or 300 miles.

Q: Did you ever make contact or see any German submarines?

Adm. W.: We never saw any German submarines ourselves. As a matter of fact, we did see several objects that we thought were German submarines' periscopes, but we were never able to actually identify them. We saw also several tracks of torpedoes, which fortunately missed us.

Q: Was your ship equipped for submarine warfare?

Adm. W.: Yes. That was an interesting affair in that when we first arrived in Queenstown, the British navy yard workmen came on board and immediately removed the depth charges which had been placed on American destroyers by our own American dockyards, because the depth bombs which had been placed on the American destroyers weighed 50 pounds and were very crude affairs.

They had a line attached to them which, when the depth charge was kicked overboard, it dropped to a depth - a predesigned depth, and exploded. But none of us thought it really would do a submarine any damage. The British installed tracks on the stern of each destroyer, each carrying about 15 300-pound depth charges with hydraulic mechanisms, which enabled these depth bombs to be released from the bridge, and, of course, whenever we saw anything suspicious, why, we would drop these. There were also Y guns which were installed on the after deckhouse which enabled us to drop a pattern of depth charges - we'd fire four at a time with the hope of catching the submarine.

As a matter of fact, instead of a pattern of four depth charges, we fired a pattern of six because in addition to the Y gun, we had a so-called Thornycroft thrower on each side of the main deck aft, which enabled us to fire six at the same time.

Q: Were any of the ships ever in collision that you were...?

Adm. W.: Yes. The Benham was run into by a British sloop called the Zinnia. The British had a class of ships which they called "sloops," but they were of course men-of-war, not sailing ships, and this occurred in a dense fog, and the Zinnia almost cut the Benham in two. Fortunately, she came alongside immediately thereafterwards and took off most of the crew, which lightened the ship considerably, and then towed us in to port.

Q: Was that the end of the Benham for the rest of the war?

Adm. W.: No. The Benham was then temporarily repaired and sent to Newport, Monmouthshire, England, which is very close to Cardiff, Wales, where we remained for about six weeks, and repairs were effected which restored the Benham to her original condition.

Q: That's remarkably fast work, isn't it?

Adm. W.: Yes.

Q: But there were no casualties?

Adm. W.: No casualties.

Q: Did the Benham stay at Brest for the remainder of the war?

Adm. W.: Yes, the Benham stayed at Brest for the remainder of the war and, fortunately, we had no more mishaps. We had a very active schedule, both at Queenstown and at Brest. We would be at sea for about six days and in port for only two or three days, making ready for the next sortie. The weather at Brest and in the Bay of Biscay outside of Brest, and the English Channel, was the worst that I have ever seen. You could always be sure, at that time of year, of running into a storm, and some of the crew used to get terribly seasick. I remember one young man who apparently had come from a very wealthy family, who was just so ill that he thought he was going to die and I thought may be he might, too. He came in and said to me that he just couldn't face another trip and would I consider a present if I would let him off. I said, no,, we don't do things that way in the Navy. He went to sea

Wheeler - 16

again and again, and finally completely recovered from his seasickness.

Q: Do you know whether anyone has ever been run out of the Navy because of seasickness?

Adm. W.: I think there are a good many cases on record where people have been transferred from the Navy to the Army because of it. A destroyer is a very unpleasant place to be in a storm.

Q: Those Atlantic storms, I gather from pictures and stories, must be just unbearable.

Adm. W.: Destroyers have a corkscrew motion that's entirely their own.

Q: And that time of year, wasn't it freezing in the fleet?

Adm. W.: Cold, and, of course, very wet on the bridge. Although the bridge was housed over it would be impossible to make it completely watertight. It was a pretty unpleasant experience. We were very happy when it was over.

Q: Were you detached, then, at the end of the war for return to the United States?

Adm. W.: No. Before that I must tell about my having had a choice between going to see the festivities that took place in Paris in connection with the end of the war, or of going to Scapa Flow to see the surrender of the German fleet, and I've always regretted my decision to go to Paris, rather than to Scapa Flow, but being a boy in my twenties, I suppose, I'll have to be excused for that. The celebration in Paris was like nothing that I've ever seen or heard of. It lasted for three solid days, and during that time the boulevards and streets were just thronged with people, arm in arm, singing and hurrahing and generally expressing their happiness without any thought of being tired or having anything else to do. The whole town was just given over to celebration I saw some of my classmates on the boulevards dancing with these young Parisian girls, and other fellows that I never have seen since. It was really the most fantastic thing that I think ever happened.

Q: How was the popularity of the Americans in France then?

Adm. W.: Their popularity was at the top.

I forgot to mention that before we were transferred to Brest, on one of our return trips to Queenstown we were in a frightful storm, which was so bad that we lost some of our boats, and we also saw on the horizon in the distance an object which we at first thought was a German submarine, but later turned out to be HMS _Achete_ - isn't it funny how you remember names like that - which had suffered even worse than we had. She had had most of her bridge blown overboard, including her compass, and didn't even know where she was.

Q: That's what gave her the appearance of being so low in the water that you thought she was a submarine?

Adm. W.: That's right. We escorted her to Penzance, on the southern coast of England, and then we went into Falmouth ourselves for refueling.

One of the interesting episodes that took place while I was in Queenstown was the - were - the activities of the U.S.S. Santee. The Santee was an old cargo ship, which was renamed for a very old American vessel, and she was used as a decoy for German submarines. The people on board the Santee were all volunteers from the American Navy, and the scheme was that there were sections of the upper deck of the Santee which were cut out and on hinges with guns placed behind them, so that when and if a submarine torpedoed the Santee, as was their custom to torpedo all the cargo ships they could, and then came up, as the German submarines often did - they would come up and take the captain a prisoner - as soon as the German submarine surfaced, all of these gunports would be lowered, and the guns would open fire on the submarine with the hope of sinking it. In doing this, we copied the activities of the British who had many of these so-called Q ships, or mystery ships, and they had been quite successful in this maneuver, but by the time we got into the act, the Germans had gotten pretty well onto it. The ship was torpedoed but the submarine didn't come up, and about that time the whole project was abandoned..

Q: Was the Santee lost when she was torpedoed.

Adm. W.: No, she wasn't lost. Her holds were filled with lumber, she remained afloat and was towed into port.

After the armistice, I learned that the Benham was going to be among the few destroyers that would remain in France, so I requested permission to go home on leave. This permission was granted, and I went home on the USS Nevada and spent a month, at the end of which time I learned to my surprise that the Benham had returned to Norfolk, and I rejoined her in Norfolk. Soon thereafter, which was in 1919, the Benham was one of 50 destroyers strung out across the Atlantic Ocean as guardships to pick up the survivors of any personnel from the naval planes that were making the first transAtlantic flights. We were stationed about 50 or 100 miles east of the Azores and, as history will record, three of the Navy planes met with disaster by the time the NC-4 reached the Azores, the weather was particularly bad while we were wallowing around in the Atlantic, remaining on station, we would receive for days the unwelcome signal that the remaining plane, the NC-4 will not fly today. But she finally did fly and reached Portugal safely, thereby becoming the first airplane to cross the Atlantic.

Q: Is that so? Well, how does that relate to Lindberg?

Adm. W.: Oh, Lindberg wasn't till a long time after that.

Q: How many people were on the Navy plane?

Adm. W.: I think there were about three.

Q: Perhaps Lindberg, then, was the first solo?

Adm. W.: Yes.

Q: You spoke of the Navy planes having met with disaster?

Adm. W.: Yes, three of them did reach. I can't remember exactly where they fell by the wayside, but they were the NC-1, 2, 3, and 4. I don't think there was anybody lost, but they all gave up before - by the time - they got to the Azores, except this one.

Q: Were they picked up by the destroyers? The line was effective

Adm. W.: Oh, yes.

Q: After this particular duty, did you leave the Benham?

Adm. W.: Yes. I applied for duty on the Asiatic Station and was ordered to the South Dakota, then outfitting in Portsmouth, New Hampshire. The South Dakota had been used as a transport to bring back troops from France after World War I - which we called after World War II "magic-carpeting". They had installed bunks in all of the compartments and many, many troops were brought back on her and when I reported on board, she was really a mess, not only dirty but completely sort of messed up due to all these alterations which had been made in order to enable her to bring troops back from France. I had three men in my division, which had a normal complement of 72, so we were really in dire straits for getting work done.

Q: What was your assignment on the South Dakota?

Adm. W.: I was in charge of the quarterdeck division. That included the after turret. The South Dakota had 8-inch guns, two 8-inch guns in the turret, and I had that whole after part of the ship to care for. We were in such dire straits that we had to call upon the naval prison at Portsmouth to send men down to scale the sides and paint because there were not sufficient men on the ship to clean it up and paint it. As a matter of fact, there was only one ship in the United States Navy at that time that had a full crew, and that was the USS Tennessee, which was manned by people mostly from Tennessee because Captain Upham was from Tennessee, and he had made an appeal to people from Tennessee to volunteer for duty aboard the USS Tennessee. The reason for this shortage of men was because the Secretary of the Navy, Josephus Daniels, had practically allowed anyone who wished to get out of the Navy after World War I to get out, so the ships were just practically stripped.

Q: Whether they had finished their enlistment or not?

Adm. W.: Yes, they just let 'em out, and so trying to fit this ship out was one of the most difficult jobs I ever undertook. On the 1st of September 1919, the South Dakota became, by order of the Navy Department, the flagship of the United States Asiatic Fleet, which was a very strange arrangement because, obviously, the flagship of the Asiatic Fleet was usually stationed in Asiatic waters. Admiral Rogers who had been commander-in-chief of the Asiatic Fleet had to haul down his flag in the Brooklyn, which was then the Asiatic Fleet flagship.

Q: And where was it?

Adm. W.: It was in China. It was Admiral Rogers' flagship of the Asiatic Fleet in China. But when Admiral Gleaves was appointed c-in-c of the Asiatic Fleet in New York Harbor, there couldn't be two commanders-in-chief of the Asiatic Fleet, so poor Admiral Rogers had to haul down his flag and hoist one as commander of the First Division of the Asiatic Fleet, you see what I mean?

Well, at any rate, the ship obviously couldn't sail from New York to China without a crew, and so an order was sent out practically to all naval recruiting stations to send all of their recruits to the South Dakota. They came on board in civilian clothes, in Army uniforms, in rags, and everything else, and this, of course, was very unusual because, generally speaking, enlisted men are given at least three months' training, but these were just sent on board...

Q: What was the complement of the South Dakota?

Adm. W.: ...as they were. I can't give you the exact figures, but I would say about 800 men. And these people just poured on board. They were assigned sort of helter-skelter to the different divisions. This is really an epic in naval history. I don't think it's ever happened before or since, as far as I know. They had no training, they had no uniforms. We had to supply them with uniforms and we had to teach them - in those days we slept in hammocks - not only how to get into hammocks but how to sling it afterwards. You know, you can't leave the hammocks up during the day because that's where the guns and everything else are. They all had to be slung and put in what we used to call hammock nettings, big sort of compartments that they were stowed in. And we had to explain to them how to wash their clothes. Of course, there were no laundries on board ship in those days.

Q: Even when it was under way?

Adm. W.: Oh, no, there were no laundries of any kind. They had to scrub their clothes in salt water. There wasn't enough fresh water for them to scrub their clothes in. Well, of course, these people who had had no training at all didn't like that. They didn't like to sling their hammocks and put them in the hammock netting, so what they did was, they'd just get up in the morning and throw the hammocks overboard, and rather than wash their clothes, they just threw those overboard.

Q: This was in the Navy Yard?

Adm. W.: This was on the way to Panama..

Q: Oh, you were training them under way?

Adm. W.: Training them under way, trying to, but they didn't want this training, they didn't want to do any of the things that they were supposed to do. It was the worst mess that I have ever seen in my life. There were, I think, close to 50 who deserted in Panama and we wished more had.

The next development was that we began to run out of hammocks and clothes because you can't throw over hammocks and clothes all the time and have any left.

Q: Did you realize they were doing this?

Adm. W.: Well, we didn't see them do it. They did it at night, you see. But we soon realized that we didn't have anything on board to give out any more. We were running short. It was just the most frightful experience that I've ever been through. I don't know yet how we lived through it.

Q: How many officers were there to train this number of people?

Adm. W.: Just the usual ship's company of officers. I suppose there probably were 100 officers, or something like that. Maybe there weren't even that many. I don't remember how many there were. There was the normal complement of officers who would be expected to train their men in gun drills and things like that. I remember Admiral Gleaves was a very tough disciplinarian, a real martinet, and we had only been out of New York Harbor and struggling with this mass of men, trying to get them clean and get them clothed and everything, when he looked at the captain - Captain J. M. Luby - and said, "Captain, I've never been on a ship three days in my life before where they didn't have general quarters. Sound general quarters." Well, Captain Luby sounded general quarters and you can imagine what happened. We hadn't even been in our turrets.

Q: Did anybody know what it meant?

Adm. W.: They didn't know what it meant. I tried to get in my turret, which I knew was my battle station, but I couldn't get in there. It was all filled up with stores. It was the worst thing I've ever seen in my whole life.

Q: It sounds unbelievable.

Adm. W.: It was unbelievable. If I hadn't seen it, I mean, if I were you listening to this, I wouldn't believe it.. Anyhow, we finally left Panama and went on this very, very interesting cruise down through the Galapagos Islands. We anchored off the islands and Admiral Gleaves and his staff went ashore. Nobody else went ashore. And they looked around and, let me see, where did we go from there? We went to the Marquesas Islands, which are beautiful. We did go ashore there, but it was one of the saddest experiences I've ever had, because it was explained to us that some French ship, it was a French possession you know, had come in there during the 'flu epidemic, and they had the virus on board and it hit the South Sea Islanders, and they just died like flies, because they had no immunity. We walked along the beach - they always built their huts, sort of grass shacks, near the beach, and they were all empty. People had just died off. We saw very few people in the islands at all.

Q: It decimated the population?

Adm. W.: It decimated practically the entire population. From there, we went on to...Speaking of the 'flu epidemic reminds me that I forgot to mention while talking about the period when the Benham was based at Queenstown. I remember very clearly now that the Benham was in Liverpool, having escorted some troop transports in to port, and we were waiting to escort some empty troop transports out, when the flu epidemic hit our ship, and people were laid low by the numbers. Before we left Queenstown [Liverpool?], one-third of the crew were down with the 'flu. At least a third of the officers were down with the 'flu, but we thought we could make it back to Queenstown anyhow. So, we got under way and headed for Queenstown, and by the time we got back to Queenstown, two-thirds of the crew were down flat on their backs, and I was the only officer on the ship that wasn't down with the 'flu, and as soon as I'd tied the ship up, I went to the hospital with the 'flu.

Q: You had complete charge of the ship while...?

Adm. W.: Not the entire way. They just dropped off as we went along, but by the time we went in to Queenstown I was the only one - the only officer - on my feet. There were other incidents, speaking of the flu, that were quite terrifying. I remember during the height of the epidemic, we used to quite often escort the Leviathan, with 10,000 troops on board, in to Brest, and the ships as they came in to Brest were required to make three signals to the shore station: one was the number of dead, two, was the number of hospital cases, and three, was the number of other 'flu cases.

Well, to get back to where we were about the Marquesas...

Q: Since we had stopped just for a moment, I'm interested to know whether you put on additional stores in Panama that made it possible for you to care for the hammocks and the uniforms for the rest...?

Adm. W.: Oh, yes, we took on all the stores we could get.

Q: Then, the whole trip you were still training?

Adm. W.: Still training, the entire trip.

Q: When did the problem seem to ease, where people seemed to fit in?

Adm. W.: After Manila the worst of it was over. They were all sort of getting hep to shipboard life. It was awful, but I'll tell you later.

Q: Yes, you had stopped at going ashore on the decimated Marquesas. This was all on the way to the Asiatic Station?

Adm. W.: All on the way to the Asiatic Station. Our next stop was Tahiti, where we went ashore and enjoyed being there for a couple of days. A beautiful place. I can't recall anything particular happening there. We all bought, of course, a number of souvenirs and things, and we enjoyed swimming in delightful Tahiti which, from all accounts has changed greatly during the intervening years. As a matter of fact, we used to call the principal port Papeete and I hear the travel agencies are now advertising it as Papaeete. From Tahiti we went to Samoa, Pago Pago, and we loved that. There were no tourists, no hotels, no sort of regular communications with Samoa. It was under a naval governor. It seems that before the war all these outlying places like Samoa and Midway, and all of our Pacific island possessions were under naval governors and somewhere along the line the President decided to put them all under the Department of the Interior, which I never could understand, because how could the Department of the Interior have anything to do with islands in the Pacific, but the result was that they appointed civilian governors to all these places. At any rate, when we were there, there was a naval governor and we were very cordially received. There were all kinds of native dances, and the governor's guard had very colorful native costumes and they put on a parade for us, and we took long walks out into the countryside around Pago Pago, which was just beautiful. We got coconuts, got the natives to climb up the trees and throw down these green coconuts which, if you've never tasted one, you haven't any idea what a coconut tastes like when it's fresh. The liquid in it is always cool, no matter how hot a day it is, and the meat in it is perfectly delicious and tender, not at all like the coconuts you buy on fruit stands. We coaled, of course, there. We took a deck-load of coal.

Q: When you say a deck-load of coal it brings to mind the kind of propulsion that the Navy used then. Do you want to expand on that just a little bit?

Adm. W.: Well, of course, up to that time, we had never used anything else but coal. I remember on the midshipmen cruises, they had what we midshipmen felt was a rather unpleasant custom of putting four coal lighters alongside, two on each side, and they would put one division of midshipmen into each lighter, and then we would have competitions to see who got their lighter emptied first, which was fine from the point of view of getting the coal on board, but was pretty heart-rending from the point of view of the midshipmen who had to do it.

Q: What did you use to take the coal from the ligher up into...?

Adm. W.: Bags. Enormous bags that were about three or four feet high.

Q: Canvas? Burlap?

Adm. W.: Canvas bags, and about two feet in diameter. They had rope handles, and they would lower the boom from the deck and hook the handles over the hook and hoist them up. They had another batch of midshipmen up there who would shovel it down the coal chutes into the bunkers.

Q: I see. It was real manual labor.

Adm. W.: As a matter of fact, I still bear the scar - you can hardly see it now. One midshipman got over-zealous and we were getting near the end of a pile of coal andhe mistook my forehead - I was leaning over like that - for the pile of coal and hit me right over the eyebrow with the edge of a shovel, which the doctor on board ship apparently didn't know how to deal with, so after the stitches were taken out it left a long black line there, and it wasn't till I got back to the Washington naval hospital that they reopened it and got out all the coal dust.

Q: When you took on the coal at Pago Pago, they were still, of course, using the same method? Except they didn't use the midshipmen.

Adm. W.: Oh, yes.

Q: You had midshipmen on board?

Adm. W.: Oh, no, no, that's right. We used the sailors.

Q: Is that what they called the "black gang"?

Adm. W.: The black gang was the engineer force and was generally colored. Everybody in the engineering department, which would have included the firemen and the coal passers - we had a rating of coal passers - and, well, the black gang also included the machinists and the enginemen and people like that. In other words, anybody that wasn't in the deck force was in the black gang. Which reminds me, also, that as a midshipman on our three cruises, we had to - particularly when we were youngsters, that is to say, third classmen on our first midshipman cruise - scrub the decks and fire the boilers, pass the coal, and do all the things that the enlisted men did, which was very hard work. In those days of economy, why, they actually - the Navy Department - would actually reduce the number of enlisted men on board because the midshipmen were going to do a good portion of their work. As a matter of fact, on one occasion, coming into Hampton Roads, I remember, on a midshipmen cruise, we were told that if we would put on a double watch of midshipmen firemen and coal passers, we could get in a day earlier. So we did, and we stood watch and watch in the fire room, and I want to tell you that when you stand in front of one of those huge furnaces and open the door to throw in the coal, you sometimes wonder if you're ever going to live through it. I've never felt such intense heat in all my life.

Q: One wonders how the men in those days survived at all, whose job was down there.

Adm. W.: It was a wonderful thing because - of course, in those days I didn't like it much, although I didn't protest, I didn't like it, but now I'm glad that I did it because there wasn't a single man in the Navy that did anything of that sort that I hadn't done. In other words, I knew exactly what all their problems were and I was prepared to deal with them, and deal with them sympathetically, because I had been through it. It was wonderful training. Just wonderful training.

Q: Now we leave Pago Pago...

Adm. W.: And we go to the Philippines. The Philippines at that time, of course, were under the United States, and we made that our base.

Q: The headquarters of the Asiatic Command, then, was in the Philippines?

Adm. W.: In the Philippines, that's right. There's nothing particular to tell about the Philippines, except that it was a beautiful country. The people were very respectful. There were interesting things to see. We had our vacations at Baguio, where there was an army camp, known as Camp John Hay, available to naval officers as well as army officers, where we used to go and play golf and mountain climb and have dances.

Q: That's up in the higher... elevations

Adm. W.: Up in the higher area, yes. That was really a delightful place to be. It was cool and comfortable. A good place to sort of recharge batteries.

From Manila we went to Shanghai, which of course in those days was a delightful place to be, and we were very interested in all the new things there. Shanghai being a beautiful city, built largely by the English, oft times referred to as the Paris of the East, because it was so gay and, to me, the interesting thing about Shanghai was that it was originally a very large Chinese city, but when the treaties permitted the foreigners to establish what they called treaty ports, that is, after the Boxer Rebellion one of the provisions of the treaty was that foreigners would have the right to establish settlements in many of the port towns. I've forgotten the exact number, but Shanghai was one of them. The foreigners moved in in force and they built outside of the Chinese city, on more or less new ground, this beautiful foreign type city, right on the banks of the Woosung River. Of course, the French also had a part of the city. As a matter of fact, a part of it was called the French Concession, which the French considered as French territory. It was very carefully marked off, and they had French policemen and if you were arrested there, why, you would be handled exactly as you would if you had been arrested in France itself.

Q: This was what they called the extraterritorial...?

Adm. W.: Extraterritorial rights.

Q: How many nations had those rights? Do you recall?

Adm. W.: Well, at that time, the Japanese had a concession there, the French had a concession, the Russians had lost their concession. I don't even remember - you see, this was after World War I and the Revolution had taken place, so the Russians weren't counted. The Americans and the British had gone in on what they called the International Settlement. It was not a British concession, it was a sort of an unofficial agreement between the British and Americans that they would occupy this particular area, which they called the International Settlement. It lay between the French Concession, on one hand, and the Japanese Concession, on the other. That was where, of course, most of us lived, although some Americans lived in the French concession.

Life was very comfortable.

Q: You lived ashore?

Adm. W.: No, I didn't live ashore. I was a bachelor, you see. I lived on the ship. Things were very cheap. The rate of exchange was two for one, in other words, we got two Chinese dollars for every American dollar. Then, things were cheap anyhow. We had courtesy privileges at all of the foreign clubs: the French Club, the Shanghai Club, which was a British club, and there was the American Country Club, and the American Club, and all kinds of activities. A great many cabarets. It was thoroughly delightful. The foreigner was king.

Q: How many foreigners would you guess were in Shanghai alone?

Adm. W.: That's hard to say, but I would say it would have been between two and three hundred thousand.

Q: Hundred thousand?

Adm. W.: Oh, yes, it was a big place, a tremendous place. Although I once got a letter addressed to me - I was a lieutenant in those days, as Lieutenant C. J. Wheeler, U.S. Navy, China, and it reached me. The reason for that, of course, was that thanks to these extraterritorial rights we had our own post office, so all they had to see on the letter was "U.S. Navy" and they had a roster of who was on each Navy ship and they just sent it out to the ship.

Q: You said you lived on the ship and I know, at one time, the South Dakota's name was changed.

Adm. W.: Not till later.

Q: You still were on the South Dakota?
Adm. W.: Yes, still on the South Dakota.

Q: Did you ever meet or get to know any Chinese nationals?

Adm. W.: Oh, yes, we got to know them, but not so much at that time as later. You see, I was in China twice. Later when I was out there we got to meet quite a number of people. As I say, I went to Chiang Kai-Shek's and Madame Chiang Kai-Shek's wedding, and some of the more important people there, in the universities, and people like that we knew. I can't remember their names, unfortunately. In those days it didn't seem important.

Q: Your statement that the foreigner was king is a tragedy, in part.

Adm. W.: Well, it is a tragedy from the standpoint of what eventually happened and the fact that we do believe in equal rights for everybody, but it was awfully nice while it lasted. It certainly was pleasant because a foreigner could go in a store anywhere and buy whatever he wanted, and you never used cash in China, you just signed a chit, and at the end of the month each one of these stores had agents who came out on board ship and spoke to the officer of the deck and said, "I have these chits for Lieutenant So-and-so and Commander So-and-so," and he would send down to the ward room or wherever we were, and we'd come up and settle our bill. Money was practically never used.

Maybe I'll think of something more later about that. Anyhow, while we were there we got orders to proceed to Vladivostok, and that was a very interesting story which I think very few people in the United States know about.

Q: Could you pinpoint this as to time?

Adm. W.: January 1920. Towards the end of World War I, the Czechs who, in my opinion, are very fine people who have just been the victims of the most horrible luck of any race I know of in the world. They had had enough of the Central Powers who were our enemies, you know, in World War I, and they indicated to the Allies that they would fight on our side if we could get them on our side. Of course, they couldn't go through the line of the Western Front. So the Allies undertook to - told them - that if they could get themselves to Vladivostok, they would be transported by ship all the way around to Europe and they would be able to fight on our side.

Well, during the Russian Revolution - when it broke out, they got trapped in Siberia. Russia was originally on the side of the Allies, and that was all right by them at the time they started, it was all right by the Russians for the Czechs to go through there, because they were going to fight for us. But they, the Czechs, got trapped in Siberia. *by the Bolsheviks*

Q: How many are we talking about?

Adm. W.: Oh, - there were a couple of hundred thousand, at least.

Q: This, I surely never heard about.

Adm. W.: Very few people know about that.

Q: How were they transported?

Adm. W.: They went by trans-Siberian Railway. But before they got all the way over - across Siberia, why, the Bolsheviks started picking on them and blocking their way, and everything like that. Also, the trans-Siberian Railway was breaking down. And the United States was asked to - they had this sort of consortium - and among the people that the United States were asked to send were railroad engineers to get the trans-Siberian Railway running again. So, the United States sent all of these - a contingent of troops - I think each Allied nation, that is, the Americans, we sent 10,000 troops, the Japs sent 10,000 troops, the French and English sent some troops - not nearly as many, and I think the Italians may have sent some. At any rate, they all had ships up there, too, to be there to protect their troops and also to assist in this operation. That's why the South Dakota was sent there. While we were there, incidentally, the name of the ship was changed from South Dakota to Huron. And, you talk about cold, you haven't seen anything until you've been to Vladivostok.

Q: Were you prepared for it in clothing?

Adm. W.: We had clothing. I don't know where they got it, but they had fur hats, fur jackets - no, they weren't fur jackets, but they were heavy jackets with fur collars - and we took our insignia off the front of our caps and put it on our fur hats.

Q: You should have a picture of yourself, do you?

Adm. W.: I think I have somewhere. The ship was backed in toward the shore, and we had anchors out in front, of course. Then we had a big barge alongside the gangway. But you didn't need any of that because you could walk right on the ice. A lot of people walked on the ice. You could see at one end of the harbor there, they just walked on the ice all the time. It went down to 30 below zero, and I remember when the temperature went up to 10 below, we all thought spring had come, and we went out without some of our winter gear and got our ears frozen. We had this house built on the quarter deck for the officers of the deck and it had an electric stove in it, otherwise no man alive would have been able to stand watch out on deck in that climate.

Well, there was a good deal of activity there. We were there about three months, I think. Of course, there were army troops and army nurses, and they had dances. There was always a good deal of shooting going on in Vladivostok. At night when things were comparatively still, you could always hear gunfire. People being bumped off.

Q: Who was shooting who?

Adm. W.: Well, it was just a lawless city, and there was a good deal of feeling there, as everywhere else, there are always people who are against the government. There was no real police force, no real stable government there. As a matter of fact, while I was there, the first batch of revolutionaries marched into Vladivostok and I was in command of the consulate guard. I had a company of bluejackets, and I was at the consulate with this company of bluejackets to defend the consul if these people molested him, but, of course, they didn't. In those days, people respected the United States, and they wouldn't bother with the American consulate. But they came in and they did away with a number of people, and they took over the government. But they never bothered us. So, the Americans went in with their engineers and they got this railroad running, and they brought out a number of the Czechs. Of course, as usual, we did all the work. We were the only ones that sent any transports, and as the Czech troops came out, they loaded in these transports and were sent around through the Suez Canal to the Adriatic Sea, thence to Czechoslovakia. By that time the war was over, you see, it was 1920 and they were repatriated. But, in the meantime, a number of them were there, and they had a Czech orchestra which played the most beautiful symphony music, we used to go to that quite frequently. It was in an old shed on the wharf.

Q: Have you any idea how many Czechs ever did make it to Vladivostok?

Adm. W.: No, I don't know how many got there or how many were disposed of on the way, but I know there were a lot of people involved.

Q: But we did put Czechs on American transports?

Adm. W.: Oh, yes, and sent them back to Czechoslovakia.

Q: They went around to France?

Adm. W.: To Trieste.

Q: How many American transports were involved? Do you recall?

Adm. W.: I'm sure there were four or five came there while I was there. I don't know how many more.

Q: You were in Vladivostok for three months?

Adm. W.: Yes.

Wheeler - 40

Q: That would have been the early months of 1919?

Adm. W.: 1920. You see, we left New York on the 1st of September 1919..

Q: Then you didn't stay on board the Huron much longer, did you?

Adm. W.: I was going to come to that. I was trying to be as nearly chronological here as I can. After that we visited the Japanese ports - in the latter part of March and April - just on a sort of friendly visit. But in those days the Japs weren't very friendly.

Q: Was the Huron the flagship of the Asiatic Fleet?

Adm. W.: Yes, Admiral Gleaves was the C-in-C, Asiatic Fleet. So, we visited the Japanese ports. Of course, in those days, we always wore uniform, and I remember I got leave and I went with a shipmate of mine, to visit old Japanese temples on the top of a mountain down on the island of Kyushu. We were just walking along in our uniforms with sort of napsacks on our backs and I remember one Japanese woman indicating she wanted to know who we were. We hadn't Japanese language books, and we said "Americans" and she sort of spat to one side. That's the way the Japanese felt about us. Of course, the officials were very nice. You See, that was about the time of the Japanese Exclusion Act, and they were very bitter about the United States. Well, we went to Osaka, to Kobi, Yokohama, and from there we took trips. There was nothing particularly interesting about that feature of it because anybody can go to Japan and go to all those places. We were interested in going to Japanese restaurants and the tea ceremony and the Geisha Girls, and all that sort of thing. It was all very interesting and all very colorful. I think the cherry blossoms were in bloom, at that time. It really was lovely.

Later on that year, in July - you know the Chinese war lords were continually fighting. There was no central government in China at that time, and whichever war lord had control of Peking was considered the No. 1 in the Chinese government, but that was a fiction because he only controlled what was right around him. In each province, there was a separate war lord who ruled his little province. And in July of 1920, Wu Pei Fu and Chang Tso Ling were fighting for the control of the Peking government and, as you know, we had in Peking at that time an American Legation with a full staff of secretaries, attaches, and their wives and children, and in addition a Marine guard. Now, the Marine guard was one of the features of the treaty that followed the Boxer Rebellion - and in fact similar guards were permitted at all of the other legations to protect the legation personnel. The American Minister was getting worried during this so-called revolution that the legation guard would not be sufficient to afford the necessary protection, so he called upon the commander-in-chief to send additional forces from the flagship, and Captain Barry was sent in command of another company of Marines - each large ship of the Navy has a Marine guard - to join up with the Marines there, and he sent me in command of the bluejacket detachment. We were there for two or three weeks. We were very comfortably housed in the Grand Hotel de Pekin at government expense, of course, and the bluejackets were housed over in the legation guard compound, and we all went through drills and target practice, and such things.

Fortunately nothing arose during that period to cause any trouble. In Peking most of the battles between these contending Chinese took place outside the city. So we were eventually withdrawn to the flagship.

Q: Were the extraterritorial concessions established in Peking the same as at Shanghai?

Adm. W.: I don't think so. I don't remember any concessions there, no, except of course that the legation quarter itself was a kind of concession.

Q: Yes, but the other nations, were there...?

Adm. W.: What I mean is the legation quarter housed all of the legations, that is, British, French, American, Italian, all of them were in this one section of Peking, which was known as the Legation Quarter.

Q: I see, but all nations were represented there, the same as in Shanghai?

Adm. W.: The same as in Shanghai, but only in one section. Of course, Peking is a fabulous place to visit. You know Peking is built in concentric squares and the central part is the Forbidden City. That's where the emperor and his family live, and when he was in control nobody could go in and out of there. I never went in there during the time that I was there because the young emperor was still living there. He didn't have any power, but he was still a figurehead.

Well, then, in October of 1920 I was ordered to the USS Palos as executive officer.

Q: That's P-a-l-o-s?

Adm. W.: Yes. Do you know what that's named for? That's the city in Spain where Columbus started out with the Pinta, the Nina, and the Santa Maria to discover America.

The Palos was one of two gunboats that were built from plans borrowed from the British, who had built two similar gunboats, the Widgeon and the Teal, I think they were. At any rate, there were two small gunboats like that, which were built by the British to navigate the rapids. Do you know about the Yangtse Gorges?

Q: I've seen pictures of it and read about it.

Adm. W.: Well, the Yangtse Gorges are where the Yangtse River cuts through a range of mountains in Western China, and some of the walls on each side where the river flows through are 2,000 feet high. The most beautiful scenery. I've never seen anything like it in the world. These two gunboats, the Palos and the Monacacy, were built from these plans borrowed or bought from the British, I don't know which, and I would say she was about 100 feet long. She was about 30 feet wide, and very shallow. She drew about 3 or 4 feet of water only. The reason being that she had to pass over all these rocks and because she was so shallow, one rudder wouldn't have been enough, it wouldn't have had enough resistance, so she had four rudders, all controlled by one wheel in the pilothouse, because they all worked together. The Americans who built these two gunboats tried to improve upon them, as they always do on everything, and they made a mess of it. They made closed fire rooms with the idea of being able to get more speed, in other words, to have forced draft. They were coal-burners because you can get coal all up and down the Yangtse River, and the thought was to have them be coal-burners so you could always get fuel wherever you are. And these fire rooms were shut up tight with a blower in them, with the idea that by doing that with the forced draft they could get up more speed. The current in the Yangtse, at the worst season, is 12 miles an hour. You could throw a handkerchief overboard going up the Yangtse River and have it flow by you going 12 miles an hour just by the current itself. So, in order to get up these rapids, these ships have to make at least 13 knots and even then we've only got one knot against the current. At best, we could make about 13 1/4 knots. But, in the American ships, with these closed fire rooms, it was so hot down there that no human being could stay in those fire rooms under forced draft more than half an hour. Therefore we had to have the enlisted men stand one half watches, because by the time a man was there for half an hour and by that time he was finished practically, and he had to come out and be relieved by another man. Well, that way, we would make our way slowly up the Yangtse. Of course, we only steamed in the day - because there were no lighthouses. We'd anchor at night and wait until the daylight when we could find our way. In addition, on that ship we carried nine or ten Chinese natives, five of them were boatmen, one in charge and four oarsmen, who manned the sampans. We also had three Chinese servants, we had a steward - there were only three officers on board, the Captain, Glen Howell, and myself, and a doctor, he wasn't there all the time, just those three so we all messed together. In addition to ~~that~~ the Chinese named above we always had to have one, sometimes we had two, and sometimes we had an extra Chinese in training as a pilot. There were two or three pilots, and the reason for that was that no American ever stayed on the ship long enough to learn the river. That was a lifetime job, practically. In the first place because the river is very difficult to navigate, and secondly, it changes its banks. But the Chinese knew what the river did at different seasons. So, we had the five boatman (one, two, or three pilots, as the case may be). Those pilots, for instance, when the Monacacy was down at Shanghai undergoing refit - we'd have all the pilots on board and vice versa - and then we had, as I say, the steward, and the captain had a boy, and I had a boy, and the doctor had a boy, when he was on board. Then when we would start to go up these rapids, not the whole way up the river, but when we got to Ichang, which was at the foot of the rapids, 1,000 miles from Shanghai, we would start up the rapids and I remember that when we went up the first time, we got about, oh, I should say, one day's run up the rapids and we hit what was called the "flood." The water - the snow was melting in the Tibetan ~~Alps~~ Mountains - was pouring down so fast that nothing could combat that current. It was coming down in the order of 15 or 16 knots.

Q: Was there any way you knew ahead of time you were going to meet this flood?

Adm. W.: No. Communications were very poor. So what we would do, we would anchor - we wouldn't anchor, we'd make a spar moor - at night. We would go alongside a bank - first of all, we would send the Chinese boatmen out in the sampans with a long hawser, a long mooring line, and he'd go straight out and pick out a friendly rock or tree and tie that hawser to the tree, or the rock. He'd put the end of it - it would be secured to the bow, then we would put out what we called spars, we carried them on board all the time. They were...

Q: Would they be the size of a tarpaulin pole, may be?

Adm. W.: No, not that big. They'd be about six inches in diameter, and about 20 ft. long. Well, we would put these spars out against the riverbank and secured the inboard end with lines on the ship.

Q: They were at right angles to the boat?

Adm. W.: At right angles to the ship.

Q: Oh, then as you snubbed up the line, they would jam these two spars into the bank.

Adm. W.: Yes. Otherwise the ship would go right into the bank and beat itself to pieces. Well, one night, we realized that we couldn't go any farther and we pulled over to the bank...

Q: This was because of the flood?

Adm. W.: Because of the flood, yes. So we pulled over to the bank and made this spar mooring. We always had a rule that the quartermaster had to keep a watch on the water level. He'd put over a pole from the deck where he stood watch, and the pole's all marked like, say, 11 feet, 12 feet, and so on. And I remember when I turned in that night, that over on the bank there was a little Chinese hut with Chinese families and children playing out there, and during the night the water rose at the rate of a foot an hour. So when I got up next morning, the first thing I thought of was what had happened to those poor people on the bank. They were not perturbed at all, they had picked up their house - it was all in parts, and they did this every year, and moved it up a little farther up on the bank. Wasn't that funny?

Q: Well, it was very creative of them.

Adm. W.: We stayed there about four or five days before the current subsided and, in the meantime, we ran out of everything. We ran out of coal, we ran out of food, some foods, so we sent our Chinese boatmen out because they could speak the language, and we told them to get some coal. Sure enough, pretty soon these coolies came tramping down there with bags of coal. No white man ever did any menial work out there. They were above for that. The Chinese did all the work and got what they thought was handsomely paid for it. Then, in a short while, when the Chinese came back leading a calf - you know, China's a Buddhist country, and the Chinese don't like to kill animals, particularly cows - and we only had 48 men on the ship, so the first thing we did was to see if we could find anybody who would kill the calf so we could have some veal for supper. We found two butchers on the ship, so they butchered the calf and we had some nice roast meat that night. Then, in a day or so, things cleared up and we proceeded on up to Chungking. Oh, no. We weren't going to Chungking, my mistake. Yes, we were. But I've gotten this out of order now.

I should have told you first about the time - because the first place we went was Changsha.

Q: How far is Changsha from Shanghai?

Adm. W.: About 900 miles. Well, now, shall I tell you about Chungking or go back to Changsha? We went to Changsha first.

Q: Why don't we finish with Chungking and then revert?

Adm. W.: All right. We proceeded up the Yangtze Gorges, which is 300 miles long, and we arrived at Chungking.

Q: That is the Gorge is 300 miles?

Adm. W.: Yes.

Q: Chungking is how far from Shanghai?

Adm. W.: 1,500 miles. That doesn't come out quite right, does it?

Q: My thought was that Chungking where Chiang Kai-Shek had his headquarters was about 1,500 miles up the Yangtze.

Adm. W.: It is about that. May be Ichang is 1,200, I'm not sure about that. In any case, we went up to Chungking, and there we made another spar moor and went into sort of summer quarters. This is out of order because we spent the winter in Changsha, then we went to Chungking.

Then, all we did was just enjoy life, because all we were doing...I haven't explained yet that the reason for these gunboats on the Yangtze — and there were two kinds, there were the lower river gunboats, and the upper river gunboats. The upper river gunboats, of course, were the two which I have mentioned that cruised in the area between Ichang and Chungking. The lower river gunboats cruised between Shanghai and Ichang. And the reason for these gunboats was that in that war lord period of China, you could never be sure that any area was going to be secure. In other words, if anybody was shipping cargo of materials of any kind - and one of the principal cargoes out there was oil, because at that time, no oil had been discovered in China, and so kerosene was a great necessity for lighting for all of the Chinese Navy. And when anyone shipped a cargo, why, he never knew whether it was going to arrive or not, unless there was some protection. Each country had its own gunboats. The British, for instance, had gunboats; the French had a gunboat, even the Italians had a gunboat. The Germans used to have them, and the Russians also before World War I. And their function was to protect these shipments.

Q: From their own countries? Going into China?

Adm. W.: Well, no, in their own boats, in their own carriers. The Dollar Line - well there was a little steamer that used to make this Gorges run called the Robert Dollar Second. Then, there was another one came along later, called the Alice Dollar. They were small draft and very fast and small, so that they could get through these gorges, and they carried cargo, and they say that they had the highest freight rates in the world because it was so dangerous. I was talking to somebody the other day who told me that both of them had been wrecked after I left, both the Robert Dollar and the Alice Dollar, which is easy to understand, because, you see, in navigating these gorges, the only way you could make any time at all was by staying near the shore, because the fastest part of the current came right down the middle. And if you went up near the bank, you'd get a backwash, you'd actually get a current going with you. But, of course, the closer you got to the shore, the closer you got to the rocks. That's how so many of these ships were wrecked.

Q: The purpose of the patrol, then, was really to protect American shipping?

Adm. W.: The purpose of our gunboats was to protect American shipping. The purpose of the British gunboats was to protect British shipping. The British-American Tobacco Company had representatives throughout there, and they used to ship tobacco, Every large nation had its gunboats. That was also part of this extraterritorial treaty - we were allowed to have our own gunboats. Generally speaking, when things were quiet, all that was necessary was for these gunboats to be there, but if there was any military activity at all - one war lord would be trying to rout another one out, and that frequently happened, and take over, and they'd be shooting at each other across the river or something like that - why the gunboat would actually have to convoy the cargo ships. So, that's why they were there. As a matter of fact, we used to jokingly argue with the Standard Oil, which who had places all up and down the river there, whether they were there on our account or we were there on their account. Neither one could be there without the other, except of course that we also had American missionaries and some tobacco men that we had to look out for.

Q: How wide was the river in the Gorges?

Adm. W.: Oh, it varied. In some places it was very, very narrow, in some places it was quite wide, and still, and beautiful. You couldn't really say. Sometimes it would be probably only, say, 40 feet wide. No, it would be more than that because the ship was 30 feet wide, say, 50 to 60 feet wide, but awfully, awfully narrow.

Q: When you went up to Chungking, was that the first time an American gunboat had gone that far up?

Adm. W.: Oh, no. They'd been there for years. We actually took our gunboat up 400 miles above Chungking. We went up to a place called Sui Fu and that had been visited before by American gunboats. We also went to a place beyond that called

Kiating. To get there we had to turn off the Yangtze River because Sui [Swei] Fu was the absolute head of navigation for ships of that size. You couldn't go an inch farther. So, we turned off into the Min River and went to Kiating, which was still 100 miles farther into the interior.

I must tell you a little bit about the lower part of the river. We found in Chungking - of course, there was an American consul there, a very nice chap who was madly in love with a girl in the States and he knew that we were expecting to leave that fall to come back to the States, he gave me a message to her I remember, but the next time I saw him was in Washington D.C., he was married and had three children. At any rate, we got up to Chungking and we moored there very securely, and then we each hired a sedan - the only means of transportation, chairs. We moored on the side of the river opposite Chungking. There were regular moorings that had been placed there before. The commissioned officers had four-man chairs, the chief petty officers had three-man chairs. Everything was according to rank. And the enlisted men had two-man chairs. Everybody had a chair. I think I paid $20 a month for mine, or something like that. Of course, there were a great many missionaries and a great many people from Standard Oil and Asiatic Petroleum, British-American Tobacco, that had summer places out on our side of the river. We played tennis and had tea parties and things like that. Then, later on, we took the ship up to Kiating which was 100 miles beyond Swei Fu. There the skipper, Glen Howell, a lieutenant commander, he was, decided he wanted to go to Chengtu. Now that is the capital of Szechwan Province, a couple of hundred miles, I guess, beyond Kiating. So he took off with a crowd of coolies, he had his chair, of course. Coolies carried his clothing and his food, water, and everything he needed on the trip. He was gone, I guess, a couple of weeks, and about two days after he left the senior Chinese pilot, the No. 1, came to me - he couldn't speak any English, except a word or two - and he pointed down the river and he said, "Must go, must go." I got hold of somebody who could interpret, and he said the river was going to fall and if we didn't leave right away, we would get caught up there and wouldn't be able to get out until the next spring. So I got the ship under way and we went back to Chungking and about two weeks later, the skipper arrived by chair.

Q: How long then did you stay in Chungking?

Adm. W.: We were there all summer. Then we returned to Shanghai.

Q: You went clear back to Shanghai?

Adm. W.: Yes, but that I'm going to wait on because that was the end of this cruise, you see. We left Shanghai in 1920, then it became 1921, and ...well, could I tell you now about the trip to Changsha?

Q: Yes, I was thinking we ought to do that. You made one trip each way each year? Is that what the schedule was?

Adm. W.: Yes, and we left in the fall of 1920, and we stopped at Nanking, Hangkow. I joined the ship in Shanghai, and we stopped at Nanking and Hankow, then we went on to Changsha. That's where I got off my chronology, here.

Changsha was interesting because when we went up, the river was very, very low, and we had to leave when we did, otherwise wouldn't have been able to get to Changsha, because the entrance to Changsha is through a lake, called Tung Ting, so when we went up we anchored in the early afternoon in time to play base ball on the bed of the lake which is dry at that time of year. There wasn't anything there but a ribbon of water because the water was falling. It was about November by the time we got up there. We went on to Changsha and made the same kind of a moor and we had a delightful time there because that was the location of the Yale-in-China University. Not many people know about that, but there was a beautiful university there which was run by Yale itself. There were four young men who had just graduated from Yale and they were teachers. Then there was the Standard Oil group and all kinds of missionaries. We were there from November until we left for Chungking in the spring. We took walks out in the country which I don't think had ever been visited by a white man before. An interesting feature of the visit to Changsha was that in order to keep the men occupied - one of the great difficulties that the officers have on any kind of an assignment like that is keeping the men happy - so we organized two football teams. The captain took one team and I took the other, and we practised every afternoon, and we had planned to have organization was very well set up and functioned very efficiently. There were a number of other Americans there, including doctors, and we saw a great deal of them, on national holidays and at our entertainments which, as a matter of fact, were most attended by the American colony there consisting of the American staff of the university, and the consul and his staff, and the Standard Oil men, of whom there were four or five, and their wives. There were also some British people there, including the British Consul General, and the British-American Tobacco Company had representatives there.

Q: Did you know any Chinese people?

Adm. W.: Very few of the Chinese. At that time there was very little actual socializing between the foreigners and the Chinese. There was later on. On my second cruise to China there was a good bit.

Q: The book The Sand Pebbles was written of the same...I'm not sure what date it was, but did you find that it was accurate or was it...?

Adm. W.: I'm glad you asked me that question because I started to read The Sand Pebbles and after three or four chapters I put the book down in disgust because it was a complete misrepresentation of life on a Yangtze gunboat, as I saw it. Life on a Yangtze gunboat, in my experience, was, of course, quite different from life on board any other naval ship, but we obeyed the regulations, we had no liquor on board, and there was no carousing of any kind. We had a number of Chinese, of course. We had the five boatmen that I believe I previously mentioned, together with our mess attendants, steward, cook, and mess boys. But everything was runs in a very orderly way and there was none of the carousing and sort of extraneous activities which were depicted in <u>The Sand Pebbles</u>. I realize that anyone who's writing a book about life on board a Navy ship is somewhat handicapped by the fact, that, in general, Navy ships are well run and they do obey the regulations, which doesn't make a particularly interesting story. So that if a man wants to write a bestseller about life on board a naval ship, I suppose he has to stray from the truth in order to make it interesting.

Q: Did you ever hear of any ships that were run in any such fashion?

Adm. W.: No, I never did. As a matter of fact, we had an arrangement with the British gunboats, of which there were several on the Yangtze, by which we would supply the ice from our ice-making machine on board our gunboats, which the British gunboats didn't have, and we had a standing invitation to go on the British gunboats at the cocktail hour and have cocktails with them on the understanding that we bring the ice with us.

Q: Were cocktails ever served on the <u>Palos</u>?

Adm. W.: Never, in my stay.

Q: Well, I think it's interesting to bring out those facts as opposed to fantasy.

Adm. W.: After leaving the river at Changsha, after leaving Changsha, I should say, we went down through ~~Chungking~~ Tung Ting Lake. That is a lake that is made from the overflow of the river and I believe I mentioned on the journey to Changsha we stopped at dark, as we always did, and the crew had a baseball game on a piece of land near the ship. And on the way back, the river having risen as a result of the spring floods, it so happened, I noted from the chart, that we anchored exactly on the spot where the baseball game was held on the way up.

Q: To clarify for the record: you went from Shanghai and went directly to Changsha...

Adm. W.: Directly to Changsha and spent the winter there.

Q: That would have been the winter of 1920.

Adm. W.: That's right.

Q: Then you went up to Chungking in the spring?

Adm. W.: In the spring. After clearing Tung Ting Lake, which is part of the Min River, on which Changsha is located, we got back into the Yangtze River and proceeded farther west on the Yangtze to Ichang which is the beginning of the Yangtze Gorges. Then we spent the summer in Chungking, including the trip to Kiating.

Q: And then you came back in the fall of '21? I just wanted to get that clarified. Thank you. Then I think we are, right at this point, on your return down the Yangtze.

Q: I'm sure it caused a strong impression on the people to see him do this.

Adm. W.: Terrific impression. Well, that was the kind of a man he was, and it's been my experience that that is a typical example of the honesty of the average naval officer.

After arrival at Shanghai, we received our orders and made arrangements to return to the United States via the Pacific on one of the Canadian Pacific Line Empress ships. It was interesting that this event never took place and the fact that it didn't changed my whole career in the Navy and in life as well, in this way. The night before we were due to board this Empress liner, Lieutenant Commander Howell and I, who had become great friends, had arranged to hold a farewell party at one of the restaurants in Shanghai. I forgot to mention that Lieutenant Commander Howell and I had booked passage together on the same ship, and we had a room together in the Astor House Hotel in Shanghai. As the party was drawing to a close, I offered to take a young lady home, as she lived on the outskirts of Shanghai, and left Glen Howell to close the party up. We were of course to meet later at the Astor House Hotel. When I got back to our room I fully expected Glen Howell to have preceeded me. I was therefor very much surprised to find that he had not arrived yet. I thought, however that he was a grown man and older than I was and perfectly able to take care of himself, so why should I bother about what time he came in. So I turned in my bed and went to sleep. Next morning when I awakened I saw that his bed was still empty and had not been slept in. Then I got very worried. Our trunks had already been placed on board the steamer the day before and so I began to worry about whether I should have them taken off or not. I got in touch with a mutual friend of ours, a Mr. Mason, and he and I went down to board the ship because we thought, possibly, Glen Howell might have turned in in his cabin on board ship, but there was no Howell and no one knew anything about him. So we had the trunks removed, as it was by that time only an hour or so before sailing. I had come to the conclusion that I would not sail without finding out what had happened to my friend. We then notified the Shanghai police and, to our great surprise, considering the labyrinth of alleyways and various places in which a man can be lost, the Shanghai police reported that afternoon that Glen Howell had been found in a roadside tavern about 20 miles away on the Whangpoo River.

Q: Alive or dead?

Adm. W.: Alive. It appears that he had decided as he got out of his taxi in front of the Astor House Hotel that that would probably be the last night he'd ever spend in China, and he thought he'd just have one more drink, so he asked the taxicab driver to take him to a place where he could get a drink, and the taxicab driver took him to a joint where he was given a mickey finn, which knocked him out. And then he was taken down this road along the Whangpoo River and stripped of practically everything including his clothing, except his underwear, and there he had been found by some people passing by and turned in to this tavern.

Q: They left him on the road?

Adm. W.: The man who robbed him left him on the road, but the people who found him carried him to this tavern.

Q: But he had just been left unconscious on the road?

Adm. W.: Left unconscious on the road.

Q: What time of year was this?

Adm. W.: This was about, I'd say, October. It was pretty chilly then. When Mason and I found him, he was still suffering from the effects of this drink and didn't seem to quite know what was going on.

Q: Did the police, then, take him into the police station, and that's where you found him?

Adm. W.: No. The police told us that he had been found down in this tavern, and he was still there, and we went down to the tavern and found him. We got him some clothes and took him back to the hotel and, inasmuch as there was no Empress liner leaving for a couple of weeks, we made arrangements and after getting permission from Admiral Strauss, the then-Commander-in-Chief of the Asiatic Fleet, to return to the United States by Europe, and that is what brought about the change in my after life.

Q: I just have to inquire, did Lieutenant Commander Howell

our big game on New Year's Day. So New Year's Day rolled around and we were right in the midst of this game, when the word came that the military governor had just been beheaded. Excuse me for laughing, but that was China in the old days. When one War lord felt he had accumulated sufficient strength to do so he just beheaded the reigning war lord and that was that.

Q: Did that stop the football game?

Adm. W.: That stopped the football game because we immediately began to get concerned about the Americans, whether they were going to have the proper protection. We got the crew back to the ship and sent guards out to various places and so on. On the way to the university, I remember looking up overhead and seeing on top of one of the gates to the city all the heads up there, there were several heads up there on spikes. Things happen in China that you never would imagine. For instance, there was a very nice little woman who had married the Vice Consul in Changsha, and she had just come out, she had never been to China before, she had no preparation for this. They were living in the consulate, and one morning she opened the window and looked out and there was a man out there in front who was beheading Chinese on the bund, what they call the bund, which is the waterfront.

Wheeler #2 - 56

Interview No. 2 with Rear Admiral Charles J. Wheeler
Date: 19 July 1969
By: Etta Belle Kitchen

Q: Last time we were still on the Yangtze and, in order to finish it up, I wonder if you might have some other anecdotes that would be helpful concerning your experiences on the river?

Adm. W.: Well, the Yale-in-China University was a missionary effort which was conducted, of course, by Yale University. The President of the university was a charming gentleman. He had a very attractive family and lived on the campus. In addition there were four young graduates of Yale University and I understand that two were usually changed every year. They would send out two new graduates from Yale University. The students were all Chinese.

Q: How large was the student body?

Adm. W.: I would guess anywhere between 300 and 500. It was a small effort, but a very effective one from all I could learn.

Q: Was it a four-year college?

Adm. W.: Oh, yes, and they had a very fine hospital in which I was hospitalized after getting a blister that turned into blood poisoning, and I had marvelous care by Chinese nurses and their assistants. So that, from my standpoint, the whole

Adm. W.: After leaving Chungking on the return journey down-river, the captain appointed my relief who had already arrived on board, and me to conduct a complete inspection of the entire ship. This was done because the American guboats were the only vessels on the Yangtze River that were not inspected by the Chinese Customs Service. The reason for that is that the Navy regulations do not permit any foreign organization or person to inspect U.S. naval vessels. The Navy ships were, therefore, constantly under suspicion of transporting opium which, unfortunately, sometimes they did because the officers didn't know that it was on board.

Q: Would it have been brought on board by the Chinese?

Adm. W.: It would have been brought on board by the Chinese people of whom, as I said, we had ten or twelve in various capacities. All these Chinese lived in the very after portion of the ship, where we also had some stores - reserve supplies, you might say - and it was usually in this area which was not frequented by Americans, officers or men, that the opium was hidden, and, as I said before, our skipper, Lieutenant Commander Howell, did not want any untoward incidents to occur with regard to the transporting of opium. In obedience to his orders, I began at the bow of the ship and my relief began at the stern of the ship, and we conducted this inspection. Before very long, my relief discovered opium hidden in 50-gallon drums of coffee. It was packaged in small cakes and wrapped around with tinfoil or something of that nature, and the coffee had been poured in over it - that is, placed over it, so that it wasn't - it would not be - noticeable to anyone who was not conducting a careful search. All of this opium was brought up on deck and the captain placed a guard over it, a sentry.

Q: Do you have any idea how much there was?

Adm. W.: It was estimated at that time that the opium would have been worth in Ichang $50,000, in Shanghai $100,000, and in America $500,000. The opium was a kind of a sticky material which had to be covered, as I said, by tinfoil or something like that. I don't recall actually the number of packages that there were, but there were many.

The Chinese, of course, were very wrought up about this. As a matter of fact, some of them could be seen crying on the fantail, which is what we called the after part of the ship, and we were afraid that in spite of the sentry there might be some violent activity on board. As we passed through the Yangtze Gorges, where the current, as I previously mentioned, is very swift, the captain had these packages thrown overboard one by one, so that there could be no question of any of this getting to Shanghai, or any other port on the Yangtze. I always thought that this was very commendable on the part of our skipper because the Chinese Customs Service does pay a considerable sum when caches like this are found and brought to the attention of the customs authorities. But Captain Howell decided that he would forego any reward that he might receive in order to prevent any violence occurring on board the ship.

completely recover?

Adm. W.: He recovered after a few days and we found that we could get passage on a Chinese coastal steamer to Amoy, strangely enough, our first stop was Amoy, which is the place where I was married eight years later. We also stopped at Swatow and Hong Kong. From Hong Kong, we visited Canton and the only thing I can remember there of interest was our visit to the City of the Dead, which was a kind of a cemetery where the Chinese kept their dead in coffins above ground until the Chinese soothsayer informed them that it was a propitious time to bury them.

From Canton we took another steamer to - from Hong Kong, we took another steamer to Singapore and, at that point we made a rule that we would, upon arrival in any new place, hire a taxi and rive around and if we didn't like the looks of the place, we would leave as soon as possible, and we didn't care much for Singapore. We did have dinner at the Raffles Hotel. Before that we had discovered that there was a British India steamer leaving that night for Rangoon, so we booked passage on that, the last two remaining berths, as a matter of fact, and set sail for Rangoon, where we spent several days and we found very interesting, but nothing out of the ordinary. From Rangoon we went to Calcutta, and we didn't care too much for that, so we arranged to take a train after dinner that night for Agra, where the Taj Mahal is located. The only interesting experience that came out of that journey was we didn't realize that at that time the sleeping cars provided no bedding. All they had was what looked to us like shelves running fore and aft along the car, and each of the other travelers, mostly Englishmen, of course, had their bedding roll with them. Of course, we had no bedding rolls and we were the butt of English jokes by these other travelers who finally took pity on us and lent us a blanket a piece, in which we rolled ourselves up and turned in on these shelves which were otherwise only hard boards.

Q: Were there dividers between the passengers?

Adm. W.: No. It was an open car. Then, we were surprised, having always thought of India as a very hot country, at how cool it got that night and were very thankful for the blankets. When we arrived in Agra, we were faced with the same difficulty because not only the railroad trains had no bedding, but many of the hotels had no bedding. The Englishmen, having had the custom wherever they went, were carrying their own bedding rolls. Somehow or other we managed to get fixed up, so we were fairly comfortable and, of course, did all the sights, including the Taj Mahal which, it goes without saying, is a very magnificent building. We learned for the first time, and I don't think many people know that Shah Jahan who built the Taj Mahal for his wife, with whom he was very much in love, had also planned to build another Taj Mahal for himself across the river, built of black stone, and these two buildings were to have been connected by a silver bridge, but the populace resented this terrific expenditure and he died before anything more was completed, and both his wife, Mumtaz and himself are buried in the Taj Mahal.

From there we went on to Delhi and did the sights there, which, of course, are well known to many travelers. I think the thing that impressed me most was that it was obvious that the Indians had thought of air conditioning long before we did because they had, in their palaces, water troughs running through their principal rooms, through which running water was always flowing, and this, of course, added materially to keeping the temperature down - one of the earliest forms of air conditioning. From Delhi we went to Rangoon and took our ship from there, which carried us as far as Port Said, stopping en route at Aden and Suez. From Port Said we visited the Holy Land, which is about like it has been described by many others, but we did have an interesting experience when we got to Port Said, from which we were going to Alexandria. We had left our luggage alongside the porter's desk and went in to have lunch before our ship was due to sail, but it appeared that another ship which was sailing about the same time but a little earlier than ours had a number of passengers who had collected round this porter's desk about the time that we were having lunch. And when we came out from lunch our luggage was gone, and we were informed by the porter that the only thing that could have happened to it was that it had been picked up by some of the people who were leaving on the earlier ship. So we hastily got a taxi and rushed down to the waterfront, got a water taxi, and chased this ship down the harbor.

Q: It had already departed?

Adm. W.: It had already departed, but we waved frantically at the bridge. The captain paid no attention to us at first, but we kept at it and he finally stopped the ship and lowered a gangway, and we went on board and found our luggage at the purser's desk.

From Port Said we went to Alexandria and then to - the ship stopped at Piraeus, from which of course we visited Athens on the way and Smyrna, thence through the Dardanelles to Constantinople. One interesting feature of the trip was that my friend, Lieutenant Commander Howell, and I had packed our uniforms at the bottom of our trunks and we posed as rich Americans traveling around the world, and we had lots of fun with the girls along the route.

My first glimpse of Istanbul, then called Constantinople, was from the porthole of an Italian steamer at anchor near Leander's Tower in the Bosporus. In the early morning of November 28, 1921. Nothing was visible except the tops of the minarets of the hundreds of mosques which dot the area, as the surface of the city, the Bosporus, and the Golden Horn were covered with a thick blanket of fog. Little did I know at that time that I was to make my home there for three years. Constantinople, at any time, is fascinating but it happened at that time to be an area in which the entire history was to change its course from what it had been for the past hundreds of years. My former shipmate and I, Glen Howell, were not expected and so we hired caiques, which is the term for native boats, and were rowed ashore to the dock where we engaged Turkish porters called hamals, who loaded our baggage into a

Turkish victoria called an arriba, by means of which we were transported to the Pera Palace Hotel. We had planned to spend only a few days in Constantinople and were going to see as many of the sights as we could. That evening, while we were dressing for dinner, a friend whom we did not even know was in Constantinople knocked on the door and came in with the astonishing news that Admiral Bristol would like to see us the next morning.

Q: Where was Admiral Bristol? What was he doing there?

Adm. W.: Admiral Bristol was the high commissioner of the United States to Turkey. He was not called ambassador because the United States and Turkey had severed relations soon after World War I broke out, and they had not yet been resumed. So Admiral Bristol had the title of high commissioner, but he carried out all the duties of an ambassador.

We told Ham, which is the name that all of his friends knew him by - Hamilton Bryan - that we were planning to go out and see the Russian restaurants and all of the sights of the night life of Constantinople that evening. He said that he knew them all and would be glad to escort us around, which he did. The next morning when we were supposed to go and see Admiral Bristol at 10 o'clock, neither one of us was really in the mood, having been up a large part of the night, and my friend Howell absolutely refused to go because, he said, he was going to get back to the United States as soon as possible because he was trying to persuade a girl in New York to marry him. I said I would go and talk to Admiral Bristol, which I did.

I would like to correct the sequence of our first day in that soon after we arrived at the Pera Palace Hotel and got unpacked, I remarked to my friend, Glen Howell, that I wanted to go and make a call at the American Embassy, which was only a few doors away. Howell agreed with that, and so we presented ourselves at the door of the Embassy where we were confronted with the doorman dressed in gold braid and a very fancy uniform, who was called the kavass, and we gave him our cards to deliver to Admiral and Mrs. Bristol. I was rather astonished, actually, when he took the cards and went off with them, because my experience with embassies has been that they generally just lay them down and say that the ambassador or his wife, or whoever it is, is not there. The result of this, however, was that in a few minutes the Kavass came back with an invitation from Admiral and Mrs. Bristol to join them at tea, which we did. After staying a little longer than the usual 20 minutes prescribed for an official call, we left and went back to the hotel. While dressing for dinner that evening, Lieutenant Bryan whom I mentioned before, came to our door and informed us that Admiral Bristol would like for us to come and see him the next morning at 10 o'clock. We replied that we would take that matter under consideration, but that right now we were getting ready to go out and see the town, and Bryan offered to escort us, which he did, as previously stated.

The next morning I went over to see Admiral Bristol and was invited to remain on his staff as aide and flag lieutenant. I was completely taken aback at this because, being on my way home, where my mother and father were expecting me, I did not plan to be delayed. So I asked Admiral Bristol how long he thought I would remain in Constantinople if I accepted his kind offer. He said, well, not more than six months. The extraordinary part of that was, however, that I stayed three years and he stayed almost three years after that. But the three years that I spent were among the most interesting and delightful of my entire naval career. Mrs. Bristol had been a school mate of my mother's in our home town of Mobile, Alabama, which was the reason for my desire to go and call on both Admiral and Mrs. Bristol that afternoon. Mrs. Bristol was a very lovely, attractive lady and our family and hers had known each other for many years in Mobile, which at that time had changed very little from the way it had been many years before. Mobile was under five flags at various times in its history, and a good deal of the foreign atmosphere in appearance and customs and manners was still preserved, so that those of us who come from Mobile have a very real bond.

Having spent most of my time since World War I either in Guantanamo, Cuba, where the fleet trained during the winter, or in the Orient, I was not aware of the tremendous changes that were going on in the Near East. After World War I was over, Mustapha Kemal became the dominant figure in Turkey. He, as will be recalled, was the hero of the Dardanelles during the Gallipoli Campaign. A man of middle class origin with very few advantages in his education, he had a fixed desire to free Turkey from the yoke of the sultans, and left no stone unturned to that end. After the two leading characters, who were mere puppets of the Germans in World War I, escaped Turkey, Mustapha Kemal began his campaign to overthrow the sultan and his government.

Q: What was the sultan's name then?

Adm. W.: Mahomed VI. The Treaty of Sevres, which was designed to settle the differences between the Allies and Turkey, really called for the dismemberment of Turkey. There would have been nothing left of the Sevres Treaty, except Anatolia, which is the part of Turkey in Asia Minor, and Constantinople. All of eastern Thrace, Macedonia, Syria, Palestine, Mesopotomia, Egypt, and all of the countries bordering the Mediterranean which had been under Turkish jurisdiction, would have been dismembered from Turkey. In addition, the crowning blow provided for the Greeks to occupy the city of Smyrna. The city of Smyrna was to Turkey what New York is to the United States: it was the leading commercial port, and the Turks, under the leadership of Mustapha Kemal, determined that this was not to be. However, under the guns of British battleships, the Greeks landed and occupied Smyrna. Not only that, they began incursions into Anatolia as far as the Sakarya River, which is not far from Ankara, where Mustapha Kemal made his headquarters.

Q: We know the capital now as Ankara, don't we?

Adm. W.: It was known in those days as Angora, and is now called

Ankara.

Q: But, at that time, Constantinople was still the capital?

Adm. W.: At that time, Constantinople was still the official capital, where the Sultan Mahomed VI resided.

Q: Why was it moved to Ankara?

Adm. W.: Because Mustapha Kemal felt that as long as the capital remained in Constantinople it would be subject to foreign influence and intrigue, and he was not going to have any of that. He wanted to have complete control of the government and he felt that he couldn't as long as the capital remained in Constantinople.

Q: So that somewhat gives us the political situation that existed when you went there?

Adm. W.: That's right. Admiral Bristol had been ordered to Turkey in 1919 as an observer. Before World War I, there were a great many Americans in Turkey, some of whom were connected with relief organizations, some were missionaries, and a good many were connected with tobacco firms, which imported Turkish tobacco from the shores of the Black Sea.

Admiral Bristol arrived in Constantinople on board the Schley, a destroyer, in January 1919. He was known in naval parlance as the Senior Naval Officer present, which conferred certain prerogatives upon a naval officer that his mere rank does not. His reports of conditions there, his cooperation with Americans, were so good that he was soon thereafter made

Wheeler #2 - 74

High Commissioner, which, as I said before, was the only title he could be given at that time, because there were no diplomatic relations with Turkey, but he was our Ambassador in everything but name. Admiral Bristol had a staff of nine naval officers, of which I was one, two military attaches, two commercial attaches, a counsel of embassy, a first secretary, a second secretary, and one or more third secretaries.

Q: And where were all of these housed?

Adm. W.: All the staff officers had their offices in the chancery which was just behind the Embassy. The American Embassy was located of course, in Constantinople before World War I began. This building belonged to the United States and was being used as a consulate when Admiral Bristol arrived, but his activities were so extensive that the consulate was soon moved out to another address, and he took over the entire Embassy. My duties were those of aide and Flag Lieutenant, and as such, I lived on the top floor of the Embassy and had charge of the admiral's automobiles, his barges, his orchestra his servants, his appointments; and also attended him wherever he went on official occasions.

Q: That gave you a wonderful opportunity to see all phases of Turkish life, social and official as well, I assume.

Adm. W.: Exactly. That's right. His naval officers consisted of a chief of staff, at that time Captain A. J. Hepburn, who later became commander-in-chief of the United States fleet, assistant Chief of Staff, Lieutenant Commander T. C. Kincaid, who later became the hero of the second Battle of the Philippine Sea, a flag secretary, a communications officer, an intelligence officer - the other members of the naval staff were not particularly outstanding, as I can recall, but the first secretary of the Embassy was Allen Dulles, who later became the first chief of the Central Intelligence Agency. Major Sherman Miles was the military attache. He was well known in Army circles. Gillespie, who was the commercial attache, was well known as a traveler in Near Eastern lands. I don't recall any more who were later heard from, but it was a very fine cohesive staff, all of whom worked very, very well with Admiral Bristol, and they all adored him. Gillespie was later killed in Perala for photographing a religious ceremony.

One of the unique features of this period in Constantinople was that practically all of the leading figures among the foreign diplomats and military men had their wives with them, which together with the Turkish imperial family and some of the leading Greeks, French, and other residents, really made a glittering society.

Q: Where were the social events located?

Adm. W.: The social events were so numerous that it's almost impossible to describe them. There was something going on every night, either at some embassy or on board some ship or at someone's private house. In addition to that, there were theatrical performances given by both the Turks and the Greeks, and a number of very beautiful Russian cabarets, and people, as we were all much younger in those days, and there was a great deal of activity everywhere. There were receptions, dinners, suppers, charity bazaars, every conceivable sort of entertainment, which took up oftentimes five evenings a week, and in addition to that, in good weather, there would be picnics to one of the lovely places in the area, which were beautiful for picnics, such as the Black Forest, which lay on the north side - the northwest side - of Constantinople between the city and the Black Sea, which was a favorite picnic spot. There were the Princess Islands in the Sea of Marmora, which had many beautiful locations for picnics to which we often journeyed in the Admiral's barge. It seems a little difficult to remember all these places, but I remember one evening particularly which I shall never forget as long as I live. It was the occasion of the dinner given for Admiral and Mrs. Bristol in the old Russian Embassy at Bebec, which was a town on the western side of the Bosporus, where the Russian Embassy was located. This embassy was on the top of a hill overlooking the Bosporus, and this party took place on a beautiful moonlight night in the summer, which I never expect to see duplicated. The party was given really for Mrs. Bristol who had headed up the Russian Relief for Czarist refugees who had come to Constantinople from both the Denikin and Wrangel evacuations from southern Russia. When I arrived in November of 1921, there were literally thousands of these Russian refugees in evidence throughout the area. As a matter of fact, one old Turkish barracks, which had been evacuated by the Turkish troops under the terms of the armistice, was made available to the Russian refugees. This particular barracks was on the Asiatic side and there were many of them living on the European side. For example, Many the leaders of the Czarist refugees lived in the Russian Embassy in Constantinople, which was in the downtown area, and in order to accommodate more of the refugees they had even hung blankets as partitions in the ballroom of the Russian Embassy. Now, I've got a little off my story, because I was telling about this party which took place in the old Russian Embassy grounds above the city of Bebec.

The dinner was a typically Russian dinner, where they began at 8 o'clock with what they called cold sakuskas, cold cocktail relishes. About 9 o'clock they served hot sakuskas or cocktail relishes. The actual dinner began about 10.00 p.m. There were seven or eight courses. During this entire evening wine was served throughout the dinner and there were Russian entertainers, dancers and singers, who performed throughout. The scene was particularly outstanding in that the moon shone through the trees down on this table which was located in a garden at the entrance of the Embassy building itself. The whole affair was so beautiful and romantic that, as I say, I never expect to see it duplicated. Well, at any rate, after the dinner was over, I took the arm of a very attractive young Italian girl, who was the daughter of the Italian general commanding the Italian forces of occupation in Constantinople. She was a particular friend of mine and had been invited on my account. As a matter of fact, there were many people who thought that I was engaged to her, including Mrs. Bristol, but Mrs. Bristol, who, as I said, had been a great friend of my mother's was not about to have me become matrimonially entangled with any foreigner, came up to me and took my arm, took me away from this young lady and said, "No, you don't. You're walking down to the landing with me, Julian," thereby probably preventing an almost certain foreign alliance.

Q: You really had intentions of becoming engaged to the girl?

Adm. W.: Not actually, but I mean - at that time I didn't really know, but I was quite smitten.

Q: You were young and impressionable.

Adm. W.: Yes. Well, now let me see. Speaking of this young lady reminds me that I omitted to mention at the beginning that when I arrived in Constantinople, the city was occupied by the Allies, that is to say, the French, British, Italians, and Greeks had both troops occupying the city and naval ships at anchor in the Bosporus. This had followed the surrender, of course, of the Turks at the end of World War I, and was intended to safeguard the city throughout the period of the negotiations following the end of the war. The British commander-in-chief, General Harrington, was also in command of the entire allied forces of occupation. We, as Americans, had no troops in Constantinople, but we did have a number of naval ships which had followed Admiral Bristol as he gained influence in Turkey as High Commissioner. As a matter of fact, he had two titles - he wore two hats, that is to say - he was not only High Commissioner to Turkey, but he was also in command of the U.S. naval detachment in Turkish waters at that time. It consisted of about 20 destroyers, a repair ship, destroyer tender, a provision ship, and the naval yacht Scorpion. The

Scorpion was his flagship. It had been in Constantinople throughout the war in an inactive status. Before World War I, it was known as a stationnaire. Each of the leading powers had a similar ship retained in the Bosporus at the command, so to speak, of the diplomatic representatives of their country, and the purpose of these ships was to assure the safety of the embassy personnel. This had been agreed upon at an early treaty, when the Turks had threatened some of the embassy personnel, and the great powers felt that in order to be sure that their embassy people would be safe, they insisted on having these naval yachts.

Q: And that was before World War I?

Adm. W.: This was before World War I, yes. So when World War I was over, these ships were recommissioned and retained in the area until the final treaty was agreed upon. Admiral Bristol flew his flag from this Scorpion which remained in the area and did very little cruising because of the fact that it had been laid up for so long and it needed considerable repairs.

Q: Did the men on the destroyers have their familites there?

Adm. W.: No. The men on the destroyers did not. Some of the officers had their families come over at their own expense, but there were not very many of those.

Q: Mainly the Americans [women], then, were related to the Embassy staff?

Wheeler #2 - 80

Adm. W.: Mainly the Americans were related to the Embassy staff, *connected* except for the businessmen, relief workers and missionaries.

Q: How did the Turkish people react to this occupation by the various national powers?

Adm. W.: They obviously didn't like it but they couldn't do anything about it because they were a defeated nation, and they had no way to avoid it.

Q: Did you know any Turkish people?

Adm. W.: We knew quite a number of them. Prince Osman Fuad, whose picture is over there, *in my study* and his wife were particular friends of ours. She was an Egyptian princess before she married Prince Osman Fuad, who was the fifth in line to the Sultan. It was before *the Sultanate* it was done away with. They were a delightful couple, and we often had them to dinners and receptions, and so forth, at our Embassy. We also had many other Turkish friends who were equally delightful and quite friendly with Americans. The prevailing idea in the United States of the terrible Turk is a great misfortune because throughout my entire period in Turkey I never saw any evidence whatsoever of the so-called terrible Turk. They were an educated, thoroughly charming, delightful, and friendly people.

Q: Did you ever know Mustapha Kemal?

Adm. W.: I never met Mustapha Kemal, but I did go on the train with Admiral Bristol and Mrs. Bristol, and Lieutenant Commander Kincaid and his wife, and Pierpont Moffett, who was third secretary of the Embassy, from Scutari, which was on the

Asiatic side of Constantinople, to Ankara, stopping en route at Afium Kara Hissar, Konia, and several other interesting places. At that time, the American Embassy had in Ankara a representative who was really one of the secretaries probably attached to the American Embassy in Constantinople, but had been delegated by Admiral Bristol to represent him with the new government in Ankara. Admiral Bristol and one of the secretaries went and had a conference with -- more or less a friendly meeting -- with Mustapha Kemal, but there was nothing much more to it than that. After that meeting, in Ankara, though, we continued on by train over what had been planned as the Berlin-to-Baghdad Railway by the Germans in their so-called "drach nach osten," which according to my understanding means the push towards the east, and we went on eastward to Tarsus, where we saw the place where Jonah was supposed to have been buried, and then we boarded a destroyer and visited Rhodes, the island of Rhodes, where we were all entertained by the Italian governor, as Rhodes at that time was under the jurisdiction of Italy. From there, we went to the island of Patmos, which is where St. John is supposed to have seen the revelations in a dream at the monastery at the top of a hill there. We had a rather unusual incident there. Admiral Bristol had sent me ashore in the first boat to Patmos to make arrangements to -- for him and his party to get up to this monastery by donkeys, and I had no sooner landed on the dock, and I had a Greek interpreter with me, and a perfectly strange man came up to me and said, "Is the beautiful Helen Moore Bristol on that ship out there?" And I said, yes, "How did you know that?" He said, "Well, we heard that Admiral Bristol was coming and, you know, I used to run a fruitstand in Mobile, Alabama, on the corner of Conception and St. Francis Streets," which I remembered very well indeed, and he said, "If there's anything I can do, I'd be very happy to arrange for your visit." So, he did. He arranged for the donkeys which took us up to the monastery. And an almost even stranger coincidence was that there was another officer on the ship on which we were traveling who also came from Mobile. So we had a friend take a picture on the island of Patmos in the Mediterranean of the four Mobilians.

Q: Then did you return to Constantinople?

Adm. W.: We returned to Constantinople after that and about that time, as near as I can remember, we - I had a very interesting trip to a place on the Asiatic side, just opposite Therapia, known as the Polish Village. This village is about 10 miles or so inland from the Bosporus. It's entirely inhabited by Polish people who fought on the Turkish side in the Crimean War and were given the land as a reward for their part in helping the Turks in the Crimean War. They were given this plot of land, which is quite extensive, in perpetuity without taxes. It was the strangest feeling riding, as we did, into this area to find a complete Polish village, with Polish-style houses and thatched roofs, contrasting of course with the rather run-down types of Turkish dwellings which we'd seen elsewhere in the area. The occasion for that was a hunting trip where a number of the staff of the Embassy personnel including

myself went out to shoot deer and wild boar. We spent the
night with some of these Poles who treated us very cordially
and fed us delicious Polish food, which was quite a change for
us and was very acceptable.

Q: How large a Polish settlement was it?

Adm. W.: Well, I don't know exactly, but I would guess there
must have been 400 or 500 people there, at least, if not more.
But they kept pretty much to themselves. It was a farming
community, and they I think subsisted large on what they
themselves grew.

Q: That's an item of history that is new to me.

Adm. W.: There are so many of these thing unfortunately -
yes, I think it is unfortunate that they're new [not better known]. One of the
pleasantest experiences that I had was a duty of going out to
meet tourist ships which came in, usually, during the latter
part of February and throughout March with tourists from the
United States on board. They were the big ships, like the
Mauretania, the Homeric, and the well-known transatlantic
liners of that time, which were taken off the transatlantic
run in winter because of the lack of patronage and sent on
these Mediterranean cruises. Many of these passengers had [who were VIPs]
letters of introduction to the VIPs on board [Admiral Bristol], copies of which,
of course, had previously been sent to Admiral Bristol. These
letters of course were from the State Department and when these
vessels arrived, why, Admiral Bristol would give me the
copies of the letters which the State Department had written

to him, and I would take his barge, go out, circle round the ship, thereby creating quite a lot of interest on the part of the tourists, and as soon as they lowered a gangway, as they always did because the ships were too large to go alongside the dock, I would go on board and look up these VIPs, such as the President of United States Steel, and others of that type, including one of the partners of the Brown Brothers, Harriman and Company who, incidentally, was a cousin of mine. I would ask them to attend a reception which Admiral and Mrs. Bristol were giving for them at the embassy that afternoon, which they of course, were delighted to do. Then I would offer my services while they were there and, of course, since they were only there for a few days at a time, they were all very anxious to see the sights, and I would invite them to go ashore with me, where we would be met by several of the embassy cars, and we would go from sight to sight and from mosque to mosque, and other places of interest to satisfy their sightseeing curiosity. As a matter of fact, I think before I left Constantinople I could very easily qualify as a licensed guide.

Q: What were the sultan's palaces in Constantinople...?

Adm. W.: I'm glad you asked that because the sultan, actually, before he was evacuated from Constantinople lived in Yildiz Palace, which was really on the outskirts of Constantinople, in a fairly quiet location, and he remained there in seclusion most of the time, except on Fridays, which is the Moslem religious holiday. You see, in Constantinople there were three holidays. There was the Moslem holiday on Friday, the Jewish holiday on Saturday, and the Christian holiday on Sunday.

Q: That's still true. In Mesopotamia last year, I was impressed that any day you go you find part of the city closed. What did he do on Fridays?

Adm. W.: On Fridays he would have what he called a selamlik, and that was a visit to one of the mosques to pray, and he would be accompanied by his entourage and would travel in a victoria and would be escorted into the mosque by his entourage, where he prayed. The reverse procedure, of course, would take place when he came out. He visited a different mosque every Friday, and when he went back to his palace, there was always an opportunity for VIPs, such as members of the embassy, if they wished to, they could get a card and go to the palace and have coffee, not with the sultan himself, but with his courtiers in one of the palace rooms. They had Turkish coffee with them which was quite an experience, especially for visiting tourists.

I believe I have thus far failed to mention that after Mustapha Kemal gained power in Anatolia, the Turkish sultan, Mahomed VI, realized that Constantinople was becoming a very unhealthy climate for him, and he therefore asked the British commanding general, General Harrington, to assist him to escape. Arrangements were made, therefore, for the sultan to leave in the early morning in the British battleship Malaya - HMS Malaya - and it is believed that he went to Switzerland, although I never heard of him after that.

Wheeler #2 - 86

Q: Well, who was the sultan who went to pray each Friday?

Adm. W.: That was he. His name was Sultan Mahomed VI. He had grey hair and wore a very elaborate uniform of scarlet and gold like a Turkish military officer only more elaborate.

Q: Did you ever see the sultan?

Adm. W.: Oh, yes many times.

Q: At what time did he decide that he should leave for his health?

Adm. W.: It was after Mustapha Kemal had established his own Turkish parliament and had chased the Greeks out of Smyrna, and Turkish bayonets were visible in the sunlight on the hills of Scutari, just across the Bosporus from Constantinople.

Q: That seemed like a good time to leave?

Adm. W.: That seemed like a good time to leave, and - the interesting thing, however, that occurred then was that immediately after his departure, Mustapha Kemal, who is now called the ghazi, which means the conqueror, came out with an edict to the effect that the normal successor to the sultan would not be called the sultan, he would be called the caliph. The sultan, of course, previously had two functions. He was the governmental ruler of the Ottoman Empire, and he was also the head of the Moslem religion, in other words, you might say the pope of the Moslems. We all wondered whether Mustapha Kemal could get away with that, because we felt that there might be some repercussions on the part of very devout Moslems because they had been so accustomed to having the sultan be also the caliph. The incident, however, passed off without any difficulty whatsoever.

Q: Does "caliph" have a meaning?

Adm. W.: Caliph is pope. The caliph is the head of the Moslem religion in Turkey. And when the Ottoman Empire included Syria, Mesopotamia, Palestine and Egypt he was the religious head of all three countries.

Q: But the people didn't seem to...?

Adm. W.: The people didn't seem to mind it at all. The man who would have become sultan in the ordinary course of events was Abdul Mejid, and he is the one that became the caliph. He took up his residence in the Dolma Batche Palace, instead of Yildiz, and was seen on many occasions. As a matter of fact, both of his aides, Captain Ekrem Bey, his military aide, and Nazim, his naval aide, were good friends of mine. I used to go oftentimes with Admiral Bristol when he went to call on Abdul Mejid. Well Abdul Mejid didn't suffer a much better fate than Mahomed VI, because, later on, when the Nationalists, which is the name for the party that Mustapha Kemal founded, gained still more power and were able to demand that the Turks - that the Allies - leave Constantinople as a result of the Lausanne Treaty, Abdul Mejid was notified at 10 o'clock one evening that he had two hours to gather up such possessions as he could take with him, including one wife - he had to choose one out of four that he had, and it's interesting to note that he chose the youngest one, who had been the daughter of one of his gardeners - and he and his wife and such possessions as the two of them, I suppose, could carry with them were put into a car, and he was taken to the Bulgarian border, where he was put on the train for parts west. I think he also went to Switzerland and, as far as I'm concerned, was never heard of again. The remaining imperial princes and princesses were given two weeks in which to clear out, and they could only take with them such things as they could carry in their hands, or baggage, and everything they left behind was confiscated by the new Nationalist government. I remember a very sad occasion when we all went - when I say "we" I mean the staff of the embassy, including Admiral Bristol - to the station to see these imperial princes and princesses off to their destinations. Many of them, including Ozman Fuad and Princess Kerime, his wife, were very great friends of ours, and it was really quite a tearful occasion, because these people, of course, were leaving their homes and, insofar as they knew, for ever, leaving most of their possessions behind.

Q: I want to ask you one question: it has been my observation that many times, military people live in but are not necessarily part of a political situation. Now, in your situation, how much were you aware of the transition from the sultanate to the republic?

Adm. W.: We were quite aware, because we knew a great many of these officials who were quite close to Mustapha Kemal. Adnan Bey and his wife, Halide Hanoum, were great friends of Admiral Bristol whom he entertained at the embassy and I met them all.

Q: You say that the people whose names you're giving me now were friends of Mustapha Kemal?

Adm. W.: Friends of Mustapha Kemal, of the new regime, and there were others. I can't remember all of their names, but we were pretty well informed as to what was going on, which is one of the things that made it so interesting, because of course I was the one who arranged for all of these appointments. As a matter of fact, another interesting incident of my career - of my Constantinople career - which began very early in the game because one of the questions asked by Admiral Bristol when he first invited me to serve on his staff, was if I could speak French. I said I could speak a little Naval Academy French, and he said, "Well, you'd better brush up on it." Eight languages were spoken in Constantinople altogether. English was spoken among the foreign colony quite generally, although French was still the diplomatic language, and was the language used between the Turks of the sultan's regime, rather than English, which was used by the Nationalist regime. A day or so after I took over the duties of flag lieutenant, the Sublime Porte, which was the name given to the sultan's office of foreign affairs, called up and this Turkish gentleman, in absolutely perfect French, asked me if he could have an appointment with Admiral Bristol. Fortunately, I was able to see that through, but that one experience was enough to impress upon me the need for brushing up on my French, so I took about five lessons a week for several months, three at the Berlitz and I had a French - Swiss-French - woman who gave lessons come to the embassy several afternoons a week and give me French conversation, so I was able in a few months to handle occasions like that and also to carry on a conversation at official parties and things like that, although not very fluently, I could get by sufficiently to carry on with my job.

Q: You were very much aware of the political changes being made...

Adm. W.: Very much aware. We were kept informed through these contacts that Admiral Bristol had. Admiral Bristol was a very remarkable man. He was a very fair man, a very straight-laced man, and he never trimmed. That is to say, he would never move from side to side in order to gain what he thought was favor with that side. It was a very difficult position, and I knew this, because, as I say, I was the one who made these appointments. He would have people come to see him who were on the side of the sultan's party and, then, sometimes, the very next man who would come in to see him would be on the side of the Nationalist Party. Oh, there were a great many things on the rolls there that required sort of legal adjudication.

Q: Did the United States government try to wheel and deal in...?

Adm. W.: They never tried to wheel and deal in any of this. They were absolutely straightforward in this thing, and the result was that Admiral Bristol was greatly admired by everyone. I don't know anyone, even his enemies, if he had any, I don't recall any, but if he did, but I mean even the people that were not on the same side that the incoming government was on, respected him enormously, because they knew they could absolutely trust him. They knew that he was absolutely square, and that he could be depended upon. His word was as good as gold.

Q: How did you feel about the opposing party?

Adm. W.: Well, my sympathies were all with the Nationalists. I think nearly all of our sympathies were with the Nationalists, because the sultan's government, of course, was just a sort of historic regime which had lost power. The people were not behind them. The only adherents he had were the sort of palace gang, you know, and, of course, the imperial family - they were all behind him and like that. But the great bulk of the people were supporting Mustapha Kemal, and I think everybody realized that that was the way things were going.

Q: The sultan really represented ancient civilization almost, didn't he?

Adm. W.: Yes, despotism and that sort of thing. And the surprising thing was that we had these very close friends on both sides. We had them because, actually, they knew that we had no axe to grind. We were not trying to get anything from the Turks, and we were only there to look out for the - for our interests, which as I said before, only had to do with some businesses and some missionaries and relief workers and people like that.

Q: Did you ever see any of the sultan's palaces inside?

Wheeler #2 - 92

Adm. W.: I went through all of them.

Q: Were the sultans living there then?

Adm. W.: No. The palaces in which the sultan lived were never opened to be shown, but after he left, why, they were opened up, and we were specially invited to go and see the palaces, not as tourists but as members of the embassy.

Q: The one now which has such fabulous collections of jewels and fantastic objects of indescribable wealth, I am told, used to be a harem.

Adm. W.: Well, that is probably the seraglio. The seraglio was never occupied by any sultan while we were there. That was over in what we used to call Stamboul, that was the Turkish section of the city.

Q: Did you ever see a harem?

Adm. W.: I went through a harem at the seraglio, yes. It wasn't occupied, but of course you've been through there and you know what it's like. It's a museum really is what it is.

Q: And was it a museum when you saw it?

Adm. W.: No. Well, I mean, it wasn't used. It was a place to see on any sightseeing tour. One of the fabulous experiences that I had was going to Santa Sofia on what they called at that time the Night of Power. It occurred during Ramadan, which is the most prominent Moslem festival, and at that time Santa Sofia was a mosque. Of course, as you know, it had been built many hundreds of years before as a Christian church, which is where it got its name - Santa Sofia - but the Turks had covered up all of the murals and converted it into a mosque.

Q: But it was built with minarets originally, wasn't it, even though it was a Christian church? Were the minarets added later?

Adm. W.: The minarets were added later. But on this night of Ramadan, we had special seats - and when I say "we" I mean the embassy personnel - up in the balcony, and as we looked down on this multitude of Turks - I don't know what the capacity of that Santa Sofia was, but there must have been thousands of Turks, two or three thousand, at least - praying on their knees, praying to Allah, and the place was all lighted up, of course, and there was an air of sort of festivity about the whole thing. Although dignified festivity, if you know what I mean, it wasn't gayety or anything like that. It was a religious festival, and it was really a very impressive. Of course, no one will ever see that again, because a short time after I left, Santa Sofia was closed as a mosque and all of the brass plates covering the beautiful frescoes and mosaics and things inside were removed and renovated, and it's one of the show places of Constantinople. One of the people who was there after I left told me that, and it shows the way the Turks do things, this place had been used as a mosque the day before, and the next day people went over to look at it and there was a sign hanging outside, "This museum is closed."

Overnight they tried to make a museum out of it. One of the other interesting sights over in that same neighborhood was the cisterns. Did you see the cisterns?

Q: No, I don't identify it by that name.

Adm. W.: Well, the cisterns were an underground waterworks which had been built in the time of the Eastern Roman Empire to retain water in case the city was besieged. You could go down there - they had artificial lights - and row around. The water was still there, which is interesting from the standpoint of thinking back to the old days and how they had to provide for every contingency like sieges and things like that.

Q: Those old walls are so fascinating, I think.

Adm. W.: Yes, I think they are. As you probably know, Constantinople was taken by the Turks, the Ottoman Turks, in 1453. The Turks had captured most of the surrounding country before that. You can see on the Asiatic side of the Bosporus the remains of a fort called Anatoli Hissar, which means Anatolian Fort, I imagine, and right directly opposite are the remains even better preserved of another fort which the Turks built called Roumeli Hissar, which means European Fort. Then, when the - so that, in effect, the entire city was surrounded before it actually fell to the Turks, and one of the defenses that the Constantine defenders made was to have a chain extend from the Constantinople side of the Golden Horn, which is an inlet of the Bosporus, to the Stamboul side, with the idea of preventing Turkish boats from cruising up the Golden Horn and attacking - outflanking it, so to speak, don't you see. I couldn't see the chain, of course, but I could picture the whole campaign, so to speak, from my room at the top of the embassy, which overlooked the Golden Horn.

Q: That would have been to the west of you?

Adm. W.: No, that was to the east, as I recall. Then, of course, the final assault on the city was through the walls on the land side of Stamboul. Stamboul, at that time, was the main part of Constantinople. What is now the new part of Constantinople, I don't think was very much used at that time. The main city, as I say, was in Stamboul.

Q: Around where all the big mosques are.

Adm. W.: Around where the big mosques are. They show you now where the hippodrome used to be, which was used of course in the days of the Eastern Roman emperors.

Q: It's an unbelievably fascinating city, isn't it?

Adm. W.: Yes.

Q: It's been fought over by how many civilizations?

Adm. W.: It certainly was. Speaking of the sultan and his family reminds me that after the sultan left, it was rumored that two of General Harrington's aides, I mentioned General Harrington was the allied commander of the forces of occupation, had been appointed keepers of the sultanas, because of course the sultan didn't take all of his wives with him either. The caliph only took one, and I don't know how many the sultan took, but he had a good many more than the caliph did, so there were some left behind, and it was rumored in the area among the foreign colony that these two boys were appointed keepers of the sultanas. About that time a very charming lady [Mrs. Stedman] who was a great friend of Admiral and Mrs. Bristol came to Constantinople to visit them. She was the widow of a very wealthy man who had been in the tobacco business, and she was quite an excitable person, wanted to see everything and wanted to be in on everything, and so we thought we'd have a little fun with her. We cooked up a scheme by which she was to meet one of the sultanas, through the good offices of one of General Harrington's aides. Mrs. Stedman was actually living in the Pera Palace Hotel, which as I said earlier was only a few blocks from the embassy. So it was arranged that this meeting should take place in one of the Pera Palace Hotel rooms on a certain afternoon when the sultana would come to tea. So we got the two aides, British aides who were great friends of ours, and we dressed up one of Admiral Bristol's aides, who was a very goodlooking, small chap, who had often played the part of ladies in the masquerades shows at the Naval Academy. We dressed him up as a lady, complete in black dress with Turkish tcharchoffs and everything like that - tcharchoffs, that's a headgear. So, at the appointed time, Mrs. Bristol and I escorted Lieutenant Commander Merrill into the Pera Palace Hotel. Admiral Bristol would have nothing whatsoever to do with this. Mrs. Bristol was in on it, and she and I escorted Merrill dressed as the sultana to the Pera Palace Hotel and to the suite that Mrs. Stedman was occupying. She had invited many of her friends. There were at least ten or fifteen and maybe twenty of the embassy staff sitting round the sitting room in this suite. I knocked on the door and Mrs. Stedman saw the "sultana" there all dressed up in Turkish costume, and she bowed and scraped and said "how-do-you do" in her atrocious French, which was pretty hard to take. Then she went around and introduced everybody to the "sultana," you know. Well, that part was fine. It went off fine.

Q: What did the man - how did he speak?

Adm. W.: He spoke in French.

Q: Did he disguise his voice or something?

Adm. W.: Yes, he disguised his voice. It was very well done. He didn't have much to say, you know, but he said a few things like "Enchanté" or something like that. Then the sultana was seated and Virginia Stedman asked everybody if they'd like to have a cocktail, and they all said yes. Then she asked the sultana if she'd have a cocktail. Well, of course, the Turks are not supposed to drink but we knew they often did, and Tip Merrill who was playing the part of the sultana was not known for refusing drinks. In fact, I don't think he ever had been known to refuse one. Up to that time, everything had been very decorous and everything like that. Virginia Stedman thought this was the sultana and she was just so thrilled. She was all atwitter, you know. When she invited Tip Merrill to have a drink and he said, no, somebody snickered. That was just more than anybody could stand. Then the cat was out of the bag, and I felt so sorry for Mrs. Stedman. It was really a mean trick. She just burst into tears. We all had a lot of fun out of it anyhow.

Q: Did she ever forgive you?

Adm. W.: Oh, yes. She went on around the world and in Calcutta she met the American Consul, whose name I can't remember, and was married there to him. She came back to this country and was flying high, wide, and handsome, with all her money and his prestige. I think he was later minister or ambassador to some country. Then they were both killed in a terrible railroad wreck. An awful comedown.

Well, from the naval standpoint, it might be interesting to note that Admiral Bristol's dual assignment as high commissioner and commander of the naval forces in Turkish waters led to some rather amusing contretemps in this respect, that, At that time, we had a battleship in the Mediterranean carrying the flag of the commander, U.S. naval forces in European waters, a holdover from the commander, U.S. naval foces in European waters in World War I. This command was later abolished, but again reinstated after World War II. It still exists as the commander, NATO forces in European waters. But the commander of U.S. naval forces in European waters was a Vice Admiral and, as such, he was entitled to 15 guns, but Admiral Bristol, who was high commissioner with the rank of ambassador, was entitled to 17 guns. And so when the commander of naval forces in European waters came in to Constantinople, he was junior to the high commissioner, although he had three stars and Admiral Bristol only had two. The commander of the naval forces had to call on Admiral Bristol first, and when Admiral Bristol returned his call, Admiral Bristol got 17 guns, but when - that was the end of the crisis insofar as the Vice Admiral and the high commissioner were concerned. Then, Admiral Bristol as the commander U.S. naval forces in the Eastern Mediterranean would call on the commander U.S. naval forces in Europe, and he only got 13 guns. Wasn't that funny.

Q: Yes. I hope the people in charge of the salutes knew in what capacity each one was calling or receiving.

Adm. W.: Then, of course, when Vice Admiral Long called on Admiral Bristol he got 15 guns, because it was the reverse.

One of the interesting sights of Constantinople in those days and I imagine it still is, was the Constantinople bazaar.

Q: The Grand Bazaar?

Adm. W.: The Grand Bazaar, which is a medieval edition of a modern shopping center...

Q: And larger than anything even in the world today, don't you think?

Adm. W.: I don't know if I'd go that far. It looked pretty large. I don't know what it's like now. It wasn't so terribly large then, but in any case, you could buy anything there from a shoe string to diamonds, or Persian rugs or what have you. We used to go there quite often on a Saturday afternoon or sometime like that when we didn't have much else to do. Before the military situation heated up there, we had a lot of time to more or less enjoy ourselves, and we'd often go, just friends, you know, and knock around. That's where I bought most of my Turkish rugs, you know, Persian rugs. We had great fun because, of course, nothing was bought until we bargained for some time. As a matter of fact, I remember one time the staff of the High Commissioner were going to buy Admiral and Mrs. Bristol a quite handsome Persian chest. I've forgotten how much it was, but we started in some months beforehand and I think it took us about the better part of four months to buy that chest. We finally got it for what we thought was the right price. We knew that many of these bazaar merchants ourselves, and they knew us and, as we lived there, they couldn't put over much on us.

Q: Did you wear uniform?

Adm. W.: Oh, yes. When the American tourists would come in February and March on the cruise ships, we used to get awfully mad at these Constantinople bazaar tradesmen because they would sell our friends on these ships the new Turkish embroidery stuff which we thought was just perfectly horrible, and charge them perfectly outrageous prices. Then, as often happens, after Admiral and Mrs. Bristol and the embassy staff had entertained all these VIPs for several days, why, they would invite us out to these cruise ships to have dinner and say farewell, and they would always proudly bring out this stuff which they bought at the bazaars and we would have to oh and ah about it. Then, we'd go to the bazaar the next day and give these merchants hell for cheating our friends, and they would say, "Oh, but you know, we have to live. We have to live." One of those occasions when we went out to the ship for a party it was really quite amusing, and I will say, on our part, quite audacious, because - I think it was the Mauretania that was in - and a friend of mine, Captain Churcher of the British army, who was one of my best friends, and I had just gotten fancy dress costumes made as reproductions of the Cossack costume. We'd gotten everything, including some of the old medals that were being sold in these antique shops, you know, and they really were quite outstanding. And we were very anxious to have a place to wear them.

Q: And a handsome pair, I'm sure you were.

Adm. W.: Oh, I wouldn't say that. So we had the audacity to get in touch with a purser whom we had met out on this ship several times, and suggest to him that instead of having an ordinary dance on their last night in Constantinople, they have a fancy dress ball, and they did. So that was our opportunity.

Q: I bet you were a hit.

Adm. W.: I look back on that and I think, is it possible that two kids could have that much nerve, you know.

Q: Everybody enjoyed it, didn't they?

Adm. W.: Oh, everybody turned out in fancy dress, too.

Q: When you were in Istanbul, were the streets jammed with people?

Adm. W.: Oh, yes. Always.

Q: Were there women on the streets?

Adm. W.: Yes, there were women. Not too many, but there were women. Of course, at that time, the men wore fezzes and the women wore tcharchoffs. The tcharchoff is the - what shall I say - the aftermath of the veil, but it was very becoming. The Turkish ladies always wore solid colors with matching colors

Q: Women weren't wearing veils then?

Adm. W.: No, they weren't wearing veils. They wore a sort of a scarf over their heads which was tied back sort of behind their ears. It was very becoming. We'd see those on the streets, of course.

At that time, there wasn't a modern fire engine in all of Constantinople. The only way that fires could be put out would be by a voluntary company - not a volunteer company - which had a water tank pulled by a couple of mules or something like that, and some pumps, small pumps, which were carried by members of this fire organization. It was really funny because oftentimes when a house would be burning down, we'd see the owner standing outside bargaining with the head of the fire company as to whether the fire company's men would accept what the owner of the house offered him to save his

Wheeler #2 - 103

house. Meantime the house was merrily burning down.

Q: Did you ever see that happen?

Adm. W.: Yes, I saw that happen. Among other duties that I forgot to mention that I had, I was the chief of protocol for the embassy and had the job of seating all the admiral's guests in their proper places at the table. But that, in my day, was not too difficult because the people we entertained were mostly military men or diplomats, and of course the members of the imperial family, they always got precedence. But, generally speaking, I found the Navy regulations were a great help, because there were tables in there that showed how many guns an ambassador, a minister, a first secretary, consul, general, lieutenant general, and all the people like that get, and all that was necessary, generally speaking, was to see how many guns a man was entitled to and give the one that had the largest number of guns the first place. That didn't apply invariably, but it helped a lot.

We met some amazing people there. For instance, Baron and Baroness Wrangel were in Constantinople at that time, and he was of course the last Czarist defender of the Czarist regime. He was finally driven down to Yalta, where he embarked on board some Allied ship, together with his wife, and some of the more important people of his delegation. Of course, thousands of others came on other ships about the same time.

Q: Is that how the Czarist refugees reached Turkey - by ship from Odessa or Yalta?

Adm. W.: Yes, Yalta, and other Russian south sea ports. I was at dinner one night, I remember, a stag dinner, and Baron Wrangel was one of the guests. He came in in his Cossack costume and then he gave a Cossack sword dance after for the entertainment of the guests. Most interesting. He was a charming, delightful gentleman.

On the frivolous side, I perhaps should tell you about the party that we had on board the Scorpion in Therapia one summer. As I said, Admiral and Mrs. Bristol and I lived on board the Scorpion in the summer. Most of the great powers had summer embassies or legations in Therapia in addition to their regular winter legations in Constantinople proper. The Americans had no summer embassy, but Admiral Bristol used the Scorpion as his quarter in the summer and I had the pleasure of staying with him, of course. We had many delightful parties on board the Scorpion, especially in the summer time, usually on Sundays when Admiral and Mrs. Bristol would invite their friends to have luncheon on board. We used to go and meet them beforehand at the Tokatlian Hotel and have cocktails because, of course, they were forbidden on board ship, and then we would adjourn to the quarterdeck of the Scorpion and have buffet luncheon. On this occasion, Lieutenant and Mrs. Bryant were among the Admiral's guests. You may recall that Lieutenant Bryan is the one who came to see me - Glen Howell and myself - the first day we arrived in Constantinople and transmitted the Admiral's invitation to me to remain on his staff. He had a very lovely wife, and there was no talk of separation or anything, but these two used to have the worst fights of any couple that I've ever seen before or since. In fact, it was a sort of standing joke among our intimates, that is to say, the embassy family - and on this occasion it was mostly the embassy family who were there - that Ham and Margaret got into this awful fight. I don't remember what the fight was about but they were just going at each other hammer and tongs and, finally, ~~Margaret said, "Hamilton," she always called him Hamilton,~~ - oh, no, it was the other way round - Ham said, "Now, Margaret, I'm not going to let any woman in the world talk to me like that. You just can't get away with that." And with that he dove over the side. There was quite a strong current there and we were a little bit concerned for Ham's safety, but Margaret wasn't in the least disturbed. We sat there for a while and finally Margaret got up and walked over to the rail and she said, "Now, Hamilton, you come up here. I know you're down there sitting on that rudder, and you come up here. I haven't finished with you yet." Poor old Ham, who was sitting on the rudder, swam around to the gangway and came on board, of course, dripping, soaked with water, and sort of slunk down to somebody's cabin and got some dry clothes.

Q: Did that go on all the time?

Adm. W.: Well, I mean, that's the only time I know that he jumped overboard. His half-brother is Prentiss Cobb Hale, who is now the president of the San Francisco Opera.

Q: Did they still live together and still fight that way?

Adm. W.: He died in World War II of cancer.

Q: Speaking of going overboard, you mentioned earlier having swum the Hellespont?

Adm. W.: Yes - not the Hellespont, the Bosporus. It was during one of these summers that we all got the idea of swimming from Europe to Asia. So we began our swim from the waterfront in front of the Tokatlian Hotel, and we swam across the Bosporus to the Standard Oil installation which was just opposite. I don't actually know what the distance is. I would guess about three-quarters of a mile.

Q: The current's very swift there, isn't it?

Adm. W.: The current's very swift and it's very cold because it was coming out of the Black Sea, you see. Of course, we were accompanied by a friend in a boat alongside, so we weren't in any danger, but it was sort of a challenge.

Q: Was that the same place that Leander did swim?

Adm. W.: No. He swam the Hellespont, which is down at the Dardanelles. I don't believe I've mentioned yet that in July of 1922, under the leadership of King Constantine of Greece, the Greeks marched their troops up to the vicinity of Constantinople - when I say the vicinity, I mean a matter of 200 or 300 miles, but much closer than they had been before. Of course, it was a very unsettled time.

Q: It wasn't war, officially, I mean?

Adm. W.: No, there was no war. He just marched up there because, you see, the Allies, including the Greeks, they were allies of Great Britain, were in occupation of Constantinople. Our belief was that the Greeks probably thought, well, now this is a good time for us to take Constantinople because our friends are there. There had been a legend for some time that Constantinople would be recaptured when the Greeks had a king named Constantine, and they had a king named Constantine at that time. So, they were close enough to threaten Constantinople, and there was a good deal of agitation there because although Constantinople was occupied by the Allies, the British have always been friendly to the Greeks, and we didn't know - I say we, I mean nobody knew - whether the British were going to give way and let them come in and take it. They could have done that, you see. The British had by far the largest force of troops and they could have easily given way and let the Greeks come in. So there was a good deal of feeling as to what was going to happen. The atmosphere was very tense around there. This I don't think you'll ever find in history, either. This is something that probably never got in the history books. But General Harrington took off very summarily for England, and we were all waiting with bated breath to see what the outcome would be. Finally, the message came through that the Greeks - there was an ultimatum, that is, the Allied powers together having been spurred, no doubt, by the British issued an ultimatum to Greece forbidding the occupation of Constantinople. So that ended that flurry.

Q: Is that what you were referring to back a bit ago when you spoke of before things heated up, you did visiting and went to the Grand Bazaar - you said, before things heated up, and this incident is what you were referring to?

Adm. W.: Actually they heated up much more after that, because it was after that that the Greeks were driven out of Smyrna.

Q: Was this part of a two-pronged thing, Constantine went north and went into Turkey and the Greeks also went into Smyrna?

Adm. W.: The Greeks went into Smyrna a long time before - long before I got there. They were there under the terms of the Treaty of Sevres in 1920 or thereabouts.

Q: So, it was not too long apart?

Adm. W.: Oh, no. It seemed long in those days, but it wasn't really long.

Q: And it was Mustapha Kemal who stopped the Greeks from going on into Anatolia?

Adm. W.: Yes. Then he started driving them down to Smyrna and eventually drove them actually into the sea at Smyrna. Then after he had retaken Smyrna, which was his primary objective of the Turks, then his army marched north and threatened Constantinople. They didn't surround it, but as I said you could see their bayonets glistening on the Asia Minor side, on the Anatolian side. Of course, when that took place, then we really were worried about our American security, and we had plans made to bring all the destroyers in and concentrate all the Americans in the Embassy and provide escort for them down to the docks, so they could get on board, because there would have been no way to prevent the Turks from getting into Constantinople without fighting them, you see, without the Allied forces of occupation actually putting up resistance.

Q: That was the time when the sultan decided to take off?

Adm. W.: The caliph left on that occasion. The sultan had already gone. The scene was now set for the Turks to cash in on their military successes, because you see they had driven the Greeks out of Smyrna, they had marched northwest up to the Asia Minor shores of Constantinople, and they were threatening to retake Constantinople. That was really the only thing that brought the Allies to terms. You see, the Turks had refused to abide by the Treaty of Sevres. The Greeks had been put in to Smyrna under the Treaty of Sevres, but by force, you see, under the guns of British battleships. But the Turks had driven them out and they'd gone up and were threatening the Allied forces of occupation in Constantinople. So then the Turks said, all right, now you'd better make another treaty, in effect. So that was when the Allies agreed to peace negotiations at Lausanne, and that was in 1922, November, when the peace conference between them and the allies began in Lausanne. The Americans were not actually members

— they were not party to this treaty, because we had never been at war with Turkey.

Q: They were not party to the original treaty either?

Adm. W.: No. But the Americans did send a delegation consisting of Ambassador Richard Washburn Childs, our ambassador to Rome, Joseph Grew, our minister to Switzerland, Admiral Bristol, high-commissioner to Turkey. In addition there were, of course, several secretaries, attaches, and myself attached to the American delegation.

Q: In what capacity did you attend? As the aide to Admiral...?

Adm. W.: I attended to begin with as the aide, but the American Representative who sat on the health and sanitary commission was not very well, and I was delegated to act in his place.

Q: So you actually were a member of the team?

Adm. W.: I was a member of the team, yes.

Q: What other powers were present?

Adm. W.: The British, French, Italian, Turkish, Greek...

Q: Japan?

Adm. W.: Yes, there was a Japanese member...and the Russians.

Q: Who headed the Turkish delegation?

Adm. W.: The Turkish delegation was headed by Ismet Pasha, who was a general. The term "Pasha" is a rather difficult thing to describe. It was never used except in referring to a general, but I don't think it was always used in referring to a general. A Pasha was, of course, a very high title. Ismet Pasha was the right-hand man to Mustapha Kemal Pasha. When the Turkish government was first set up, Ismet Pasha was the prime minister.

Q: Wasn't Inonü...?

Adm. W.: It's the same man. Ismet Inonü is the same as Ismet Pasha. When the Turks decided to "go Western" they changed many of their names, gave up such titles as Pasha, and endeavored to follow Western customs as much as possible. That was an interesting development while I was there, in that to begin with, after the successes of Mustapha Kemal Pasha in Anatolia, there was intense feeling of nationalism. Everything had to be very Turkish, the language, the dress, the customs, and everything accented the Turkish theme. A short while after I left, they completely reversed that. Mustapha Kemal issued an edict that fezzes should be done away with, tcharchoffs should be done away with for women, and the entire Turkish language became Arianized - I don't know whether that's the word for it or not, but I mean Westernized, that's a better term. They stopped using the Arab script, that is, officially, and used our own type of letters and figures - our figures are Arab, aren't they?

Well, among the other famous people in Lausanne at that time were Lord and Lady Curzon - Lord Curzon, of course, was the British representative, Sir Horace Rumbold, who was the British ~~representative~~ High Commissioner at Constantinople, and Lady Rumbold, Monsieur Bompard, the French delegate, Marquis Garroni, who was the Italian high commissioner in Constantinople, but was also the Italian representative in Lausanne. Another very interesting character, of whom history has a long record, was Monsieur Venezelos of Greece, and Monsieur - or perhaps I should say, Comrade Tchicherin, who was the first foreign minister of the Soviet government. He was there as the Soviet delegate. Ismet Pasha was the Turkish representative. While this conference was going on, it was interrupted by Christmas, which was the occasion for declaring a vacation, and most of us went to Paris. Admiral and Mrs. Bristol and I were all invited to visit the Lamotte Belins in Paris. Mr. Belin was the first secretary of the American Embassy there. I was about to accept this invitation, when I received what I thought was a better one from a friend of mine who was an official of ~~Morgan Hodges~~ Morgan Hanjes banking concern and told me that he was leaving very shortly to visit his wife on the Riviera, who was an invalid, and urged me to take his apartment on the left bank of the Seine, which he said was fully staffed and fully stocked with a wine cellar. After feebly protesting, why, I accepted this invitation and, as you may well imagine, had a perfectly glorious time. Among my contacts was a beautiful Russian girl, a ~~Miss~~ Princess Russie Mdvani, whom I had known in Constantinople, but who was then living in Paris with her family, consisting of her mother and father and her brothers, who were later known as "the marrying Mdvanis." Russie and I attended a number of functions together, danced at a number of cabarets, and generally had a good time. I was amazed when I came back to the United States later and read in the papers about all the furor over the Mdvanis, because I had seen them in their very modest apartment in Paris and I don't think any of them had a cent to their names, other than what was necessary to buy the minimum of food, clothing, and shelter. As a matter of fact, these boys were all from Georgia, in the south of Russia, and that is a country where most people other than peasants were called princes or princesses and the boys made a very poor impression on me.

Q: Maybe the precursors of the hippies?

Adm. W.: But they came over here with their title of prince and proceeded to get away with claiming that they were big shots and married a number of our very attractive American girls...

Q: and wealthy...

Adm. W.: Yes...which was certainly very unfair, I thought. Russie Mdvani, whom I knew was a lovely unpretentious girl who later married a Spanish artist, Jose Maria Sert, and lived in Spain for a number of years before she died about 15 years ago.

Q: And then you returned to Lausanne?

Wheeler #2 - 114

Adm. W.: We then returned to Lausanne, but the conference broke up short thereafter, as it seemed to be impossible to agree on the abolition of the capitulations, the status of Mosul, which is where the oil fields are located, and the straits agreement, relating to the control by the Turks over the passage of ships, including warships, through the Dardanelles. One dispute that was settled was the exchange of populations, which was one of the most curious provisions of any treaty in history, I believe. It provided for the physical transference of most of the Greeks who were living in Turkey to Greece, and most of the Turks who were living in Greece to Turkey.

Q: What numbers were involved, do you know?

Adm. W.: I think there were on the order of 200,000, or something of that sort. Everybody thought it was a pretty cruel thing at the time, but apparently it was all for the best.

Q: Well, in our time, we've done this at Cyprus, in our...

Adm. W.: Have we? I didn't know they'd actually transferred any people.

Q: Well, I thought,, to send Greeks from Turkey to Cyprus and vice versa.

Adm. W. W.: We did? Well, I didn't bother about it too much.

Q: Yes, I remember seeing pictures of them waiting to be

evacuated.

Adm. W.: These capitulations which I mentioned are an interesting phase of the emergence of Turkey from the old times to the new. They extended way back to the days of the Venetian supremacy in the Mediterranean. I couldn't begin, at this time, to trace the history of the capitulations, but I do know that they did include, among other things, the right of foreign nations to keep a stationaire, a naval yacht in Constantinople as a concession to the Embassy personnel. There were also provisions which enabled foreigners to give greater protection to their nationals than they would have gotten under Turkish law, and this of course was considered a great ignominy by the Turks.

Q: Was this similar to extraterritorial provisions in China?

Adm. W.: Yes, same idea.

Q: What was the result of it? As far as Turkey was concerned?

Adm. W.: The Turks won, and the capitulations were abolished. The Lausanne conference, after breaking up, was resumed on April 23 with Minister Grew as our observer, and concluded its work on July 24, 1923.

Q: Did Turkey recover any land?

Adm. W.: Yes. They retained a much larger slice of territory around Constantinople.

Q: Its present-day boundaries?

Adm. W.: Its present-day boundaries, yes. They gained some concessions from the Europeans in Anatolia, such as rights and things like that, but they didn't regain any territory because all of us - any territory comparable to what they'd had before, because, you see, all those countries like Syria, Mesopotamia, Palestine, and so on, were given their independence.

In the spring of 1923 I visited Odessa in Soviet Russia, in one of our destroyers which had been participating in the American relief administration. The American relief administration was set up by the President of the United States to assist the Russians after the terrible famine that they had there in 1922, in which millions of people died of starvation, and the American government appropriated 20 million dollars to furnish wheat to the Soviet government to help them because of their, as was claimed by the Russian government, poor crops. Actually, I think it was due more to the fact that the Russians were trying to Sovietize the farms and that didn't set so well with the Russian farmers. In any case, we had destroyers in each large port in the - Crimea - to assist in the distribution of this wheat. It had come over on American merchant ships and the captains of the destroyers would act as sort of liaison with the Russian representatives and the American relief administration's representatives in the ports.

Q: Was this on the Black Sea and up north, and on to Vladivostok?

Wheeler #2 - 117

Adm. W.: Oh, no, only in the Black Sea, as far as I know. That's the only thing that came to my attention, anyway.. I went as a matter of fact to Odessa, that's the only port that I saw. I was interested in the fact that, at that time, most of the monuments in Odessa were headless because the Soviets had knocked the heads off these Czarist monuments. We were also shown around by a Russian communist by the name of Margolis whose name for some strange reason I happen still to remember taking us to dinner at his house, which he said had formerly belonged to him but was now divided up into eight apartments. We asked him how the Communism was working out because we had heard that there was no money being used in Russia, at that time, and the people were just given tickets which they could use to get bread and go to the opera, get clothes and things like that. No money was in circulation. He, I think, was afraid to speak openly but we gathered that the trouble with the system was that the people had plenty of tickets but by the time that - I mean a lot of these people would be standing in line after all the bread and food had given out, so that it was far from perfect and, of course, as everyone knows they eventually gave that up and started to use money again.

Q: Were you impressed with the appearance of the Black Sea itself? It sounds so bleak to hear the words, Black Sea.

Adm. W.: No. To me it was just like any other sea. Of course, it's more shallow than the ocean or than - it didn't have that blue color that... the Mediterranean has.

Q: No, it does have a darker hue, doesn't it?

Adm. W.: Yes, it really does. After my return from Odessa, Captain Maurice Churcher, Royal Artillery, of the British Army, who was a great friend of mine, and I made a trip to the battlefield of the Dardanelles campaign as a guest of the commanding officer Squadron Leader Blount, who was also a friend of Captain Churcher's. We were especially fortunate in this arrangement in that we were taken everywhere and shown everything, being flown around to all the various points of interest, and saw everything worth seeing. The battlefields were very impressive in that the terrain was overgrown with a kind of a wiry weed which made progress through them almost impossible and which, I think, eventually defeated the British in their attempt to capture Gallipoli. It's interesting to note that whereas the British made two attempts to capture the Dardanelles, they both failed. The first attempt was by the Navy, which attempted to force the straits - the Dardanelles - and you could, at that time, still see the wreckage of some of their ships on the beaches at the south end of Gallipoli - I mean the southern end of the northern shore of the Dardanelles. Then, their next attempt, of course, was on the other side, which they failed to take because, as I say, of this - of the terrible loss of life and the master strategy of Mustapha Kemal Pasha.

Q: But you say the actual natural growth there was to a great extent responsible for their inability to move the troops, I presume?

Adm. W.: Absolutely. It was terrible.

Q: I never heard that.

Adm. W.: It was terrible to get through. It really was. It was hard to walk through even when you didn't have somebody shooting at you. Later that year, Consul General E. L. Ives, brother-in-law of the later to become famous Adlai Stevenson, Consul General R. C. Treadwell, who was making an inspection trip of the U.S. consulates in the Near East, Lieutenant Commander Kincaid, later to become the hero of the Battle of the Philippine Sea - the Second Battle of the Philippine Sea in World War II, and I embarked on the destroyer MacLeish and visited the leading ports of the Eastern Mediterranean. Among these were Mytilene, Smyrna, Rhodes, Messina, Alexandria, Nicosia in Cyprus, and Beirut, from which we went on a side trip to Damascus, Balbec, and Alexandria. Thence we visited Cairo, Memphis, Luxor, and the Valley of Kings, including Tutankhamen's tomb. Returning to Constantinople, we stopped in Athens and Salonica, the birthplace of Mustapha Kemal.

Q: Where is Salonica? I thought that was in Greece.

Adm. W.: Yes, it is.

Q: Mustapha Kemal was born in...

Adm. W.: He was born in Salonica. On July 10, 1924, the U.S. Army Air Corps planes making the first round-the-world trip stopped in Constantinople for a rest and fuel. Among the pilots was the then Lieutenant Hap Arnold, who was later to become a five-star general and chief of the Army Air Corps in World War II.

Q: When you'd see these men, did you have a sense of destiny about them at all? Or did they just seem ordinary people?

Adm. W.: No. Just ordinary people. Of course, there's a great deal of ability that goes with this, as you well know, and I would be the last to want to cut them down. Also there's a tremendous amount of luck in this thing. I mean being in the right place at the right time.

Q: Men perhaps raised to greatness or to the occasion.

Adm. W.: Yes, they rise to the occasion. Of course, if they didn't have the stuff, why, they wouldn't rise to the occasion. But the Navy's selection system has such a vast method of choosing people for promotion that, in my opinion, almost anybody who has been promoted to a high-ranking job will deliver the goods. I mean, there are very few cases of failure. I can't remember any right now. I do know a case of an admiral who was also the victim of a circumstance, who - maybe I'm not getting this in the right context - but this man - you may have heard of Admiral Ghormley - he was in command of the - at the time of the four cruisers - sunk near Guadalcanal in World War II.

Q: I know what you mean, but I do think we're getting out of

Wheeler #2 - 121

context because if you tell it now I want you to repeat it when we get into the Pacific.

Adm. W.: Yes, well, we'll let that go, but the point I was trying to make is that I think that because of the selection in the Navy, nearly all of the people who are selected have the ability and the courage to meet any occasion that is demanded of them.

Q: Yes, I think we ought to pursue this, though, when we get into that area, because I want to ask you more questions and your comments, and I don't want to make this too long.

Adm. W.: Later - did I tell you about going to Ankara with Admiral Bristol?

Q: You spoke of going on the train and he went to meet Mustapha Kemal and then you went on in the ship.

Adm. W.: We went on to Afium Kara Hissar and Konya, Adana, then through the Taurus Mountains and Tarsus, where we saw the tomb of Jonah...

Q: Yes, you did mention that, and you went on by ship to Patmos, I believe. You really had an opportunity that few men have had.

Adm. W.: Yes, that's true. Now, this is getting down to the very end. About the middle of August 1924, Admiral and Mrs. Bristol and his entourage, including me, embarked on the naval yacht *Scorpion*, which in the meantime had been thoroughly overhauled, for a six-week cruise in the Mediterranean and a motor trip.

Q: This always sounds like you were going on a wealthy man's cruise, doesn't it?

Adm. W.: Oh, yes. Well, we were living like millionaires. No doubt about that.

Q: Did you realize then the opportunities you were having?

Adm. W.: No, we took it as a matter of course. It was all just in the day's work, you know.

Q: It could happen to anybody.

Adm. W.: I look back on it now and it seems like a dream.

Q: Were you aware of the poverty of the countries you were visiting?

Adm. W.: Yes, we were. Although I don't think the poverty there was anything comparable to what I later saw in China, or saw before in China the first time. No, there was no great emphasis on great poverty. Of course, there were always poor people. You always will have them.

Q: You didn't feel there was any great contrast between you as an American and the other people living in this part of the world?

Adm. W.: Well, I think there was, yes. It depends on what people you're comparing them with. I mean there was certainly a great contrast between the way Admiral Bristol, Mrs. Bristol, and I lived when you compare it with the natives, but there wasn't any great contrast between the way we lived and our friends live in the United States, for example. I don't think there was any more contrast between us and the natives than there is between us and the poor people over here. I don't think that the people in those countries were suffering any. They weren't affluent, no, but they had plenty to eat and plenty of clothing. I didn't see any indication...

Q: I remember after World War I...

Adm. W.: ...did you, on your trip?

Q: Yes. I was aware of it.

Adm. W.: Where?

Q: In Turkey, in Istanbul. But I remember after World War I the starving Armenians, which we always related to Asia Monor, then Turkey. Remember in World War I, people were raising money for the starving Armenians?

Adm. W.: Well, I'll tell you about the starving Armenians. I'm very sorry for anybody that's starved, but the Turks hated the Armenians because the Armenians always stayed home - you remember in years past, long ago, people were always fighting wars. I don't believe in fighting wars, but they were fighting wars, and the Turks used to go out to defend their country and the Armenians stayed home and got their businesses, and proceeded to wax fat and take advantage of the Turks in every way they could, so that the Turks just hated them, and they proceeded to do what anybody, I guess, under the circumstances would do. They eliminated some of them. I'm not in favor of that, but I do see the mitigating circumstances. The Turks are, in my opinion, a very fine people. They are - they give you their word and you can absolutely depend on it. They're clean and straightforward, dependable. The Armenians, on the other hand, are sneaky, many of them, they will cheat you if they can, and, in my opinion, they're not nearly as trustworthy as the Turks.

Q: Until this very minute, in this conversation, I never had wondered why that phrase "the starving Armenians" became such a universal phrase, because as a child I heard it and I just - was it because of the Turks' attitude toward them?

Adm. W.: You see, there's a good deal of religion that goes in on that. The Turks are Moslems, and we over here, of course, are Christians, at least supposed to be, and the missionaries were all in favor of the Armenians *whose religion is Christian* and they hated the Turks. They couldn't convert the Turks.

Q: Did they convert the Armenians?

Adm. W.: Yes. Well, the Armenians were mostly Christians anyway. I talked to a dear old gentleman who was the head of the American Bible Society in Turkey - Dr. Peet - a wonderful old gentleman. Of course, we had schools over there, we had the Constantinople College for Women, we had the American College

Called Roberts College

for men there - ~~I've forgotten the name of it right now, but it will come to me~~ - The Turks were very generous about allowing American missionaries to open schools here, there, and anywhere. They shut down later on, but for many, many years they had no restrictions - in other words, come in here and teach our children, we dare you to make them Christians. And, as I say, the American Bible Society had been out there for years, and I asked dear old Dr. Peet one day, I said, "Tell me frankly, have you ever converted any Moslems?" And he said, "No."

Q: Why should we?

Adm. W.: Well, except that it's a part of the Christian doctrine to go out and spread the word.

Q: Yes, I know, but basically, they have theirs - to each his own, you know.

Adm. W.: Well, we began this cruise on the Scorpion - oh, the high commissioner's car was carried on board and later unloaded in Venice - and our first stop was at Mount Athos in Greece. Mount Athos is a very interesting place in that it's the site of many monasteries and churches of the Greek Orthodox Church, and nothing female is allowed in this area.

Q: Even chickens.

Adm. W.: Well, I wondered about that. How do they get more chickens? At any rate, Mrs. Bristol and the other ladies who were traveling on the Scorpion were very much put out that they weren't allowed to go ashore there, but we went ashore, looked all around, and had luncheon there. *as guests of the monks*

Q: Did you go up to the top of the mountain?

Adm. W.: Yes. Well after stopping in Brindisi for fueling, we went on to Venice, where we were met by our American naval attache, Captain Castleman and his wife, and also Mr. Young, who was the consul in Venice, and his wife. After playing around in Venice for a while, including the Lido, going swimming and all, why, we took off through the Italian Alps, through the Brenner Pass, and the southwestern part of Germany to Vienna. I remember passing through Germany on a Sunday afternoon, we saw the German villagers having their folk dancing in native costumes and it really was a beautiful thing to see. In Vienna we were entertained by the American minister and his wife, and in return Admiral and Mrs. Bristol gave a dinner for them.

Q: Were these on orders that you were traveling, or on leave? I mean what Navy relationship did you have taking this trip?

Adm. W.: I was aide to Admiral Bristol. I didn't have to have any. As long as he went, I went.

Q: Did he have orders to do this?

Adm. W.: He had permission.

Q: Permission, and he chose his own route?

Adm. W.: Oh, yes. You see, he was under orders from both the

State Department and the Navy Department. But he was actually more under the orders of the State Department than he was the Navy Department. But he got permission from both to make this trip. You see, this was in the nature of a vacation for him, but it wasn't for me because I was on duty accompanying Admiral Bristol.

Q: Nice duty.

Adm. W.: Yes, nice work if you can get it. At any rate, I do remember another interesting feature passing through Germany. It was during the period of that rampant inflation, remember, and I remember looking in a store window in some town in Bavaria and I noticed that there were numbers, placards with number on each article in this men's clothing store, like, for instance, there'd be a "6" on a pair of shoes, there'd be a "5" on a hat, there'd be a "25" on a suit, and down in the very front of the window there'd be one card which was a multiplier, and the way you found out how much each article was was to multiply the number on the suit or whatever the article was by the multiplier in the front to find out what the cost of the thing was. The reason for that was that the exchange was changing so fast that they had to change the card several times a day.

As I say, Admiral Bristol decided to give this dinner in Vienna for the minister and his wife. All during this time I was the cashier for the whole - the accountant, you might say - for the whole trip, and there were five or six of us whose accounts I kept. It was really something because I think there were about five currencies that were used and I had to convert them all to dollars and cents, or to the currency of the country we were in, and then I'd tell everyone of course, I paid by way on that trip. I mean I didn't charge the government for that. Then, I'd tell Admiral Bristol what his share was, and he'd hand me out $100 or $200, and that's the way I kept books for them. But in Vienna, I'll always remember that when I paid for the Admiral's dinner, it cost six million kroner, which is the only time in my life that I've ever been a millionaire and I guess the only time I ever will be.

In Budapest we - Admiral Bristol called on Admiral Horthy. I didn't go with him that time. Mrs. Bristol and the rest of us went shopping, I think. At Trieste we reloaded the Admiral's car on board the <u>Scorpion</u> and had a leisurely trip down the Dalmatian coast, stopping at Spalato, which I think is now called Split, Ragusa, now called Dubrovnik, I believe, and Cattaro. From Cattaro we motored to Cetinje, the capital of Montenegro, the most winding road I've ever seen, as we went right up the side of a hill, climbed right up the cliff. Cetinje was the cutest place I've ever seen. It looked like an exact copy of a scene from the Prince of Graustark, it had a little opera house and it had a little sort of a village green, a town hall, and the whole thing was in miniature and beautifully kept. It was lovely. The next port of call was Corfu, a feature of which was the Kaiser's winter palace, and then we went through the Corinth Canal to visit the Oracle of Delphi. Then I say here, while we were away from Constantinople, the Turkish constitution was adopted on August 20th. This, in effect, completed the formation of the new government and marked the end of the revolution begun by Mustapha Kemal five years earlier. One of the most remarkable features of this thing was that it was almost a bloodless revolution. I mean when you stop and think of the revolution in France in 1789 and in Russia in 1918, it's amazing to think that Turkey, which we had always heard referred to as being run by the "bloody Turks", there was nothing like that. Oh, undoubtedly, there were a few people snuffed out, but I mean to say there was no mass killing.

Q: Before we leave, I have two questions about the Treaty of Lausanne: were the Turks pleased with the eventual results of that treaty? They did live with it, I assume.

Adm. W.: Oh, yes. At that Treaty of Lausanne, they just wouldn't give on things that they didn't want. They just made sure that they were going to get the kind of treaty they wanted or they quit.

Q: Which, I guess, proves that when you make a ridiculous treaty, it's of no value. It's like making a rule when no matter what you are you can't enforce it.

Adm. W.: I forgot to mention that in 1923 - I think it was the fall of 1923 - after the signing of the Lausanne Treaty, the occupation of Constantinople was over, and all of the occupying powers were required to leave under the terms of that treaty, and they did leave. They all left on the same occasion, and there was sort of a military parade down at the dock at Tophane, I don't know whether that's what they call it now or not, but there's a big plaza there. The French, British, and Italian ships were all loaded previously and then the commanders and their staffs had this sort of a review there at the dock, and then they took off in their barges for the ships, and then the ships got under way.

Q: It must have been colorful.

Adm. W.: It was very colorful but, you know, it was very sad because, in effect, it was a defeat for the allies.

Q: Was it?

Adm. W.: Well, yes, in a sense. They had had to completely scrap the Treaty of Sevres, which was what they wanted, and accept the Turkish demands in the Treaty of Lausanne. But it was a fair treaty.

Q: The various allies were leaving a Turkish country to the Turkish people.

Adm. W.: That's right.

Q: So it was sad in the way that it was the end of an era. And you were certainly there at the most delightful, colorful era.

Adm. W.: This was In the fall of 1924, after we came back from this trip to Venice and the Italian Alps and back through the Corinth Canal and ~~all, and~~ I got orders to return to the United States. That was the second set of orders that I had received to return. The first set Admiral Bristol had canceled and he was going to have the second set canceled until I told him, thank you very much, but I think if I'm going to expect to get promoted in the Navy, I've got to have some sea duty.

Q: I want to ask you one other things now before we leave this: did you or do you have the feeling that you personally accomplished anything during the negotiations at Lausanne?

Adm. W.: I think so. I mean, I think my presence was felt in connection with the health and sanitation facilities. I attended those meetings regularly, and I had my views. Of course, I wasn't a doctor but nevertheless it was quite common sense the things that were being discussed there.

Q: Did you sit in as an observer, or did you, in fact, participate?

Adm. W.: Well, we all sat as observers, but we could give our views. Oh, I suppose in one way out in Constantinople, why, I was part of the team, and I will say this, that I think all of the good will that Turkey has had for the United States since that time was generated by Admiral Bristol, assisted, of course, by the members of his staff.

Q: I think that's a very important point to make, and I'm glad that we didn't leave this without having that expression of opinion.

Adm. W.: It's very difficult to pinpoint any of those things. I understand from the papers that there has been some anti-American feeling in Turkey now, but I'm sure that that is the same kind of feeling that is being generated in this country by people who are anti-government. The feeling between the Turks of stature and the Americans runs very deep, and that I'm convinced, was generated, as I say, by Admiral Bristol, because he was universally loved by everybody. It was a fantastic thing. Oftentimes, as you well know, there are even Americans who object to the views and the actions of some of their own people. Not so in Constantinople. Later on in China when I went with him, as we will discuss later on in China, it wasn't necessarily the case. There were some Americans over there who were opposed to Admiral Bristol.

Q: How many years did Admiral Bristol represent the United States in Constantinople?

Adm. W.: He represented them about seven years. The better part of eight years, I should say. Well, soon after I got my orders, Admiral and Mrs. Bristol gave me a farewell party, at which I think they invited about fifty people to dinner, and it was an occasion which I shall never forget. I had so many friends and they were all so good to me that it was really, for me, a very sad occasion.

Q: You had been there, let's see, that was your first... assignment of any length at one place.

Adm. W.: Yes, I was there longer than I'd ever been anywhere in the Navy before. It was almost exactly three years.

Wheeler #3 - 134

Interview No. 3 with Rear Admiral C. Julian Wheeler

Date: July 20, 1969

By: Etta Belle Kitchen

Q: This is landing-on-the-moon day, and an appropriate day to continue our interview with Admiral Wheeler, and, Admiral, I guess yesterday we just left Constantinople.

Adm. W.: Correct, Etta Belle, and after leaving Constantinople I was ordered to return to the United States via the USS Henderson, a transport which had shortly before arrived in Ragusa to transfer personnel from the United States to the flagship of the commander-in-chief of the naval forces in European waters. Before joining the Henderson, however, I went aboard the naval yacht Scorpion and acted as executive officer and navigator on board her en route to join the Henderson in Ragusa. On the way we stopped in Brindisi, Italy, for fueling and, as the commanding officer immediately went on leave to join his wife in Rome, I became commanding officer during his absence. An amusing incident occurred there in that as soon as we arrived the Mayor of Brindisi came on board the Scorpion to make an official call, which I returned later in the day. On that occasion, the Mayor invited me and several of my officers to attend a performance of the opera that evening given in Brindisi. Unfortunately, we were a few minutes late in arriving and the opera had already begun, but at an appropriate intermission the orchestra struck up "It's a Long Way to Tipperary," and I noticed everybody in the audience was standing up. The Mayor looked at me and said,

"Eet ees for you." So, of course, I stood up, but why an American should stand up for an English song like "It's a Long Way to Tipperary" I have yet to know, except that possibly inasmuch as the Star-Spangled Banner is only played for high-ranking officers, they figured that "It's a Long Way to Tipperary" would do for a lieutenant, even though he was the commanding officer.

Q: I thought, maybe, that was the only music they knew besides the opera.

Adm. W.: As soon as we arrived at Ragusa, I transferred to the Henderson, but in the meantime had the pleasure of meeting my room mate of the Naval Academy, Lieutenant Charles P. Cecil, who was later promoted to admiral, but killed in an unfortunate landing in one of the South Pacific islands, later during World War II.

Upon arrival in the United States, I had two months' leave, and then joined the USS Nevada in Long Beach, California, a short time before the United States fleet made its historic trip to New Zealand and Australia. The fleet was divided into two parts, one half of which visited Wellington and Sydney, the other half visited Auckland and Melbourne. I was in the half that visited Wellington, and from there we had the opportunity of touring the area known as Rotorua, which is where there are very interesting hot springs and other sights interesting to tourists. Our visit to Melbourne was very pleasant and quite interesting. The Australian Navy really outdid themselves in arranging for our comfort. Before we docked

Australian
~~British~~ naval officers came on board with passes to theaters, street railways, and almost everything in town, except taxis. We felt after having ridden in a few taxis that may be that was the way they made up the free passes to everything else, as the taxis were quite expensive. We were taken on tours and widely feted by hostesses, both in and out of Melbourne. I remember one occasion when I was duty officer on the <u>Nevada</u> one hostess called up and pleaded that we send three more officers to attend a dinner that she had planned. I told her that there were no more officers available, and she said how about sending her some chief petty officers.

Q: She really wanted to make up her complement of guests, didn't she?

Adm. W.: She was desperate for some naval guests. On another occasion which I shall always remember, the four battleships which were tied up alongside the dock, two on each side of the dock, decided before we left Melbourne that we should do something to return the hospitality of our hosts in Melbourne. So it was arranged with several of the dry-goods stores to send their clerks out to the dance which would be held on, I think, the evening before or maybe two evenings before our departure. Invitations were sent out to each individual with the thought that there might be an attempt to - on the part of some people who were not invited - to get on board, and the policeman who were stationed at the entrance to the dock to collect these tickets to make sure that only the invited guests would arrive. This party, of course, was for the ships' companies and we had arranged for dance music on each one of the ships. That was widely publicized and the interest on the part of young women in Melbourne was terrific. I remember watching from the deck of the Nevada as these people arrived on the dock, across which a line had been stretched with policemen stationed at the entrance. Within the first ten minutes, the line was completely demolished, the girls rushed the dock, and made for the ships completely without control - the police completely lost control. On board the Nevada we endeavored to stop them, or at least to limit the number that came on board, at the gangway but we later found that there were so many on board that the level of the ship had sunk to the point where the sailors were pulling the girls in through the portholes, as we had some larger portholes in the superstructure which, by that time, had descended to the point where they could be reached from the dock.

Q: I did not realize that that could happen on board a battleship.

Adm. W.: I didn't either. The party was obviously a succes, but it was rather frightening because, actually, it was the only time I've ever known in the Navy when we lost control of a ship. There were so many people on board that we just had great difficulty in preserving order and preserving control over the various parts of the ship to which these visitors were not supposed to be admitted. But everything passed off successfully.

Q: Were they permitted in the crew's quarters?

Adm. W.: Oh, yes, they went in the crew's quarters. They went about everywhere, but there were no injuries. A few things were stolen, but nothing of any great consequence.

Q: I'm sure that was the least of your concerns at that point. How did you get them off?

Adm. W.: Well, they dribbled off around midnight. I mean, I suppose some of them had parents and their parents came for them. The music stopped and the party was obviously over, so they were more or less swept ashore.

Q: Do you have any idea how many came aboard the four battleships? It seems like it would be in the thousands?

Adm. W.: There were thousands. I don't think anybody could possibly have made a count, because, you see, they didn't just come over the gangway, they came in any way they could.

Q: You seem, Admiral, to be a catalyst for interesting and unusual experiences.

Adm. W.: That, to me, was quite unusual.

Q: That's an item of history that I would suggest has never been recorded before.

Adm. W.: No, I doubt if it has..

Q: What was your job on the Nevada?

Adm. W.: I was fire-control officer. I had charge of a division that really controlled the fire of all the turret guns, and that was very interesting in that the men who operated the fire-control instruments had to be above average, not only in conduct, but in mental ability, as one of the stations under my control was the plotting room. So I arranged with the executive officer that as each new draft came on board ship, I would give them an intelligence test and only the ones who made the highest marks in the intelligence test were assigned to my division. So we had really a very unusually high type of people in it...Incidentally, I almost forgot to mention that the then Ensign Rickover was in my division, and he was assigned as plotting room officer, in charge of the activities down there. In particular, he operated what we called the Ford range keeper and, in my opinion, the Ford range keeper was the forerunner of the present-day computer. It was an instrument made by the Ford Instrument Company, as I recall, not the company that makes automobiles, the one that makes instruments. Known data, such as our ship's course and speed, the force and direction of the wind, the temperature of the powder in our magazines, and everything else - I may have skipped some, but I think those are the principal items - that we fed into this Ford range keeper. Then we also cranked in such data as estimated course and speed of the enemy. All of this information was sorted out in this machine, which produced the estimated range and direction of the enemy ships, which, of course, was electrically transmitted to the guns, which were fired from the foretop, where the operator of the instrument up there kept it trained on the target...

Q: Was this done automatically?

Adm. W.: All automatically, and the guns were fired and with this data, of course, it was expected that the greatest number of hits would be made.

Q: Who said when the guns would be fired?

Adm. W.: The gunnery officer in the conning tower pressed the key, which actually fired the guns. In answer to your question about Ensign Rickover, who was in my charge at that time, he was a very interesting character, a taciturn individual, who had very little to say to anyone. I would have almost said that he was not very good tempered.

Q: I think that's probably a correct statement.

Adm. W.: After each meal, in the ward room, instead of sitting around and chatting, playing acey-deucey, which was the Navy's favorite game on board ship, otherwise known as backgammon, or bridge, or some game of that sort, he would immediately retire to his room and sit there and study. In view of his later accomplishments, we can't criticize him too much for that, but he certainly was not the affable type. He had very few, if any, friends on board ship, and was not, on the whole, what is generally considered a good shipmate.

Q: Were his intellectual attainments apparent in the way he did his job?

Adm. W.: Oh, yes. It was obvious that he was a genius, from

that time on, I mean, it didn't take long to figure out that he was - and that was the reason I assigned him to this job because he was obviously the best man in the division, if not in the ship, for that assignment.

Q: How many guns did the Nevada have?

Adm. W.: Let me see, I think it had - I can't really remember now - but I think it had ten 14-inch guns.

Q: It must have been an exciting - well, that's not the right word, but certainly a memorable when they all fired at one time. They didn't ever actually fire at one time, did they?

Adm. W.: Yes, they would fire at one time. They could only fire broadsides, that is to say, athwartships. The after guns could fire aft, but, generally speaking, when the forward guns - if the forward guns - fired directly over the bow, or the after guns fired directly over the stern, it created strains on the ship, which sometimes caused below-deck damage. As a matter of fact, the effort in preparing for battle was always to get the enemy ships on the beam so that you could fire all your guns at once, and, of course, the enemy would try to prevent you from doing that. But the most desirable situation was to, what we called, cross the enemy's T, by being able to fire all of your guns at him, whereas he could only fire his bow guns at you.

Q: How many turrets were there, aside from the big guns?

Adm. W.: Well, there were no turrets for the smaller guns in those days, there were only broadside guns, the 6-inch, and I think there were about 10 or 12 of those, five or six on each side, but they were not in turrets.

Shortly after my return to the United States from Australia, I was ordered to be the district communications officer in the 12th Naval District...

Q: Then, before we leave that, where was the Nevada based?

Adm. W.: At Long Beach.

Q: That was her home port?

Adm. W.: That was her home port.

Q: And she was part of what?

Adm. W.: She was part of the battleships divisions of the battle force in the United States fleet. The battle force was that portion of the United States fleet which was based on the West Coast, and the scouting force was that portion of the United States fleet which was based on the East Coast. Every so often - periodically, I should say - they would be combined into the complete United States fleet, and that is what happened when they went to Australia.

Q: Was Admiral Jackson at that time...?

Adm. W.: Admiral Jackson, as I recall, at that time, or if not at that exact moment, was soon thereafter given command of the battle force. I'm not sure whether he had command of the battleship divisions or the battle force, but his flagship was the USS California.

The duty in San Francisco as district communications officer was very interesting. I served as - I had charge of the all naval communications stations on the West Coast, in northern California, from Point Montara, which is about 20 miles south of San Francisco, to Crescent City, which is near the northern border of California.

Q: You were between the 11th and the 13th naval districts, then on the West Coast and extended east...

Adm. W.: Well, my activities did not involve any stations to the eastward, as all of our naval stations were on the coast. We had a large transmitter at Mare Island and the receiving station was in the 12th naval district headquarters, which were located at 100 Harrison Street in San Francisco. It was on the 7th floor of the Marine storehouse building at 100 Harrison Street.

Q: The entire headquarters was able to be on one floor?

Adm. W.: That's right. While there, we also developed high frequency communications, the first in the history of naval communications, between Honolulu and San Francisco. I received a nice letter of commendation for the work that we did, as this work was entirely outside of the official installation for the carrying on of communications between San Francisco and Honolulu, and thence westward to the Orient.

Q: When you say Honolulu, do you mean Pearl Harbor?

Adm. W.: Pearl Harbor, yes. The naval radio station, of course, at that time was at Pearl Harbor. I enjoyed the inspection trips which I used to make up and down the coast, and had many pleasant contacts with Admiral Washington, who was then commandant of the 12th Naval District, and Mrs. Washington, who lived in the commandant's quarters, later occupied by Admiral Nimitz, on what was then called Goat Island, which is now called Yerba Buena Island. I was only there a year in that assignment, but during that time, I remember that the fleet came in to San Francisco and I had the pleasure of meeting the young lady who afterwards became my wife on the quarterdeck of the California, Admiral Jackson's flagship, when he gave an afternoon reception on board that ship. The young lady, Doanda Putnam, whom I afterwards married, was returning from school in the eastern part of the United States and was a guest of Admiral and Mrs. Washington, who were very close friends and relatives, as a matter of fact, of her mother and father. Her mother and father were in Amoy, China, where Mr. Putnam was consul general, consul, not consul general. After I had been there about a year...

Q: I wanted to ask you if you had a presentiment that she was going to be Mrs. Wheeler?

Adm. W.: None whatsoever. As a matter of fact, it so turned out that we went out together on the same ship to the Orient, where she joined her mother and father, but I still had no thought that she would ever belong to me.

Q: If she was as cute then as she is now, I'm sure she was charming.

Adm. W.: Thank you so much, she was. As I started to say, after I had been in this assignment for about a year, I was quite surprised to receive a radiogram from Admiral Bristol inviting me to be his aide and flag lieutenant when he assumed command of the Asiatic fleet. By this time, he had completed his assignment in Turkey, which, as will be noted from what I said before, was almost three years after I left him in Turkey, and had been ordered to command the U.S. Asiatic fleet. This invitation caused me considerable concern because, although I was devoted to Admiral Bristol and appreciated the compliment of the invitation, I was worried for fear that I would get too much staff duty on my record, as it is known that too much staff duty is not viewed with favor when it comes time to be promoted. I took the matter up with Admiral Washington, who understood my predicament as he had been Chief of the Bureau of Navigation, which at that time was the bureau that handled naval personnel, and we were trying to figure out a polite refusal when my orders arrived to take this job. In other words, the predicament I was in was answered by the definite orders which, Admiral Bristol confessed later on, were sent because he suspected I was probably mulling it over.

Q: You had discussed it, anyway, as I recall, when you left Turkey?

Adm. W.: Yes...

Q: He'd asked you to stay on, so he knew your problem.

Adm. W.: Yes.

Q: Well, that, then, of course, ended your district communications duty?

Adm. W.: Yes. My relief arrived, and I turned over my job and quarters that I had lived in in San Francisco to him, because of the quick departure from San Francisco.

Q: Did you find your own quarters, or did the Navy have quarters there?

Adm. W.: Oh, I found my own. The interesting feature there is that among others who went out on the same ship, the Dollar Line President Garfield, were Captain and Mrs. Castleman, Captain Castleman was on his way to Shanghai to be Admiral Bristol's chief of staff, and Mrs. Washington asked Mrs. Castleman, who was a friend of hers, to be chaperon to Miss Putnam on their way to China, which is what took place, and we all sat at the same table on the way out. I remember one amusing incident was that Captain Castleman invited Miss Putnam to have cocktails with him and his wife on a certain day, which was the day we crossed the international dateline, and of course there was no such day because that day was skipped. I think it was a great shock to her when she realized that she'd been tricked. But after arrival in Shanghai, we all met Admiral and Mrs. Bristol who had proceeded from Constantinople, across Russia and Siberia and came down from one of the ports -

I think it was Vladivostok - in Siberia to assume command of the fleet, which he did on the 9th of September 1927. By that time all of his staff had arrived, and the flag was hoisted on board his flagship, the USS Pittsburgh, in Shanghai Harbor.

Q: Did you have any sense of going back to a familiar area when you returned to China?

Adm. W.: Very much so. Actually, it had only been eight years - no - six years since I had left there, and very little change had taken place in the situation, the political situation, in China at that time. I also had a very warm feeling about being with Admiral and Mrs. Bristol because of having really been - lived as a member of their family in Constantinople, in the embassy I was eating all my meals with them, so I was really almost like their son. I might take a few moments to describe the situation in China, both at that time and the time I was there before, inasmuch as I don't believe I covered that very well on the occasion of my first visit to China.

China, at that time, was really in the hands of the war lords. Of course, the Republic of China had been proclaimed in 1911 and, incidentally, Admiral Bristol, who had been in China at that time in command of the U.S.S. Albany, had been the first to fire a salute, the first foreign vessel to fire a salute to Yuan Shih Kai, the then-new President of China.

Q: Would that have been Sun Yat Sen's time?

Adm. W.: I think it was Yüan Shih-k'ai, but I wouldn't be sure about that because I wasn't there. But the situation had deteriorated considerably since then, and the Peking government which took over at that time gradually lost control of the rest of China, and each province or section was ruled by the most powerful military man in the area at that time. They - even the war lords attempted to preserve the illusion of a civil government by setting up what they called the civil government, and they were the military government, but they actually ran their province or their area. Of course, that resulted in a very autocratic form of government, completely dictatorial, and resulted in a great many local wars between these competing war lords, as each one would like to extend his territory beyond his own boundaries of control. The situation was, therefore, quite chaotic, as one may easily imagine. At that time, at least, there was little, if any silver in China, and the only silver that I saw in circulation was imported from Mexico and coined into silver dollars, or 20-cent pieces, or whatever was in circulation at that time. Actually, many of the silver dollars still had the imprint "Republicana Mexicana" on them. The Chinese hadn't bothered even to melt the silver and recast it in their own design.

The Chinese were very reluctant to accept any paper money. They wanted hard money and not only that, but they weighed it and examined it very carefully to see that none of it was counterfeit. They claimed, for instance, that six

20-cent pieces made of silver had the equivalent of one silver dollar. So that if you took a silver dollar to the - to an exchange place, of which there were many all over China, in almost every block in the cities, you would get, not five 20-cent pieces, but six.

Q: What do you mean by a 20-cent piece?

Adm.W.: It was like our 25-cent piece. But the silver dollar was believed to have more silver in it than five 20-cent pieces of their own currency, so they gave you six. There was also another peculiarity which I noticed: the Chinese would always thump a dollar on the table to see if it rang true and oftentimes they didn't because the Chinese would make sometimes what was called a "three-piecey dollar." To do this they would use a very sharp knife, cut around the inside of the edge of the coin, remove all of the silver, and fill it with lead, and put the top back on the coin, which is, of course, where the term "three-piecey dollar" arises. In other words, the top part, the bottom part which had been scoured out, and the lead disc which they had put inside, which made the three parts.

Q: It hardly seems worth the effort.

Adm. W.: It wouldn't be worth the effort in this country, but of course labor in China is so cheap that anything that they could gain by that, why, they were tempted to do.

Q: I never heard that described before.

Adm. W.: A lot of people don't know about that. Well, to get back to the war lords, I've mentioned, I believe, once earlier that two of them, Wu Pei Fu and Chang Tso-lin, were warring together at the time when I was attached to the Huron in 1920 and was ordered by the captain of the Huron to Peking with the - a company of bluejackets to reinforce the guard because these two Chinese war lords were fighting with each other for the control of Peking. Also the principal reason for the gunboats on the Yangtze, at that time, and even at this time, during my second visit, was because the war lords had control of various sections of the Yangtze River, and any cargo which was being shipped to the upper river was subject to being confiscated by any one of the various war lords in control of that section of the river en route to their destination. The American gunboats were therefore used to escort American vessels, such as the Standard Oil shipments. The Robert Dollar Line had two vessels operating in the Yangtze Gorges, the Robert Dollar II and the Alice Dollar, and I think I mentioned that they had the highest freight rate at that time of any in the world, not only because of the dangers of the cargo being confiscated by the Chinese war lords, but also because of the navigational dangers en route. So that the whole country was completely disorganized, and there was no central control. Chiang Kai-chek had organized an army in the south, the Canton area, and had marched north and regained a measure of control and had established his headquarters in Nanking.

Q: What year would that have been? On your second tour?

Adm. W.: On my second tour, yes. [in 1927] But that government did not control the whole of China by any means. It controlled most of the southern part of China, but not the whole of China. Soon after arrival in Shanghai and after Admiral Bristol had taken over the command of the U.S. Asiatic fleet, he took Mrs. Bristol and me to Peking to call on the American minister and to see the sights around the Peking area. We were widely entertained by the minister and by other friends in the area, including a Mrs. Calhoun, who was the widow of a former American ambassador to China. She lived in a beautiful Chinese home, which had been furnished with her exquisite taste, and entertained many Americans and other friends of hers who came to Peking. I remember one of the parties that she gave at the summer palace, which is a good illustration of how we lived in China. We all met at her house about 11 o'clock in the forenoon and were driven out to the summer palace which was one of the favorite resorts of the Empress dowager. There were no restaurants or places where one could have a meal, so Mrs. Calhoun's servants took the entire requirements for a beautiful luncheon out ahead of us...

Q: How did they travel?

Adm. W.: They traveled - er, I'm not sure because I didn't see them on their way, but I think they probably went out in cars - I mean one of her cars. Some of them may have gone in rickshaws or sedan chairs, but I think probably, on this occasion, they went out in cars. In any case, when we arrived at the Summer Palace they had set up ~~this beautiful~~ what might ordinarily be called a picnic luncheon, except that it was served in the most elaborate fashion, with cocktails and relishes and three or four courses, all done by her servants, of which she had a goodly number. It was a very colorful and delightful occasion. That reminds me also of the fact that when I was executive officer in the Palos, when we were in Changsha, the captain and I would frequently give luncheons and dinners in a Chinese temple - dinners - about ten miles away, and all it was necessary to do was to tell Yonkai, who was our chief steward on the Palos, that we were going to have 12 people for dinner at this Chinese temple on a mountain about 10 miles away and be sure that it would all be ready by 7 o'clock. And that was the end of our worry in connection with the ~~thing~~ affair. We would go at the appointed time together with our guests in sedan chairs, and the tables would all be set, the cocktails would all be ready, and everything served in a beautiful fashion, comparable to what you would have today at some of the best restaurants in San Francisco. I mention that as showing the way we lived. As one looks back on it, it seems almost, as you say, incredible. But those days unfortunately have gone for ever.

Q: Well, again, fortunately or unfortunately.

Adm. W.: It depends on your point of view. The interesting thing is that these Chinese servants did not resent that. At least, they certainly did not appear to resent it. They were

Wheeler #3 - 153

very faithful and very anxious to please. They were well paid, of course, by their standards, and they couldn't have been more agreeable. I recall, for instance, when I went back to China the second time, the boy that I had had on the <u>Palos</u> when we were up in Chungking, he lived in that area, heard that I was back in China and he came all the way down from Chungking to see me and bring me presents.

Q: That must have been very touching, wasn't it?

Adm. W.: I mention that only to point out that there was no feeling of antagonism by the Chinese against us at all. There were the friendliest relations between us.

Q: Did you finish with your party with Mrs. Calhoun? I don't want to not finish that.

Adm. W.: Well, I think after the party was over, we broke up and went sightseeing, looked round the summer palace, the most interesting thing, of course, at the summer palace was a marble boat, which was a summer pavilion made of marble in the shape of a boat, which the Empress dowager had had built with the money that had been appropriated by the government to build a Chinese battleship. She was quite a gal.

Q: She must have been.

Adm. W.: After our return to Shanghai, I had the pleasure of attending the wedding of Mae Ling Sung [Soong] and Chiang Kai-chek on the 1st of December 1927. The wedding was conducted in the Majestic Hotel in a very beautiful setting, which was only marred by the cameras and equipment that was set up right on the stage where the wedding took place. This was actually the second wedding in that the bride had insisted that they be married in a religious ceremony - in a Christian ceremony. She herself was a Christian, Chiang Kai-chek was not, but he agreed to that arrangement.

Q: Was he anything?

Adm. W.: He was whatever the Chinese are, probably a Buddhist.

Q: Then, this was a second and civil ceremony?

Adm. W.: I think it was probably a Buddhist ceremony. It was the ordinary type of Chinese wedding.

Q: Before you leave that. What did she wear, what costume?

Adm. W.: At this wedding she wore a typical Chinese costume, which is the high-necked gown with the kind of slit skirt, you know, that they wear. I don't really remember what color it was. I suppose if I were a woman I probably would have.

Q: Was it brocade, satin, or what?

Adm. W.: Very elaborate brocade. I imagine it was probably white, but I don't recall. The Chinese wedding color, of course, is red. So it was a toss-up. From the Christian standpoint, why, of course, it would have been white, and from the Chinese standpoint, it should have been red. So it was probably red. Mae Ling Soong, who became Madame Chiang Kai-chek, was one of a very famous family of Soongs. One other sister, of course, married Sun Yat Sen, and she threw in her lot with the Commies and was not a party to Chiang Kai-chek's government. Another daughter married Dr. H. H. Kung, who became minister of Commerce and Industry in Chiang Kai-chek's government. They were particular friends of mine, and we have somewhere among our possessions a pair of silver vases which the Kungs gave us for a wedding present. There was a brother, T. V. Soong, who was the minister of finance in Chiang Kai-chek's government. As I say, it was quite a noted family in Chinese history at that time. I have the feeling that Chiang Kai-chek, who was basically merely one of the war lords and not very different from any of the rest of them except that he was more successful, but when he married Mae Ling Soong a change seemed to come over him and he was influenced, I'm sure, by his wife who indoctrinated him with the ideas of what a good government should be, and he set up the best government which China had had for a long time, and would, in my opinion, have made a very successful head of state in China had not the United States failed to back him up after the end of World War II.

Q: I want to ask some more questions. At their wedding, were her sisters present?

Adm. W.: Yes. Except Mme. Sun Yat Sen.

Q: Did she have many attendants?

Adm. W.: No. As I recall, she didn't have any attendants. At a Chinese wedding, I don't think they do. I don't remember seeing them, in any case. The people on the stage at one end of the ball room of the Majestic Hotel, as I recall, were limited to the principals, the bride and groom, the priest, and the cameramen and their equipment. There was nothing like we have, such as a procession and a marriage ceremony of our type. It's a long time ago, as you know, and I don't recall exactly what they did, but they followed, I think, the Buddhist ceremony in this marriage.

Q: What did Chiang Kai-chek wear?

Adm. W.: He wore a uniform - just the uniform of a Chinese general.

Q: And how many people attended the affair?

Adm. W.: Oh, there must have been several hundred. This was the official wedding, you see.

Q: Then did they go out or were they acclaimed by people, or what happened afterwards? Do you recall any activities or festivities?

Adm. W.: No, I don't recall any festivities. They just left. I don't remember whether they left before we did, but there was nothing like we would have. No lining of the sidewalk and throwing rice and things like that. They just sort of disappeared.

Q: Do you know him well enough to evaluate his character?

Adm. W.: No. No, I didn't know him that well, but I would

- er, my conclusion from what I know that he did in China after he married Mae Ling Soong, was that he had very good intentions. He was a patriot and he had the best interests of China at heart. Oh, I don't think he was perfect. I mean, none of us are, for that matter, but I think, as I said before, that he was by far the best of the war lords and he certainly fought a very determined war against the Japanese, he was an avowed anti-Communist, and I think it is a great pity that we did not give him the support he needed to take over the entire government in China. I have the feeling that he would have done an excellent job, and I regret to say it, but I feel that the United States has a big burden to bear for its failure to back up Chiang Kai-chek and not let him become the ruler of China. Our government, I'm sure, was influenced by some of the Americans who, including General Marshall, who were sent out to China to dicker with the Communists, after which our government withdrew the supplies which had been sent to China for - to give to Chiang Kai-chek to fight off the Communists. That, in my opinion, led to the take-over of China by the Communists and all of the trouble that we have suffered from since that time.

Q: Strange in history why decisions were made as they were.

Adm. W.: Well, the unfortunate part of it was that the people who made these decisions, I don't think they really knew what they were doing. I don't think General Marshall knew the Chinese nearly as well as many other people who had lived in China and who had sized up the situation correctly, but, of course, their information and experience was not taken advantage of, so that the decisions were left up to people who really didn't know what they were doing.

Q: As I recall, Marshall had never been stationed there, had he?

Adm. W.: I think he'd been stationed there in Tientsin quite a long time before that, for some comparatively short time, but it had been a long time before and I don't think he understood the situation at all.

Q: Well, we live with now, what we have to live with, I guess.

Adm. W.: Well, on January 15, 1928, we sailed for the Philippines, where we spent most of the winter. That was very interesting and very pleasant. General MacArthur was there. By that time he had retired from the United States Army and had been given the rank of Marshal in the Philippine Army - no, my mistake, that didn't occur till later. When we arrived he was in command of the Philippine Department of the United States Army and had his headquarters in or near Manila, I've forgotten exactly where his headquarters were located. We also enjoyed visiting Baguio, which was a delightful spot up in the mountains. The army had a camp there, called Camp John Hay, which was really in the nature of a rest camp where people were sent for a vacation and to recuperate after they had been in the Philippines for a long time and were suffering from the heat. Baguio was delightfully cool and pleasant. They had a golf course there and we had delightful quarters, in the club. We spent some few weeks up there, and Admiral Bristol, of course, was entertained by the governor who was later Secretary of State, in other words Mr. Stimson.

Q: How many ships went - the entire Asiatic Fleet went to the Philippines?

Adm. W.: Not all of them, no, because some were stationed - we usually had one or more ships in each, what we called, treaty port. Under the treaty which followed the Boxer Rebellion, the Chinese were forced to agree to open up a limited number of ports to foreign commerce, and it was the policy of the United States to keep one of our ships in those ports most of the time. The need for this was shown by a story which my father-in-law told me about an occasion when a Chinese bandit in the Amoy area was anxious to cause the foreigners some discomfort, and so he captured a missionary and threatened to kill him. The missionary was one of our missionaries who was living up in the interior, and the war lord had threatened to kill this missionary. Whereupon, Mr. Putnam, who was to become my father-in-law, sent word to this war lord that if he didn't release the missionary, why, he, the consul, would get the commanding officer of the destroyer to send a group of sailors up there and get the missionary back. The war lord didn't like this threat, and Mr. Putnam wasn't quite sure but what possibly even that might make the war lord dispose of the missionary, but he didn't, and eventually, the missionary was released and came back to Amoy. But the presence of American naval ships in these treaty ports exercised a very steadying influence on the Chinese who were tempted to take advantage of foreigners who were in those ports doing business, and also to protect the missionaries who were scattered all through the interior.

Q: So one ship would be left in each port, and the rest of the fleet went to Manila. For the winter, or...?

Adm. W.: For the winter. The submarines had a regular routine. They spent the winter in Manila and the summer in Tsingtao, which is a port on the Shantung Peninsula, which became known in World War I because one of the terms of the settlement after the Boxer Rebellion provided that the port of Tsingtao should be made available to the Germans. In fact, the Germans exercised complete control and they built a little settlement there which looked for all the world like a German settlement. They even installed a battery of heavy guns to protect it against the Chinese, should they decide to retake it. That came into prominence again in World War II when the Japs who were not on our side, as they were in World War I, laid siege in World War II to Tsingtao and captured it from the Germans.

Q: Did the Germans keep it even after World War I?

Adm. W.: ~~Yes.~~ No.

Q: ~~Oh, I see. Right through to World War II.~~ When did submarines join the fleet? When did they first become part of the fleet?

Adm. W.: Oh, that was before my day. I remember the first submarine I ever saw in the Navy was the old Holland, which was one of the first submarines we ever had, I think, tied up to a wharf in Annapolis. It was not in commission, but the Navy had been operating submarines experimentally some time before I entered the Naval Academy as a midshipman. I don't know exactly when they began.

After leaving the Philippines in March of 1928, we went to Canton twice. The flagship went to Hong Kong, where we were entertained by the governor general and his wife, and by ~~many of the visiting~~ - many of the British ships which were at anchor in Hong Kong at that time. I also accompanied Admiral Bristol on the visit he made to Canton, and also on the cruise up the West River, the mouth of which is near Hong Kong. In the spring of that year, in May, the flagship made a visit of friendship to Yokohama, from which we visited Tokyo and were also entertained by the minister and the naval attache and other friends that we had in that area. Also the various officials of Tokyo and Yokohama. Later on, after leaving Tokyo, we went to Peking again. I don't recall exactly what the occasion for that was, but it does seem to me that there was some occurrence in Peking which required the commander-in-chief to be present for consultation with the American minister, and we left hurriedly to get to Peking as quickly as possible by going by train from Tokyo to Shimonoseki, where one of our destroyers was waiting to take us to Tientsin.

Q: You don't remember what occasioned that?

Adm. W.: I can't remember the occasion, but I know it was a very touchy situation that was arising, but which was amicably settled later on. From there Admiral Bristol and his staff, including myself, visited Tientsin, where the Admiral inspected the Third Marine Brigade. The Army had had a force of infantrymen in Tientsin for a long time - I think ever since the Peking Rebellion - the Boxer Rebellion - but for several years before we got to Tientsin on this occasion, we had stationed a brigade of Marines there in order to afford more protection to our Americans who were living in Peking and that part of the country, the principal function of which was to keep the railroad between Peking and Tientsin open. The Third Brigade of Marines was commanded by General Smedley Butler, who was quite a well known character at that time. I believe he afterwards became mayor of Philadelphia - no, not mayor. I believe he was chief of police. They didn't call him that, but...

Q: Something like that.

Adm. W.: Returning to Shanghai, we participated in the commissioning ceremonies of the USS Panay, which was later to become well known when it was fired on by the Japanese. The Panay was one of four gunboats which were being built at the Shanghai shipyards to replace the Monocacy and the Palos, the two upriver gunboats, and several of the other gunboats which had been captured at the end of the Spanish-American War. They were obviously ready for the scrap heap, and so our government had had these four new gunboats built.

Q: How long did the U.S. keep gunboats on the Yangtze?

Adm. W.: They were kept there right up until the Japanese took over in World War II - or, before World War II, as a matter of fact, the Japanese eventually conquered most of that part of China.

Q: Because the Panay was there right up until the early days, wasn't it?

Adm. W.: That's right, and of course the whole thing was scrapped. I wasn't there at the time, but all the gunboats were taken over by the Japs and later by the Communists, when China fell a victim into Communist hands. We don't know what their eventual fate was.

On the 1st of December we participated in the coronation and naval review in Tokyo Bay.

Q: I want to hear all about that. I'm sure it was fascinating.

Adm. W: Yes. Each foreign flagship of the British, French, Italian navies stationed in the Far East, as well as our own, were invited to participate in this review. The ships were lined up in Tokyo Bay in six or eight lines, extending for some distance down the bay, and the Emperor on board HIJMS - His Imperial Japanese Majesty's Ship - Haruna, which was one of the old warships that had a traditional flavor for the Japanese, passed down between the lines, so that he could see all the ships and they could see him. The review was marred somewhat by bad weather. In fact, plans were made to postpone it for a day if the weather was so bad it couldn't be held, but it wasn't necessary to do that.

At the appointed time, the Emperor came down to Tokyo and embarked in a launch and was taken out to the Haruna, and there was much fanfare and saluting and all that kind of thing while he boarded the Haruna and made this trip round and in between the lines of warships. The commander-in-chief had invited many of the VIPs of Tokyo and their ladies down to witness the review from the decks of the Pittsburgh. They were served luncheon and were to have left some time in the afternoon, but the seas were so rough that after one woman fell overboard trying to get aboard the launch, it was decided to keep them for dinner. As a matter of fact, some of them were kept on board all night because it was dangerous to transport them ashore in small boats.

Q: Did you fish her out?

Adm. W.: Oh, yes. We don't let anybody drown around naval ships.

Q: How heavy were the seas?

Adm. W.: Oh, they were, I suppose, about six or eight feet high, which is pretty rough. There had been an aerial review planned for the same time as the naval review. In other words, hundreds of planes were to fly overhead as the Emperor was cruising down the various lines of ships. But the weather was too bad, so that was called off. Incident to this review, there were, of course, a tremendous number of festivities, both ashore and afloat, dinners at the embassy, dinners by the bay of Tokyo, garden parties in the Emperor's palace grounds, geisha parties in Yokohama, so that by the time this thing was over - it last three or four days - we were all pretty well bushed. But it was a fantastic thing to see, and quite in contrast to the only other naval review which I attended in 1934, which was held off Sandy Hook by President Franklin Delano Roosevelt. That was the type in which the reviewing ship was stationary and all of the ships being reviewed passed in review. In other words, you see the difference?

Q: The latter of which you speak is the usual course for personal review, although one frequently sees pictures of people trooping the line and so on. But to get a little more graphic idea of the Tokyo Bay picture, you had listed I think about six nations that had ships there.

Adm. W.: Yes, and they were all given honor places at the head of the line. I mean, everyone of course wasn't at the head of the line, but there was one line at the head of which were all the foreign ships. Admiral Bristol's flagship was at the very head of the line because he had the highest rank of any foreign Navy commander, that was the four-star rank, whereas the British had as the commander of their naval forces in the Orient only three stars.

Q: How many lines were there down the bay?

Adm. W.: There must have been six or eight, may be more.

Q: Do you have a picture of it?

Adm. W.: I have a picture of it and I will show it to you.

Q: (Admiral Wheeler has just shown me a report of the coronation review, which I've asked him to let us attached as an appendix, also a chart showing the route of the Imperial flagship and how it made its review, and we also expect to have a copy of that.)

Adm. W.: During the ceremonies attendant upon the coronation naval review, I had the pleasure of accompanying Admiral Bristol to dinner on board the flagship of the Japanese combined fleet with the commander-in-chief of that fleet. The dinner was given on board HIJMS Nagato, and it was a very formal and beautiful occasion. I recall that as we stepped on board the Japanese flagship, screens had been erected around some of the guns which were visible from the quarterdeck, so that the guests could not see them, and we were shown directly down into the Admiral's cabin, where the dinner was held.

Q: Do you think the screening was for security?

Adm. W.: For security, which shows that the Japanese were not about to let us in on any of their secrets, at least parts of the ship which they considered as secret. In front of my place at dinner, in addition to the menu which was made on silk, was this favor, the import of which I have never known. I do, however, recognize the symbol of eternity which shows these little whirligigs...

Q: I'm looking at a - it appears to be silver?

Adm. W.: Yes.

Q: A silver medallion on a small ebony stand in the shape of an inverted teardrop...

Adm. W.: Yes, a very good description, surmounted by a gold star.

Q: And there are beautiful engravings on both sides. Do you recognize the Japanese words on the back?

Adm. W.: I do not, no.

Q: And on a smooth surface on the back of this beautiful little item is some Japanese writing. And that was your place card?

Adm. W.: Each one of us had one of those. The dinner was accompanied by string music, and the conversation was quite interesting.

Q: What was the language spoken?

Adm. W.: The language was English. Practically all of the Japanese commanders spoke English, and many, many of the local people speak English because English is taught in their schools, was taught even then. The other guests included the commanders-in-chief of the other naval forces, so that there was probably more rank assembled in that cabin than I have ever been with at any time before or since.

Q: How many people attended?

Adm. W.: There must have been 15 to 20. The cabin was completely full - occupied by this table where we were all accommodated. I will refer again to the Nagato in my description of my visit to Tokyo after the surrender on board the Missouri in World War II.

Q: Before we leave the coronation ceremony, I'm wondering if you remember the name of the Emperor?

Adm. W.: Yes, it's the same Emperor we have now. Hirohito. This was the beginning of his reign.

Q: He did not have an Empress, then, I think.

Adm. W.: I don't recall, but in any case she did not participate in the...

Q: Did you meet him in any of these ceremonies?

Adm. W.: No. He was, at that time, considered almost a deity. I believe that Admiral Bristol may have met him, but no one else.

Q: Could you see him? Was he close enough for you to see him?

Adm. W.: Oh, yes. We could see him on the Haruna.

Q: And his costume was?

Adm. W.: He was in a naval costume - full uniform.

Q: Who would have performed that coronation? Would it have been a religious ceremony?

Adm. W.: I couldn't answer that. Of course, the coronation didn't necessarily take place at that time. What I mean is within that exact period. The naval review might have been a week or a month or so before or after the coronation, but it was one of the ceremonies attendant upon the coronation. Of course, the Japs [anese] are very proud of their Navy and wanted to take that opportunity to advertise it, I suspect.

Q: Did you observe how many Japanese ships there were in the harbor that day? I notice from your chart that it was many, many.

Adm. W: I would say there were about 100 at least, but some of them were quite small.

Q: Could you tell what vintage they were?

Adm. W.: Well, the battleships and destroyers and cruisers, many of them were fairly new, but many of the smaller ships looked quite old and not very useful.

Q: Did you have any sense on that day that there was a forecast of an attempt at naval power by the Japanese?

Adm. W.: Yes. My attention was called to it by the fact that they were attempting to prevent us from seeing anything on the flagship, except what we had to see on the way to the admiral's cabin, by the screening.

Q: Would you have paid any attention to it, otherwise?

Adm. W.: Probably not. But I think all of us in the Navy, in our Navy, knew - or had a feeling - at that time that eventually we were going to have to fight Japan. Later on, when I was at the War College, practically all of our war games were oriented against Japan.

Q: Well, it must have been an exciting and a memorable event.

Adm. W.: Yes, indeed it was. After this, we - in January - we set sail again for the Philippine Islands, only this time Admiral Bristol prescribed a war game to take place around Guam, the object of which was to - for our fleet to capture Guam. This was, as I say, a war game, and the ships were deployed around Guam in such a way as to destroy the guns on Guam, of which there were very few and very ineffective - in other words, when we went ashore later on and visited the gun sites we were impressed with the fact that there really were no adequate defenses in Guam at all. In other words, our government had not seen fit to really fortify Guam. There were a few feeble efforts to place a few relatively small guns at what might be considered strategic points, but they wouldn't have had any real value.

Q: How large a force was on Guam?

Adm. W.: I would say not more, according to my recollection, than a few hundred Marines.

Q: Any civilians?

Adm. W.: Oh, yes. Guam was at that time under the Navy. There was a naval governor.

Q: Like the Philippines?

Adm. W.: Like the Philippines - no, the Philippines didn't have a Navy governor, they were governed at that time by Mr. Stimson.

Q: What was his position?

Adm. W.: He was governor-general of the Philippine Islands. But the governor of Guam, as was the governor of Samoa, American Samoa, - all of our outlying possessions in the Pacific at that time had, with the exception of the Philippines, a naval governor.

Q: Oh, a naval governor. That was the distinction between Stimson and the other man.

Adm. W.: That's right. Stimson was a civilian. The naval governor, of course, had a naval staff and there were a number of Navy enlisted men there. The duty in Guam, however, was not considered very choice, although there was one attraction. There was an old naval collier called the Gold Star, the USS Gold Star, which used to bring provisions from the outside world to Guam and, once a year, when she made a trip to China to get fuel and supplies, the naval personnel who had been there at least a year were permitted to make the trip at no expense to themselves except, of course, for their mess bill.

Q: Who won the war games? Were you able to conquer Guam?

Adm. W.: We had a critique and there was a great deal of palaver about it. I don't think it ever was decided who won it, as it frequently isn't in these cases. I've attended many Navy critiques and about all they do is to discuss who did what, and why, and when, and what effect it would have had. But obviously Guam could not have been taken without a large landing force, which we did not have. There was a company of Marines on board the flagship. The Marines, of course, are usually the ones who do the landings. We had no landing force and we had no landing craft, which were not really developed until World War II, just before World War II, so I don't think anybody really won, although I would say that possibly our maneuvers may have helped to inform the Navy Department of the inadequacy of the fortifications in Guam, although nothing was done about it.

After this war game, we returned to the Philippines and stopped en route at Jolo, in the Sulu Islands, which is a part of the Philippines and locally governed by the Sultan of Sulu, who has a most remarkable palace built up on sort of stilts like most of the Philippine homes, but he was not there when we arrived, so we didn't meet him. We also stopped at Davao, which was a very busy port and was the shipping point for hemp, the plant from which hemp rope is made. The plant is very much like a banana tree. I've forgotten the name at the moment. There were a tremendous number of Japanese who lived there and were growing rich off of cultivating hemp, which was used, of course, in the making of rope and other fabrics. There was so much money being made down there that I recall that one of the officers on the staff decided that he would like to get in this game himself. He went around among the other staff officers, including myself, on board the ship and tried to get us to join him in putting up money to finance a plantation down there. I wasn't about to be sucked into that and I've often wondered what happened to his investment because of course soon after that - at least, not long after that - the Philippines fell into the hands of the Japanese, so I'm afraid he. lost everything.

Q: An absentee landlord isn't very successful anyway.

Adm. W.: While in Manila we saw General MacArthur at a wedding of a member of his staff, a young lawyer on the staff of governor general Stimson who was married to the sister of a naval officer, who was also in Manila. This was the occasion for a very beautiful wedding breakfast held at the Polo Club just outside of Manila, which General MacArthur attended.

Q: Did you ever meet him?

Adm. W.: Yes.

Q: What was your reaction to him at that point?

Adm. W.: My reaction to him was that he was pretty hard to take. I say quite freely that I think General MacArthur was -

well, let's put it this way: I think that to begin with Mr. Winston Churchill was the greatest man who has lived in my time. I think that General MacArthur was the greatest military man that has lived in our time. But, from the personal standpoint, I think as I said that he was very hard to take, he was not at all affable, he regarded himself - or gave the impression, at least, of regarding himself - as next to God, very unapproachable, and he apparently had a keen dislike for the Navy, which many officers who have served with him will corroborate, although when he commanded the Southwest Pacific area in World War II (which is another story) apparently he went out of his way to cooperate with the commander of the Seventh Fleet, who was subordinate to him in the operations round the Philippines. So that I'm sure that you would find a number of naval officers who would disagree with the statement that I made previously. But I do think that he was not very fond of the Navy, which is unfortunate because the two services should stand together.

I do think, however, that General MacArthur was one of the greatest men of our age from a military standpoint, and I think that if he had become president of the United States, this country would have avoided many of the woes which we have suffered since that time.

Q: I think those are interesting comments. In spite of his personal characteristics, you felt that still he could have been a great leader of our country?

Adm. W.: I'm not in any doubt about that at all. I'm sure of it.

When talking about the Philippine Islands, I neglected to mention that one of the guests at a dinner which Admiral Bristol had on the flagship, which I attended, was General Aguinaldo, who was well known in the early part of this century, as he led a rebellion in the southern Philippine Islands against the Americans soon after the Philippines were conquered from Spain.

After leaving the Philippine Islands, Admiral Bristol took the fleet to Hong Kong...

Q: Before we leave that, I think I should ask you, since this General Aguinaldo led an insurrection against the United States, how had his status changed so that he became a guest aboard Admiral Bristol's flagship?

Adm. W.: Well, the insurrection, of course, was put down, and a lot of time had elapsed between this insurrection and the time that we were there, which was on the order of 28 years, and by that time his rebellion had been overlooked and he had become rehabilitated and was generally accepted in Manila society.

Q: Was he part of the Philippine government?

Adm. W.: No. He was a retired insurrectionist!

Well, as I was saying, after leaving the Philippines, Admiral Bristol took the fleet to Hong Kong, where we had another visit with the governor general and his wife, and from there we went to Quemoy, where the fleet was anchored not far from what is now well known as Quemoy and Matsu. As the island of Matsu - the island of Quemoy, as a matter of fact - is almost within the limits of the harbor of Amoy. Soon after our arrival, the American consul, Mr. Putnam, came on board to call on the commander-in-chief, who, of course, returned his call, and soon thereafter the commander-in-chief and I and some other members of his staff were invited to the American consulate for dinner. We went by the admiral's barge to the landing, which was very close to the American consulate, and arriving perhaps a little earlier than we were expected, the door was opened by Miss Putnam, whom you will remember I had met before in San Francisco Harbor and who had traveled with me on the way to Shanghai in 1927. In the meantime, Miss Putnam had gotten a little older and I was immediately attracted to her. As a matter of fact, I thought she was the most beautiful girl I'd ever seen. So, three days after that I invited her to a - she invited me - to a picnic at a Chinese temple not far away, and on that occasion I did the smartest thing I ever did in my life by proposing to her.

Q: That was rather precipitate wasn't it?

Adm. W.: It was precipitate in one way but, on the other hand, of course, I had met her over two years ago, so I knew her better than anyone normally would after three days of re-acquaintance, you might say.

Q: I want to introduce Mrs. Wheeler now, because she's with us, and I'd love to ask you what your reactions to now-Admiral Wheeler were then? And I might say she's as beautiful a girl now as she was when he met her.

Mrs. W.: Well, thank you, Madam, allowing for the passage of 40 years, My reaction to him when I met him in San Francisco was that he was a very attractive man, but he couldn't possibly have been less interested in me, and when I saw him again in Amoy I still found him very attractive, but I was very annoyed that night that he came to dinner because I had another date, and Father made me come to the dinner because he needed me to balance the table. So, the whole thing, I think, took both of us by surprise.

Adm. W.: Tell about what - how you disposed of your date.

Mrs. W.: No, I don't think the Naval Institute could possibly be interested...

Q: I am, though, so you go on and tell it.

Mrs. W.: I don't see why that should go down in history.

Adm. W.: Go ahead, dear.

Mrs. W.: Well, he had asked me for a date and, of course, there were no movies or anything like that. There was no place to go but the club for a date in Amoy. It was just a little island. So I suggested that we go to a Chinese temple which could be reached by boat, and was a very attractive spot, and the picnic could be put up at the consulate. But I had no free time because the fleet was there, so in the afternoon when he asked me for that night, I said, yes, I would go with him, but it was very awkward indeed because I didn't have that time free, I had a date with a young medical officer from one of the destroyers in port. I was quite worried about it because Julian was coming at 2.15, and I had this date at 2.00 with this young medical officer. So the next morning I went over to the American Hospital, which was right next to the consulate, and I sat in the waiting room and waited to see the head of the hospital, Dr. Strick. I was ushered in, finally, to his office and he said, "What's the matter with you?" And I said, "Nothing, except that I'm in this jam about these two men, and I would like to get rid of the doctor." "Well," he said, "what do you expect me to do about it? My waiting room is full of people who are sick. Just go on, get out, go away." I said, "Well, doctor, I thought, may be, if you arrived about 2.20 after Julian gets there and took the doctor over to see the hospital, then we could make a getaway." He said, "Go out," and he just opened the door and threw me out.

Well, about 2, the doctor arrived that afternoon. At 2.15 Julian arrived. At 2.20, Dr. Strick arrived, and he said, "I've come to show you my hospital," and the last I saw of the young medical officer was when he was being invited out, saying, "But I don't want to see the hospital."

Q: But he went?

Mrs. W.: He went.

Q: Thank you, Mrs. Wheeler, I think that's a nice side line on how the Admiral met you.

Adm. W.: Well, to go on with this story. It so happened that a month or so after that, Mrs. Putnam and her daughter, my fiancee, arrived in Shanghai while the flagship was there, to buy her trousseau, and Admiral Bristol said to Doanda, "Doanda, is everything about your wedding, the way you'd like to have it?" She said, "Well, there's only one thing that I'm disappointed about, Admiral, that is that Julian tells me that, contrary to the usual custom, there is not going to be an American destroyer in Amoy at the time of the wedding, which will be June the 20th." Admiral Bristol said, "I'll fix that," he said "I'll send a destroyer there for the wedding, so that you can have your arch of swords," which was the reason she said she was disappointed that no destroyer was going to be there. So, at the appointed time, why, Admiral Bristol ordered this destroyer to take me to Amoy in time for the wedding, and when the wedding took place the captain of the destroyer was Ted Chandler, the son of the former Admiral Chandler, was my best man and all of the other officers except the one who was required to stay on board by Navy regulations because he had the duty, were my groomsmen.

Q: I would suggest that perhaps the only wedding in history for which a ship of the United States fleet was ordered to duty to officiated.

Adm. W.: It was a beautiful wedding and everything went as planned. After it was over, we learned that the ship upon which we had planned to begin our honeymoon was not going to arrive in Shanghai because of a strike on the Dutch East Indies

Line, so we had to take a Japanese coastal vessel, which was not going where we had planned, but which stopped at ~~Kirun~~ Keelung, a port of Formosa, from which we proceeded to Taipei, the present capital of the Chinese Nationalist government. We were only there for a short time - a day or so - and then the little Japanese steamer on which we were passengers sailed for Shimonoseki, where we took a train for Kyoto. While in Kyoto we arranged for a trip through the Nakasendo Highway, which is a part of Japan sometimes referred to as the Japanese Alps, and it so happened that a trip very similar to this was made by my bride's mother and father on their wedding trip some 30 years before. Wasn't it about 30?

Mrs. W.: It was in 1899. It was the exact trip. Father had mapped it out, using his Baedeker guide book, except that they started in Yokohama and they had gone by rickshaw and chairs and various primitive conveyances, whereas we went by train, and we were met in the stations of these outlying places by cars.

Adm. W.: As a matter of fact, in each of the towns along this route that we took, we were met I think by the taxi, as it seems to me that there was only one car in each little Japanese village that we visited. Our first stop...

Q: I'm surprised they had roads large enough to accommodate a car.

Adm. W.: It was surprising. Our first stop was at the village of Gifu, from which we went out to see the cormorant fishing, which, as some already know, consists of the fishermen in small boats carrying lighted, burning, faggots in iron baskets on the bow of these little boats, which attracted the fish, and they had cormorants on leashes which were made fast to the boats. As the fish were attracted by the lights, the cormorants would dive for them and catch the fish in their bills, but they were unable to swallow them because the cormorants had rings around their necks which stopped the fish from going down their gullets, and the fishermen would remove the fish and throw them in the boat to be sold later on. This was, of course, a very interesting experience. Then we stopped in these native villages, which had very attractive Japanese inns, usually alongside of a babbling brook with beautiful country scenery, and we ate the Japanese food, we slept on the Japanese floors on futons, or Japanese pads...

Q: How did you communicate?

Adm. W.: We had a little Japanese book for tourists which helped a good bit, but we apparently had no difficulty. They seemed to understand what we wanted. I remember at one place they had a pond in the basement and also a cage with birds flying around in it, and we just pointed to what we wanted and they proceeded to catch them and cook them for our dinner.

Mrs. W.: A lot of them were built in near hot springs or right over hot springs, and we went down to bathe right in the water from the hot springs.

Q: Was this the occasion when you were speaking of bathing? I think you should tell that.

Adm. W.: Yes. When it came time for a bath, my wife went down to the bathroom, which consisted of a fairly sizable tank embedded in the floor so the top was level with the floor, and a faucet with running water on one side. The Japanese method of taking a bath was to soap oneself before getting into the tank, then rinse off, so that when you got into the tank the water wasn't contaminated with the soap or anything. But my wife didn't understand about this, and she got into the tank, apparently, before getting the soap off which upset the little Japanese attendant very much, and she spoke about it to the owner of the inn, who rushed right in to the bathroom, completely disregarding the fact that my wife was taking her bath, and told her that she had done wrong.

Q: Did you understand the communication?

Mrs. W.: No. I had a choice. The bath was sort of like a pool - a small pool - and it was fed by hot springs, and I had a choice of being parboiled like a lobster or getting out in front of this man, and there was nothing that mother or Emily Post or anybody had ever told me about how to deal with a situation like that. So, finally, when I couldn't stand the heat any longer, I grabbed my kimono and rushed upstairs and told Julian that this man had come in when I was bathing, and he went down and was furious. He came back looking very, very cowed, and he said, "Apparently, you were the one that was wrong, you have no manners at all, you have contaminated the bath for everybody else, and they were just trying to tell you."

Darling, are you going to tell about how we were followed by naval intelligence?

Adm. W.: Oh, yes. From there we went to Lake Chuzenji, which is a favorite tourist spot, then on to Yokohama. I neglected to mention that almost as soon as we arrived in Japan and began traveling by train, we noticed a young Japanese military officer...

Q: In uniform?

Adm. W.: ...in uniform, who always seemed to be on the train and in the same car with us. It puzzled us for a while until we finally figured out that he was probably a security officer who was trailing us. That was evidently the case, because he was there throughout the time that we were in Japan on the train, except on one occasion he didn't appear for a long time, and we were quite worried about him. We were afraid that he'd missed the trail and was going to get into trouble. He finally showed up and all was well.

Mrs W: We had quite a time persuading the Japanese to let us follow this itinerary that Father had worked out, because it was off the beaten track and it wasn't what tourists generally did, and at that time it was inconceivable to them that the aide and flag lieutenant to the commander-in-chief would take a trip through Japan for no better purpose than a honeymoon. They were sure, I'm sure, that he was there on some foul intelligence purpose, you know. So this man, finally, toward the end, I think he got very bored with us because he realized we were just honeymooners. Just before we got into Tokyo he apparently had missed the train, but he made it just the last station out of Tokyo, and we were most amused.

Q: How did the Japanese people seem to feel toward you? Did you have any feeling of that sort?

Adm. W.: They were very pleasant with us, except as Doanda has said. They were very opposed to our making this trip through the native villages...

Q: How did they make that known?

Adm. W.: They just put up all kinds of objections, at the tourist office, and in talking with some Americans who lived in Japan later on, they said they thought a part of the reason was that there were no foreign-style hotels in that region, and the Japanese were a little ashamed.

Q: You didn't then have a feeling that the Japanese were opposed to Americans?

Adm. W.: We had no feeling that the Japanese were opposed to us as I mentioned that I thought they had been when I first went to Japan in the early 1920s, ~~which was the period just following the Japanese exclusion act.~~ The only feeling that we had on this occasion was that the Japs were probably very anxious to find out all they could about us because they saw the probability some time of war between Japan and the United States. But that was not shown in their attitude toward us.

Mrs. W.: May I say something next?

Adm. W.: Yes.

Mrs. W.: Wasn't the Exclusion Act passed about 1923?

Adm. W.: Yes.

Mrs. W.: Well, Father was consul in Foochow at that time and he was a friend of the Japanese consul. I mean they played bridge together and that sort of thing, and when the Exclusion Act was passed, he went to call on him, and the consul was not at all anxious to receive him. When Father came into the room, he got up from behind his desk, and Father came over to him, and said, "I have come to you, not as the American consul, but as John Putnam to tell you how terribly sorry I am for what my country has done as a private individual." The consul did not hold out his hand, and he was shaking all over and he said, "Putnam, your country will live to rue this day." At that time, they were very, very bitter. That's how it hit him.

Q: Well, I wanted you to tell me, just because of the ending of the last tape, of the feeling that you had that the Japanese weren't anxious to have you take the route you did on your honeymoon. Would you please repeat that?

Adm. W.: The Japanese were not a bit anxious to have us take the route that we did through the Nakasendo Highway, and my explanation was that, as later explained by a number of Americans there, that they did not want us to stay in Japanese inns. They only wanted Americans to stay in foreign-style inns, because they were a little ashamed of the native hotels and didn't want foreigners to live in them. And my wife gave an explanation of the other reason.

Mrs. W.: Well, they couldn't seem to understand that the reason we wanted to take this trip was that we were following the itinerary of Mother's and Father's wedding trip in 1899, as mapped out by Father in his Baedeker guide. It was inconceivable to them that the Aide and Flag lieutenant to the Commander-in-Chief would be taking a trip to outlying districts in Japan, or anywhere in Japan for that matter, without being on a mission, and as I said before, I'm quite sure, had us followed by an intelligence officer.

Adm. W.: Well, from Lake Chuzengi, which is at the end of our journey in Japanese inns, we went to Tokyo and stayed there several days, then on to Miyanoshita, Nara, and Miyajima, and finally joined Admiral Bristol, Mrs. Bristol, and some of the other members of our staff and their wives at Unzen, which is a well known resort for sulphur baths and not very far from Nagasaki, where the atomic bomb was dropped.

Q: What was the date of your wedding?

Mrs. W.: June 20th, 1929. My Father gave me away. We were married in the consulate. Father gave me away and witnessed it, as he would have to do for any American citizen to make a marriage legal, which is rather unusual, I think.

Adm. W.: Well, to go back a little. Before our marriage, Admiral Bristol and staff were invited to the official burial of Sun Yat Sen on the outskirts of Nanking in May of 1929. This was a very interesting, though somewhat sad, experience. I remember that the first part of the ceremony involved viewing of the body, which was located in a Chinese building on the outskirts of the building, and all of us filed past his bier...

Q: Were you expected to do this?

Adm. W.: That was a part of the routine, yes. We had to file past his bier and we noted that as people ahead of us went past they got right in front of the bier and bowed, and I was quite surprised when I looked down and saw that this casket had a glass top, and here was the old gent in full view, which was quite a shock to me. Later, the casket was - I think the following day - placed on a catafalque and carried by I would say about 100 Chinese, all dressed in uniform, and borne on the shoulders of these men. The funeral procession, as are all Chinese funeral processions, was very, very elaborate. The mourning color in China is white, so white was the predominant color, and there were countless numbers of people, officials and relatives, friends, and I would judge there must have been 1,000 or 1,500 people in that procession, all on foot - that is, the Chinese were.

Q: Had he ben dead a long time?

Adm. W.: He had been dead for many, many years, but he was disinterred by the order of Chiang Kai-chek, who was a great admirer of his, and a beautiful, quite elaborate but impressive, building was erected out in the hills outside of Nanking...

Q: What was his purpose in disinterring the body?

Adm. W.: It was - he wanted to build this beautiful tomb for Sun Yat Sen and bury him there as a mark of respect and honor to Sun Yat Sen, whom he greatly admired.

Mrs. W.: Aren't the tombs of the Ming dynasty there, too? Isn't it a royal burial ground there?

Adm. W.: I can't recall that particularly. I know there are Ming tombs in Nanking as well as around Peking, but they were not prominent in this case. This tomb was tremendous and overshadowed everything else. Of course, the other tombs may have been in the vicinity and they probably were, but I can't recall that.

Q: I was wondering if Chiang Kai-chek had political motive.

Adm. W.: As I recall, Sun Yat Sen was the one that first organized the Chinese Republic.

Q: He's known as the Father of the Chinese Republic, isn't he?

Adm. W.: The father of the Chinese Republic. So Chiang Kai-chek was, of course, trying to promote the Chinese Republic and to honor it. He was a great believer in continuing the republic and not disbanding it as were the efforts of the war lords, about whom I've spoken previously, to tear it down.

Mrs. W.: I remember those Ming tombs. I think it was sort of the cradle of - well not really the cradle of Chinese history, but - they were just outside the city walls, and I think there may have been some connection.

Adm. W.: There probably was.

Mrs. W.: He wanted to associate Sun Yat Sen with a continuing ...

Q: Chain of authority?

Mrs. W.: I don't know, but I would assume that.

Q: I sense that the purpose was somewhat political.

Mrs. W.: I haven't been to Nanking since I was 15, but I do remember the Ming tombs very distinctly.

Adm. W.: After returning to Shanghai following the funeral - this took place after my wife and I were married - we were invited to a beautiful garden party given by Lord and Lady Li. Lord Li was one of the few remaining members of the Chinese nobility, who retained his title and retained his estate and lived very luxuriously in Shanghai. About that time, or just before that, an American admiral, arrived in Shanghai, whose name I'd better not mention because he will probably be remembered by a number of people...

Q: Oh, I think it's perfectly OK to mention his name because you can delete it from this later, or not, as you choose.

Adm. W.: Well, that being the case, I will mention that he was Rear Admiral T. T. Craven. I don't recall what the initials T.T. stood for in his name, but he was quite a sundowner, which is a term that we apply in the Navy to very strict and hard-to-get-along-with people. So that the initials T.T. stood for, in the parlance of the junior officers surrounding him, as Turn To, meaning that he always insisted that everybody around him should be working at top speed. He was a character in his own right, but he also had a wife who was even more of a character. She had a young daughter, about 15, whom she was very anxious to have circulate around in Shanghai society, but of course, she had not come out, that is to say, she had not made her debut and was far too young to be included in adult affairs, particularly where VIPs were concerned. This led to several very amusing incidents. The Pittsburgh was moored off the "bund" in Shanghai to a buoy which had a telephone line to the shore, and one of the telephones was on the desk in my office in the flag quarters. About this time Admiral Bristol had decided to give a dinner in honor of Admiral and Mrs. Craven...

Q: What was Admiral Craven's job?

Adm. W.: Admiral Craven had been ordered to be the commander of the Yangtze Patrol, which was the No. 2 job in the American

Navy on the China Station. So, being the aide and flag lieutenant, ~~why~~, Mrs. Bristol informed me of the names of the people she wished to invite, and I wrote the invitations on the Admiral's embossed stationery and sent them out in accordance with Admiral and Mrs. Bristol's directions. A few days after that, the telephone in my office rang and, after identifying that it was I who was speaking, Mrs. Craven said that they had not received an invitation for their daughter, Olga. I had heard about this daughter already, and I knew what the idea was of her calling me up, but I wasn't about to be involved in that kind of a dispute. So I went into the Admiral's cabin, which was next to my office, and told the Admiral about it, and he said, "Tell her that the reason she didn't get an invitation for Olga was that Olga wasn't invited," which I proceeded to tell her, and that was that. There was no reply to that on her part. She jammed the phone down and it was all over.

Shortly after that, the British commander-in-chief also decided to give a dinner for Admiral and Mrs. Craven. He hadn't heard about this business of the young daughter, so he just had the invitation sent out in the usual way to Rear Admiral and Mrs. Craven, and somehow or other Mrs. Craven got word to one of the other British officers, the captain of one of the other ships, that she would like to have her daughter invited to this British admiral's dinner. So, when this British officer got back to his ship he sent a signal to the British commander-in-chief in which he said - ~~informed~~ - ~~the British commander-in-chief~~ British Adm. that ~~Mrs.~~ Craven had a daughter. So the British

Admirals' reply was signaled, "Congratulations." Well, that story went all round the fleet in China, and the strange thing was that a good many years later on, in World War II, when I was on the staff of the British commander-in-chief, Adm. Fraser, I was thumbing through some of the books in Adm. Fraser's cabin which contained anecdotes about the British Navy, and that was listed among them.

That wasn't the end of Ma Craven, as we all called her, because she was really quite an old battle ax. In the early days of their arrival a luncheon was given for her, to which all the ladies of Admiral Bristol's staff were invited, and my wife met Ma Craven, who was only mildly polite, sort of brushed her aside, and Doanda thought that was kind of rough treatment for a lady, although she was the youngest member of the staff. At any rate, when we went to Lord Li's garden party a few days after that, I was with her this time and, of course, I was in uniform with my aiguillettes which all members of the staff wore, and we entered the garden and were walking along when we ran into Ma Craven. Mrs. Craven looked at Doanda, then she looked at me, and she was very polite this time, and shook hands and then turned to her and said, "Why didn't you tell me, dear, that you were the wife of Admiral Bristol's aide? I would have been so much more cordial if I'd known that."

Mrs. W.: That's become a family joke.

Q: I'm sure it has, and it's worse than if she'd said nothing.

Adm. W.: Well, on the 9th of September 1929, exactly two years from the day that Admiral Bristol had assumed command of the Asiatic Fleet, he was detached and, of course, so was I. We returned on board the President Jefferson and I went to duty in Washington as the head of the commercial section in the communications department of the Chief of Naval Operations' office. That was about the time of the stock crash, which cast a kind of a pall over conditions in the United States for the time being, but it had very little effect on us because we found a great number of friends in Washington, among those were many of the people who had been in Constantinople at one time or the other while I was there. As a matter of fact, we were frequently invited and sometimes gave what were called Constantinople parties, in other words, these parties were given for the people who had - that we had known in Constantinople. Among the most prominent of those, of course, was Admiral Bristol, who with his wife lived in Washington as that had been their home before World War I. He had the most interesting salons. They knew everybody in Washington worth knowing, entertained many of them at their home, and, of course, were entertained by the same people. So we met all of their friends and were quickly, you might say, inducted into Washington society. Admiral and Mrs. Bristol's home was very interesting. It was an old house on Massachusetts Avenue and was filled with artifacts and pictures and all kind of relics of their tours of duty in many parts of the world, including particularly Constantinople and China. One room, which they called their Turkish room, was really quite unusual. One almost expected to see one of the ladies of the harem pop out of the closet at any moment, because it was completely Turkish in its decor.

Life in Washington in those days - in 1929, in other words - was much simpler than it is now. There were not nearly so many people there, and consequently it was easy to get to know people, and naval officers, in particular, stood much higher in precedence than they do now. Although only a lieutenant commander, my wife and I were invited to the White House three or four times for receptions and soirees, and we were invited to Mr. Stimson's beautiful estate. As you will recall, he had been the governor general of the Philippines and he remembered me and invited me to many of the interesting events - occasions - at which he officiated and to a number of their private parties. The most interesting party, I think, that we attended was a reception which he had on New Year's Day in the Pan American Union, with most of the leading U.S. government officials and all of the diplomatic society in Washington. I remember wearing uniform full dress, I think probably the last time I ever wore it, and my sword which gave me considerable trouble while driving the car, but we managed to surmount that little difficulty and arrive on time.

Q: Where did you live in Washington at this period?

Adm. W.: On that occasion we lived in an apartment on Phelps Place just off Connecticut Avenue at California Street.

Q: And did naval officers wear uniform, then?

Adm. W.: Yes. Well, we wore uniforms to official functions.

Q: During the day though?

Adm. W.: No. The rule was not to wear uniforms. We were prohibited from wearing uniforms on duty in Washington, except for official occasions. The reason being rather interesting. Although I never saw this in writing, it was generally understood that the reason was that the congressmen had complained about the number of military officers on duty in Washington and they didn't want - the Secretary of the Army didn't want it brought to their attention.

Q: So they said after World War II, I remember.

Adm. W.: Well, after a very pleasant and interesting two years in Washington, during which, I almost forgot to mention, I had the rather extraordinary experience of having Mr. Sarnoff, who was then the head of the Radio Corporation of America, and who was a lieutenant commander in the Naval Reserve, detailed to my office for instruction in that portion of naval communications of which I was in charge. Looking back on this and considering Mr. Sarnoff's accomplishments, I'm really amazed to think that I ever was able to instruct him in anything.

Q: How old was he then?

Adm. W.: I think he's about the same age I am. He's still living, you know. Chairman of the Board, I believe, of... R.C.A.

Q: Well, I'm sure you were an expert in your field.

Adm. W.: I was only a lieutenant commander, but I did know what I was supposed to know.

Q: It would be a comment on his intelligence that he knew what he didn't know and wanted to learn.

Adm. W.: That's right.

Q: How long was he with you?

Adm. W.: Oh, just a day. He was there on active duty, which every Naval Reserve officer was required to serve two weeks of every year, and he was sent from office to office throughout the Navy Department.

Q: He was probably keeping himself apprised of what was going on in naval communications.

Ad. W.: He was following a schedule given to him by the Chief of Naval Operations.

Although the normal tour of duty was supposed to be three years, I was ordered early in October to San Diego to assume command of a destroyer, after the previous commanding officer had gotten into some kind of trouble. I had almost no notice of this and had to leave my wife and child, we had one at that time, to come out later, which they did, of course, and there was an interesting incident that occurred because of that. My wife asked me when I left to look around and see if I could find a place for us to live, which I did. I thought it was a very nice place, but when she arrived, she took one look at it and said, "How long do we have to stay here?" I probably had an idea in the back of my head that maybe she wouldn't like it because it's awfully hard to satisfy women sometimes, and I said, "Well, we only have to stay a month." She said, "Well, I'm going out and look for another place." That was fine, so she went out and found herself a place in short order, and when we went to talk over with the landlord the terms of the agreement, she said to him, "Well, I think this is fine," we had agreed on the rent, but she said, "I would like to make one stipulation." He asked her what that was, and she said, "If the Navy pay, by any chance, is reduced by ten or fifteen per cent, or whatever it is, I would like to have written in to the rental agreement, that the rent will be reduced by that amount."

Q: Wasn't she shrewd?

Adm. W.: The landlord, who, of course, had never heard of anything like that - it had never happened in the history of the country before - agreed to it without any hesitation at all. When we got home, I asked her why on earth she'd done that, and she said, "Because after you left, Captain Crosby, who was a great friend of hers - and ours - and who was also the Navy Department liaison officer with Congress, told her that there had been discussions, which had not been made public, that the army and navy pay might be cut fifteen per cent. So, she said, "I just thought I'd put that in, in case." Well, of course, it was cut...

Q: Almost immediately. Wasn't it in 1931 that it was cut?

Adm. W.: I'm not sure. It may have been a little later.

Q: During the depression years.

Adm. W.: Oh, during the depression years, yes. So, of course, we invoked that clause and got the reduction. I was very much impressed with my wife.

Q: That was very clever of her. What was the name of your destroyer?

Adm. W: The Waters. I took command of the Waters, destroyer No. 115, and I had command of her for three years. A very enjoyable cruise...

Q: This was actually your first indepednent duty, wasn't it?

Adm. W.: This was my first absolutely independent duty, and I loved every minute of it. It was thoroughly delightful. I had a fine ship's company, wonderful officers, and a very fine crew. We never had any difficulties of any kind that I can remember.

Q: That's quite a statement, for three years.

Adm. W.: We did have an unusual experience due to the depression. Roosevelt, at that time, was trying to save money, and this was in 1933, just after he became - well, he was elected in the fall of 1932 - and he became president in early 1933, and, as you recall, in the early years of his administration, he was very economy-minded, and the Navy Department decided, one, that they were going to take a number of naval officers out of active service and put them in charge of these civilian conservation camps, so I lost two of my officers from the Waters who temporarily went to this duty. The reason for that was that under that arrangement, the naval officers who were serving at these civilian conservation camps would be paid from the budget of the civilian conservation corps...instead of the Navy budget, thereby enabling the Navy to show a better record, you see. Furthermore, it was decided to put some of the destroyers, or all of the destroyers, in turn, in what was called rotating reserve. In other words, a percentage of the destroyers were sent to Navy yards with, after they arrived, two-thirds of their crew was detached, and sent to other destroyers, that were to remain in full commission for a while. Of course, those who were in rotating reserve were not being operated, and that saved money, and the crews were used on other ships, so that saved money. When we arrived in Mare Island Navy Yard, two-thirds of my crew were detached and all the officers except the Executive Officer and myself. We were there five months and during that period, the bank holiday took place. Later on, of course, we were placed back in full commission and returned to San Diego for the remainder of my tour of duty on the Waters. While in San Diego, we had the rather extraordinary experience of getting to know ex-president

Ortiz Rubio and his family. He was the ex-president of Mexico. He and his family had moved to San Diego where I think he felt the climate was more healthful, because of his unpopularity among some in Mexico. The way that we got to know them was that, Admiral Gannon, who was commandant of the 11th Naval District, didn't speak any Spanish and he knew that my wife did, as she was six years in Spain from the age of six to the age of 12, while her father was stationed there at that time, in Valencia. She speaks Spanish almost as well as a Spaniard even to this day. So, when Admiral Gannon invited president and Senora Rubio to a reception that he was having at the commandant's quarters, he asked my wife to stand beside him and talk to the Rubios to make them feel at home, which she did. She apparently made such a hit with the Rubios that they invited us over to their house for dinner, and we enjoyed that very much, and later we invited them to our house for dinner...

Q: Where did you live in San Diego?

Adm. W.: We lived in Coronado.

Q: Were you on the station?

Adm. W.: No, no. We lived 766 A Avenue in Coronado. That was the house that my wife bargained with the landlord for, you see.

Q: Were the commandant's quarters then on North Island?

Adm. W.: I think so, yes. I'm sure they were.

Q: What was the duty of the Waters at that time?

Adm. W.: The Waters was one of a division of four ships, which was attached to a squadron that consisted of a total of three divisions, or 12 ships. All of the destroyers in the battle force were stationed in San Diego, all the battle ships were stationed in Long Beach. The greater part, as you probably know, of the American fleet was stationed on the Pacific because the belief, as proved later, correct, was that our next war would be with Japan, and the ships were based in Southern California, rather than in Northern California, because the weather was so much better for operations and exercises. The harbor of Long Beach, of course, is better suited to battle ships because it's much deeper. As a matter of fact, some of the battle ships couldn't have gotten in to San Diego at that time. But the harbor of San Diego is ideally suited to destroyers and we had, oh, we must have had 60 destroyers, at least, down there on active duty, as well as a number of de-commissioned destroyers at the destroyer base. They were the ships that had been built for World War I and were not in use at that time.

Q: What was the mission of the Waters?

Adm. W.: The mission of all of destroyers there was to train with the battleships for o[pera]tions against the enemy, if and when that occured war occurred. In other words...

Q: How much were you out, and how much in?

Adm. W.: Generally speaking, we went to sea on Monday morning

Wheeler #3 - 203

and we came back on Friday evening, so it was quite a regular schedule as far as activities were concerned. Often times, we would join up with the battleships and have maneuvers with them. Sometimes, we would operate just with other destroyers, and sometimes we would have operations concerning ourselves only, such as firing torpedoes, proving our torpedoes...

Q: Fueling at sea, did you do any of that?

Adm. W.: We didn't do any fueling at sea, at that time.

Q: That became a later development, didn't it?

Adm. W.: No, we had - we knew how to fuel at sea. We fueled at sea when we went out to the islands for combined operations but there was no occasion to fuel at sea in San Diego because we went such a short distance.

Q: No, I only meant for training.

Adm. W.: Oh, the training. Well, we had enough training when we were operating with the fleet, but we didn't when we were operating from a base.

Q: Basically, when you were out your activites were training activities.

Adm. W.: Training activities. You know you can have all the finest ships in the world, but if you don't know how to use them, they're no good to you.

Q: I want to ask you at some point, and may be this is the best spot, and I'm thinking about it because you said that in three years you never had any problems, which is an incredible remark, and there are things, such as leadership, that a commanding officer must exhibit, and that a ship is a reflection of the man, all the things that we know are basic loyalty up and down, and you must have, at an early age, because you were a lieutenant commander, you were - what - 30 years old, perhaps. In 1931, you were...

Adm. W.: No. I was 36.

Q: That's still a young man, and I want to ask you at some point, either this or when you were in command of the Mobile, what your ideas of leadership are, the very characteristics that make for a fine naval officer.

Adm. W.: I think the first and most important rule is loyalty up and loyalty down. You cannot have a contented crew unless they know that you have their best interests at heart. As long as they know you have their best interests at heart, they will do anything for you, but as soon as they feel that you are trying to take advantage of them, to deny the rights and privileges to which they are entitled, you are immediately in trouble. You may remember that I said the skipper of the ship f the Waters - of which I took command, was relieved because he got into some kind of difficulty. I never have known what it was.

Q: So I gather you took over a discontented ship.

Adm. W.: Well, I don't know whether it was a discontented

ship or whether he got into some kind of personal difficulty. I don't know what that was, but I know that I never had any problem. I never had any problems with any of my crews. The crew of the Waters was a fine crew, but the crew of the Mobile was the finest crew that I think anybody ever had. Later on I'll tell you about that.

Q: Yes, I want to hear about that.

Adm. W.: The Waters was a very happy experience for me, and, as I say, I really enjoyed every minute of it.

Q: How many men did you have on the Waters?

Adm. W.: We had, I think, about 119, as near as I can remember. We had about six officer and 119 men, something like that. Not a large crew, but enough to give a lot of trouble if...

Q: Trouble doesn't need a large number. You have a lovely picture there of the men under your command.

Adm. W.: People used to jokingly refer to it as the "Quarter Past One." One fifteen, you see.

Q: Well, I think that's a wonderful comment, that you never had any trouble in three years. Did you feel that you knew everything that was going on aboard the ship?

Adm. W.: Yes. I was kept well informed by my officers. Of course, the captain of a ship has to depend upon his younger officers, on his subordinates, let us say, to be fully informed as to what's going on in the ship, because the position of the captain on board ship is quite different from anything you'd ever find in civil life. I know when I retired and came ashore, I found that people in companies like Varian and Associates, these electronic companies with which I had some dealings out here, the employees all refer to the heads of the organization by their first names. Well, to me, that was just absolutely horrifying. As a matter of fact, on board ship the captain, and particularly on a ship like, for instance, the Mobile, and to a certain extent also on the smaller ships like a destroyer, where the captain messes with his officers, the captain of a naval ship is in a position somewhat akin to God, if you know what I mean. The people are pretty frightened of him, and he doesn't have the easy camaraderie with the others that the head of a civilian organization would.

Q: It's frightening in a way, also, to know the authority you had and the responsibility. Did you feel that way?

Adm. W.: Oh, yes. I did, but it didn't bother me any.

Q: Did you ever walk around the ship? Did you walk around a great deal and know what was going on?

Adm. W.: Oh, yes.

Q: Did you ever talk to any of the enlisted men and find out what their problems were?

Adm. W.: Oh, yes, all the time.

Q: So you didn't entirely rely on your juniors?

Adm. W.: Oh, no, as I remember - I'm glad you mentioned that because I remember a case of a chief petty officer who had been on a month's leave while we were undergoing tender overhaul, alongside a tender, that is, in San Diego, and he had just come back from this leave which he was entitled to in the ordinary way, and he came to me a few days later with tears in his eyes, and he said, "Captain, I'm ashamed to ask you, but I've just had a wire that my wife is desperately ill, and I would like to ask you if I could go back notwithstanding the fact that I've just come back from leave." I said, "Why, of course you can. Under these circumstances, that's where you belong."

Q: Well, you had a warm personality and you were more understanding of him, perhaps, than many.

Adm. W.: So, he took right off. I said, "Stay as long as you think you should be there." and he said, "Thank you, Captain." and rushed away. When he came back after several weeks, his wife apparently, fortunately, had recovered, he came up to me and said, "Oh, Captain, I'll never forget what you did for me. I'll do anything for you, any time, for the rest of my life, even if it includes killing anybody." Which I thought was quite a tribute, if somewhat oddly expressed. Under the circumstances granting the leave was the natural thing to do. I mean, what else...

Q: It was natural for you, but maybe not for everybody.

Adm. W.: It was quite different from the experience I had when I was division officer on the South Dakota, which I mentioned previously, and when I heard the ship was going out to China, I asked the executive officer for leave to go and see my parents, and he - because I knew I would be gone for ~~three~~ two years, as a matter of fact, I was gone for five because of the interruption in Constantinople -and he refused absolutely. Different people have different ways of doing things.

Q: But you must recognize that the reason you didn't have any problems wasn't because the ship was different, but because it reflected what the commanding officer was like.

Adm. W.: Well, I think all commanding officers should be aware of that fact, but I grant you that some of them are not. Some skippers are, as I mentioned before, what we call sundowners. They are just terribly hard on everybody, and there have been cases that you know of probably of ships in the Navy where the crew have gone out in the middle of the night and painted the words "Hell Ship" on the side of the ship.

Q: I hadn't heard that. No, I didn't. I wouldn't want to be the skipper of a ship where that happened.

Adm. W.: Of course, you wouldn't.

Q: Let me ask you another thing. I'm interested because you're a man who does know about leadership. When you give orders, do you feel that you can give an order and forget it?

Adm. W.: ~~Absolutely~~ Not always. I'll tell you more about that when we come to the Mobile. Don't let me forget that.

I don't like to toot my own horn.

Q: I don't think you ever would.

Adm. W.: It's human nature, I suppose.

Another interesting episode was while we were still in - still living in Coronado. At that time, which was during the depression period, there were very few other inhabitants of Coronado than the Navy. In peacetime, before the depression it had been quite a millionaires' hang-out. There were a great many wealthy people there and it was a kind of a winter resort, but the depression had syphoned off most of these people, and so it was largely a Navy town. In the spring of 1934, we were scheduled to join up with the scouting fleet, which was coming round through the Canal from the Atlantic, to hold joint maneuvers with the battle force and the scouting fleet off the Hawaiian Islands. This word, of course, got around. It was not wartime, so there was no secrecy about the movements of Navy ships. There had been, even before that, a sort of an epidemic of peepers. When these ships would go out on Mondays and not come back till Friday, some of the wives would discover men peeping in their windows, and they got very frightened, of course, about that, so I said to my wife, "Well, I'm going to make sure that nobody bothers you, at least they will be driven off. I'd like you to come down to the Silver Strand and I'll bring my automatic from the ship, and I'll teach you how to fire it, and when we leave I'll leave it here with you. You can keep it on the night table right beside your bed." So we went down to the Silver Strand on a given afternoon and I picked up an old tin can and set it out about 25 or 30 yards in front of us in the direction of the ocean, and I showed her how to operate the gun, cautioned her about squeezing the trigger, rather than pulling it, and taking aim and such things. When we went through all that, I said, "Now aim at the smallest circle on this can." You know how these condensed milk cans have concentric circles. She squeezed the trigger and hit the thing right smack in the middle, so I said, "Well, I think I've been wasting my time. Apparently you're a crack shot."

Q: Had she ever shot before?

Adm. W.: Never fired a gun before in her life. I said, "Anyhow, as long as we're here you'd better take another shot and make sure that everything is all right," because I could see she was pretty badly shaken. So she fired again, and the next time it hit about half way between the target and our seat, and I said, "Come one, now, you can do better than that. Let's have another go at it." The next time she fired it right down around our feet, so I said, "Well, honey, I think that's enough." Nevertheless, I left the gun with her, and she didn't have any peepers as far as I know, but she did have an extraordinary experience with the maid. At that time we had a full-time Canadian girl who took care of our daughter, and she had a beau who was a chauffeur at the Coronado Hotel. This beau used to come and take her out evenings, but Louise, the maid, knew that my wife kept this gun right by her bed. Well, she went out one night and forgot to take her key. The maid and her beau returned about 1 a.m.

and, of course, she couldn't get in without her key and the only way to get in was to knock on the window, but she was terrified that if she did Mrs. Wheeler would shoot her. She and her beau stood off at some distance with a stick and tapped the window to wake my wife up and get her to let her in.

The next big, and last, big event of that cruise was the - oh, I forgot to mention that on this - these - fleet maneuvers off the Hawaiian Islands, we anchored in Lahaina Roads, where we later anchored in World War II prior to going out and participating in some of these assaults on the Japanese-held islands, and we had friends in Honolulu that were awfully good to us. Altogether that was a very happy experience. Soon after we returned to San Diego, the entire fleet, including the scouting fleet which had come around from the Atlantic, went back through the Canal and were reviewed by President Franklin Delano Roosevelt from one of the cruisers - I can't exactly remember which one it was. But one of the new cruisers, which was anchored off Sandy Hook, and the entire American fleet passed in review, which, I believe, is the last time the American fleet ever has been reviewed.

Q: That must have been a dramatic sight.

Adm. W.: It really was. Of course, the fleet, at that time, was quite sizable. We had a number of battleships which, of course, were very impressive. But the most impressive sight I've ever seen was the American fleet off the entrance to

Tokyo Bay just before the Japanese surrender. By that time our fleet had been greatly expanded in size.

Q: And there was drama involved in that. Were there any carriers in the fleet at that time?

Adm. W.: Yes. There were several carriers, and I'm glad you mentioned the carriers because since we've just been watching this landing on the moon and listening to the astronauts talking from the surface of the moon to us here in our living room, a distance of over a quarter of a million miles, and we heard them perfectly clearly, as I say, that reminds me of this period when we were in San Diego operating with the carriers. In those days the carriers never operated without what they called plane guards, and they consisted of one or two destroyers which followed along to pick up any aviators who met with mishaps and fell overboard. Of course, we talked to a number of these aviators when we would see them ashore at clubs and places like that, and I remember asking one of them if he found his job difficult. He said, "Well, flying the plane is nothing at all. That is just pure joy. There are no problems. But the thing that really bugs most of us is that we have to learn this Morse code." In those days the only way that planes used to communicate with the carriers was by Morse code. There was no voice. So they had to learn this dot and dash code, or be out of communication with the carriers, and they would only be a matter of 20 or 30 miles from the carrier. That was the only means of communication they had. When you compare that with what we heard today, and all that has happened in a matter of 30 years. It seems inconceivable.

I was detached from command of the Waters in New York Harbor...

Q: This was, then, right after the review?

Adm. W.: Right after the review. As soon as we went in to New York, I was detached. My time was up, and I was ordered to the Navy Department, this time as what was called Atlantic Communication Officer. But it was really more than that because I had charge of all of the U.S. naval shore radio stations throughout the world, that is, the communication end of it, not the material end. My office, of course, was in the office of the Chief of Naval Operations in the Navy Department, and we had the receiving center right there, the transmitters were located elsewhere, but we ran the whole business right there. As a matter of fact, another officer in an office next to mine was in charge of all the fleet communications, and he ran the thing from there.

Q: Excuse me, but was your office before and at this time in the Navy Department, the old Navy Department building on Constitution?

Adm. W.: Yes, the old Navy Department building, Constitution Avenue. I had a rather unusual experience - I seem to run to unusual experiences - there, in that, at this time, in other words in 1934 or 1935, there was a great deal of discussion about combining all military communications under one system. Instead, for instance, of having a separate communications system run by the army, and a separate one run by the Navy, and a separate one run by the Coast Guard, the idea was to combine them all, and, in that way, save money, which theoretically sounded like a wonderful idea, but in practice it just does not work, because as we said in our office, and I think that this was a very succinct and apt way to put it, communications are the handmaiden of command. In other words, if you don't have communications directly with your ship or with your fort, or whatever it is you are in charge of, you just don't get results. If it has to go through somebody else, one or more persons along the way may think, oh, well, this isn't so important, I'll put some other message ahead of it, and that may be the most important message of all. It doesn't seem important to the receiver, but it's terribly important to the sender. So that scheme eventually fell through, particularly after Roosevelt got over his economy ideas. In any case, while this experiment - while this theory was extant, I was given the job of running in addition to all the naval radio shore stations, I was assigned the job of taking charge of all the Coast Guard radio stations in the northeastern part of the United States. That was undertaken as an experiment. In connection with this, I had several conferences with the Secretary of the Treasury, Morganthau, who of course was in charge of the Coast Guard and in charge of their communications. The Coast Guard and the - Secretary Morganthau, were very unwilling to even try this experiment, but pressure was put on them from the White House, so it was instigated, and frankly, I never had any trouble with them at all. We had no difficulties from my end of running the ~~thing~~ experiment, that is, being in charge of running it. Of course, the Coast Guard people still manned their own stations, but they were under my orders. My orders were as few as possible because I realized that if you let people alone they run their own jobs better than when you try to run their jobs for them. So this ~~thing~~ scheme went on for about six months or so, and then I think due to pressure from the Coast Guard, the stations were turned back to them and the whole plan was forgotten. But it was an interesting experience.

Q: A forerunner of ideas on various...

Adm. W.: Yes, put that way, in that connection, I am reminded of the fact that I had very pleasant relations with these Coast Guard people, and my wife was returning from Italy where she had been to visit her mother and father, ~~and at that time we had two children~~, with our two children. She was due to arrive in Boston on a given day and, knowing that the Coast Guard usually take the pilot out or send somebody out to meet these incoming ships, I alerted the commander of the Coast Guard to the fact that my wife and family were coming in on such and such a ship, and would appreciate if he would extend whatever courtesies were proper. To my great surprise, he sent a cutter out - a Coast Guard cutter, or maybe the cutter was going out anyhow, I don't know - at any rate, the Coast Guard cutter went out, circled around the ship and all the passengers went over and looked at it and waved, they were the first people they'd seen from the United States for some time, and everybody wondered what this ship was doing, and after making a circle or two round the ship, the captain lowered the gangway, and the messenger from the Coast Guard cutter said that he'd come to get Mrs. Wheeler and her family, and they took her ashore. Which was quite an experience for her because of course all the rest of the passengers were very jealous that she was getting this kind of treatment..

Well, in 1936 I was detached and ordered to be damage-control officer, first lieutenant and damage-control officer, the job was officially called, of the USS West Virginia, which was the flagship of the battleships divisions in the battle force. I drove out from Washington. My wife had not yet returned from Italy - as a matter of fact, that was the reason I had alerted the Coast Guard officer to look out for her in Boston, because I couldn't be there myself. I drove out to the West Coast alone and joined the USS West Virginia. The most important thing that took place after I arrived there, at least important to me, was that I was sworn in as a commander in the Navy.

Q: That's a big step, isn't it, in the Navy?

Adm. W.: Well, I think the biggest thrill was when I was selected commander, which took place six months or so before.

Q: I mean the step to commander. Those three nice fat stripes.

Adm. W.: Oh, yes. Well, I served on her for about a year which was very interesting and very pleasant, but I can't recall anything unusual that happened. It was just a regular line duty, you know.

Q: That seems to be the first duty you've had on which something unusual event didn't occur.

Wheeler #3 - 217

Adm. W.: That's right. Then I was ordered to take command of USS Bridge, which was a supply ship and which I most definitely didn't want because I thought it was kind of degrading to be the captain of a supply ship.

Q: That isn't in your biography. What was the name of the ship?

Adm. W.: I never went, because while I was regretting this development, I learned from some of my friends that Admiral Hepburn, whom I had known very well in Constantinople and was then commander-in-chief of the fleet, was considering ordering me there as his aide and flag secretary, and within a very short time those orders came through, so I never went to the Bridge.

Q: And I'm sure you liked those orders.

Adm. W.: I enjoyed being with Admiral Hepburn. There were quite a number of interesting things that occurred while I was in that job. Among others the Panay incident in China, when the Japanese fired on the Panay.

Q: Excuse me, but where was the Pennsylvania then, between 1938 and 1939, when you were on her?

Adm. W.: She was on the West Coast. We were all on the West Coast. It was my initiation to one of the duties for which I really had not been prepared because it - things like this hadn't occurred. But I found, among other things, that I was the fleet press officer. It was my job to give out all information relating to naval affairs, which the press people in the Pacific area wanted to get the news about, even though it didn't occur in the ships on the West Coast.

Q: Had they had such a position before?

Adm. W.: Yes. They had had a press secretary, and I had probably been told that that was one of my jobs but I hadn't had time to find out about it.

Q: Did it later become the public relations, public information type job?

Adm. W.: It was as long as I was there, but in those days - and I think I was there about a year, as I remember - there was very little information given out by the Navy. We were called the Silent Service, in other words, we didn't toot our own horn. We didn't seek publicity.

Q: That's why it surprised me when you said press officer. I had not realized the Navy even had such a job in those days.

Adm. W.: My job was not known as being press officer. I was flag secretary, but among the duties of the flag secretary was to deal with the press.

Q: How much did your boss tell you to deal with them?

Adm. W.: He never told me at all. He never gave me anything to give to the press. The only time I had anything to do with the press was when they asked me questions.

Q: I see. When you felt you couldn't avoid answering them any more.

Adm. W.: That's right. I just had to give them something. Actually, I think I learned more from the correspondents as a result of that experience almost, than they learned from me. I found that the ones that I dealt with were very fine gentlemen, and they helped me enormously in phrasing this information which I gave out. I mean, I would tell what had happened and they'd say, well, maybe, you'd better word that this way.

Q: So you never felt they took advantage of you.

Adm. W.: I never felt they took advantage of me and I never tried to take advantage of them, and we always had the pleasantest relations. As I say, I learned a great deal. I've had other dealings with the press since then, and I'm always very happy that I had that experience because as a result of it I have never had any friction with the press. I mean I learned that if you treat them squarely, they'll treat you squarely. It's better, among other things, not to get uppity with the press. The thing is to have them on your side. If you have them on your side, why, you don't have any trouble with them. But once you get them down on you, you're finished.

Q: They can harm you more than you can harm them.

Adm. W: Right. Absolutely.

Q: Well, Admiral, every incident which you've described, the ease with which you have related to other people, and now you speak of a completely different entity in the press, I don't know if you are aware how much it's your attitude that created the response from others.

Adm. W.: Well, I think it's very nice of you to say that.

Q: It's obvious in every incident you've described. I don't know if you're aware of that in your life or not?

Adm. W.: My whole attitude, I think, is really a reflection of the way I was brought up. I really think that's the answer to the whole thing. I was very fortunate in selecting my mother and father!

Q: Do you think we've covered the 1938 to 1939 assignment?

Adm. W.: There are one or two more things. Maybe you'd like to go on here. At the end of about a year, a little over a year perhaps, I was detached and ordered to the detail office in the Bureau of Navigation, in charge of the - well I was the assistant to the officer detail officer. I was his principal assistant.

Q: That was when you were detached from the <u>Pennsylvania</u>?

Adm. W.: Yes. I reported there on February 19, and the purpose of that was, I think, to fill in the time between then and the time that I had applied to go to the War College, which was to the class that opened in June of that year. So, you see there were several months there which had to be filled in before the War College class that I had applied for opened.

Q: That is not in your biography.

Adm. W.: Really? You mean that I was detail officer?

Q: Or the War College.

Adm. W.: Well, in any case, I spent...

Q: I hate to interrupt, but when did you go to the War College?

Adm. W.: I went to the War College the 22nd June 1938. I reported to the <u>Pennsylvania</u> on May the 19th 1937, that is to be flag secretary, which was on the flagship <u>Pennsylvania</u>. And I reported to the detail office in the Navy Department on February the 19th 1938.

There was nothing unusual that occurred there. It was quite an interesting tour of duty. I learned a good deal about how naval officers were selected and chosen for various assignments.

Q: Was it still the Bureau of Navigation?

Adm. W.: Still the Bureau of Navigation, and that is where I served with Admiral Nimitz, who was Chief of the Bureau of Navigation at that time. When I went to say good-bye to him before I left for the War College, I said to Admiral Nimitz, whom I had known over a period of years and was very devoted to and whom I very highly respected, "You know, Admiral, the next time I see you, you will be commander-in-chief of the

United States fleet," and he was. It was five years later before I saw him.

Q: I want to discuss your evaluations and experiences with Admiral Nimitz. I know you had some dealings with him in the Pacific, and perhaps that would be the time to discuss it.

Adm. W.: So, on the 22nd of June I reported to the President of the Naval War College for instructions. That was a very proscribed course which I thoroughly enjoyed, especially those war games which were styled to prepare for a war with Japan, which by that time I think all of us felt was on the way. All our personal experiences in Newport were very pleasant. Through some of my wife's connections, we met Mrs. Van Allen, who was a very wealthy and well known dowager in Newport and whose daughter was a widow of one of the Prince Mdivanis, but I thought it was the better part of tact not to force my opinion of her ex-husband on her as she was still, apparently, very devoted to his memory.

After a year of instruction, I reported to the President of the Naval War College as a member of the War College staff. That assignment was short-lived because in September of 1939 - I believe it was September, August or September - Hitler marched into Poland, and a large number of naval officers, both from the class of instruction and from the staff, were detached from the War College and ordered to sea duty. My assignment was to command a division of destroyers - Destroyer Division 70, to be exact - at San Diego. This was a division of old destroyers, old World War I destroyers, which were being recommissioned for active service. I reported aboard my flagship the Crane, but I definitely did not like this assignment. I wanted something where I felt I would be more a part of the active fleet. I didn't want to hang around there and spend months fitting out an old division of destroyers which would still be old when they'd been refitted. So, fortunately, the officer who was on his way to take charge of the detail office in the Bureau of Navigation was a friend of mine, and he passed through San Diego and I had the good luck to meet him at a cocktail party, and I said, "For heaven's sake, get me out of this job. I don't like it. I don't like any part of it." And he said, "Well, I'll see what I can do." So when he got back, he hadn't been there more than a matter of a few weeks when I got orders to be executive officer of the cruiser Astoria.

Interview # 4 with Rear Admiral C. Julian Wheeler, U.S. Navy
(Retired)

Date: 16 August 1969

By: Etta Belle Kitchen

Q: Good morning, Admiral. If you will just pick up where we left off on our last interview, that will do very nicely.

Adm. W.: I'd be very glad to, Etta Belle.

The Navy was very kind to my family and me in that they furnished us transportation to Honolulu on the Matson Line. One of the things that interested me from the point of view of a naval officer was that we went on board about noon in Los Angeles Harbor and soon after we arrived at our stateroom, I noted that they had made a mistake and sent the trunk which my wife wanted in our stateroom down to the hold, although it had been properly marked. So I called up the purser and asked him to make this change, and he said he would be very glad to after 4 o'clock but that, due to the laws relating to hours of work, all the men who handled that sort of thing were off duty from noon to 4 p.m. Thinking of the many hours that I had put in in the Navy without any allowance for hours off, I thought this was an interesting side light on the American merchant marine.

Arriving in Honolulu, we were, of course, met by officers and their families from my new ship, the Astoria, and deluged with leis, which was a very pleasant experience.

Q: Where did the ship tie up?

Adm. W.: At one of the docks in Honolulu. I can't remember exactly which one. The Astoria was due to sail very shortly thereafter, so I drove my wife - my wife drove me - to the ship, and had to make her own arrangements after the ship left port to find a place to live and to get the car squared away as to license, which led her into some difficulties, in that the license we had was good until March in California but was overdue in Honolulu, and soon after she appeared on the streets of Honolulu in this car right after she had taken me to the ship, the police arrested her for driving a car whose license was overdue. It was a native policeman and my wife was quite upset over this and refused to allow him to arrest her. She said that she would take the car to the Naval Base and deal with it there, which the policeman agreed to. (She claimed the right of "military arrest" as Hawaii was a territory then.) So, when she got the car there, the Marines, in the shore patrol, impounded the car, and while she sat in the office, phoned the Chief of Police and straightened the whole matter out.

The first trip that we made on the Astoria was quite interesting in that, at that time, an airfield was being built at Johnson Island, and we had on board quite a number of civilians and also the quarterdeck was loaded with plants of all descriptions, which the Navy was transporting to Johnson Island for the Agriculture Department with the idea of planting these trees and shrubs on Johnson Island to make it more livable for the people who were building the airport and who would be living there after it was completed.

Q: Would you think it might be appropriate at this time to

describe the Astoria?

Adm. W.: Yes. The Astoria was one of our heavy cruisers - she had the usual main battery of 8" guns and eight 5" guns, let's see, ~~I can't remember exactly the armament~~, but she was one of the very latest cruisers that had been commissioned and formed a division together with three other cruisers of the same class, which was the main part of the Hawaiian detachment, a squadron of ships stationed in the Hawaiian islands, I imagine because of the strained relations with Japan at that time. Our activities consisted mostly of training exercises with each other and particularly with other parts of the fleet which came out to join the Hawaiian detachment, as I recall, in the spring of that year. I can't remember the exact date, but I do remember that we had many fleet exercises in all parts of the Hawaiian islands, and we used Lahina Roads extensively for an anchorage. The conditions - the situation between Japan and the United States at that time, as you well know, was getting more and more strained, and we were quite conscious of the activities of some of the Japanese in the area. My wife, for example, had a german hairdresser who never missed an opportunity to inquite the movements of the Astoria, and we heard later that he had been arrested as an enemy ~~a Japanese~~ spy.

Q: How had he known that you were on the Astoria?

Adm. W.: Well, I can't answer that. Actually, except that at that time I don't believe we made any effort to conceal the names of the ships that we were serving on, and I suppose that

that was information that was available to anybody who really took the trouble to dig it out.

Q: I wonder if he knew your position on the ship.

Adm. W.: Oh, I think he undoubtedly did. But the strangest affair of that kind that occurred was that we had a perfectly marvelous maid - our children at that time were of course much younger, I think they were probably about 10 and 12, or thereabouts - and we had this very wonderful Japanese maid, whose name was Yaeko, who was very fond of the children and seemed to be very fond of us. She was with us almost the entire time that we were in Honolulu until about three months before we left. To get ahead of my story a little, we left in May or June of the following year, and this maid came to us along about in February with tears in her eyes and said that she had to leave, which distressed us very much because we were all very fond of her and, as I say, we were quite sure that she was very fond of us. We asked her why, and she said she couldn't tell us. But she did leave and we got a woman whose name was Asako, who obviously had never been a maid before and knew nothing about housework, was very sulky and difficult to get along with, and was thoroughly undesirable. She never herself missed an opportunity to inquire also, not only about me but about the movements of the ship.

Q: How had she come to you?

Adm. W.: She wouldn't ask me. She would ask my wife.

Q: I mean how did you get her as a maid?

Adm. W.: Oh. We don't know how she was sent there. She just appeared as soon as the other one left. We concluded that this was all arranged by the Japanese, and shortly after she came, the former maid, Yaeko, came to see us, again crying, and said that she didn't think we ought to keep this woman. But we had to have somebody and that seemed to be the only one we could get, so we kept her, but of course my wife was very careful not to divulge any information that she thought would be of value to her.

Q: You sensed even at that time that she was definitely attempting to obtain information?

Adm. W.: We were certain that she was a "plant," and was endeavoring to find out all she could about the movements of ships.

Q: What was your position on the ship?

Adm. W.: I was executive officer. Second in command. It was a very pleasant cruise. The skipper was Richmond Kelly Turner, who had been before that assignment the Navy's representative on the War Plans Board in Washington. He was one of the smartest men in the Navy. There are no two ways about that. He had a mind that was just as keen as a razor, and he was a very firm and somewhat difficult-to-get-along-with skipper, in that he wanted to do everything himself, which left us in somewhat of a quandary, particularly after he left, in that the watch officers who had not been allowed to handle the ship themselves, were not adequately trained. So that I had to spend a good deal of my time on the bridge until the watch officers learned to do their job, through the failure of the former skipper to let them do what they were supposed to do. I'm a great admirer of Admiral Turner, but I think that he had some problem which I understand he overcame after he had attained flag rank, and we all know that as commander of the amphibious forces in the Pacific he did a perfectly fabulous job.

Q: What were his personal problems?

Adm. W.: Well, his desire to do everything himself. His lack of being able to delegate to others.

Q: Admiral Turner had a nickname later on in the war, I'm sure you're aware of that. They called him Terrible Turner, and I wondered during your association with him if you had any occasion to agree with that nickname was perhaps well placed?

Adm. W.: Well, I had one experience which might justify that nickname, although it turned out all right eventually. One morning we were expecting a materiel inspection party, of which a rear admiral was at the head, nominally, and we had just moved from the tender after two weeks overhaul in which our boilers had been allowed to die down, and in the move from the tender to the dock, the usual gust of cinders had spread cinders over the deck and I was out on the quarterdeck at the time supervising the removal of these cinders. Admiral Turner walked out and he was afraid that the admiral would come aboard to inspect the ship before the cinders were all cleared away.

So he turned to me and bawled me out in what I considered quite an unnecessary manner. In fact, in such a way as to attract the attention of some of the enlisted men standing near by. I didn't make any reply, but I was naturally pretty mad about it. After 20 minutes or so, when the ship had all been cleaned up, the inspecting party arrived, headed by a lieutenant commander, who was the admiral's representative, and they went about their inspection duties in the ship from the materiel standpoint, and the double bottoms and the areas that are usually covered by materiel inspection parties. It had nothing whatsoever to do with the cleanliness of the ship. After that was under way, why, and I had cooled down, I went in to Admiral Turner's cabin...

Q: Excuse me, but he was then a captain, wasn't he?

Adm. W.: Captain. I beg your pardon. Captain Turner's cabin prepared to have it out with him. When he saw me coming in I think he realized that he had gone too far, and he stuck out his hand and he said, "Don't say a word, Julian." And that was incidentally the first time he had ever called me by my first name. He said, "It's all right. We'll just forget it." And I said, "All right, Captain, but you know that really wasn't according to Navy regulations, bawling out an officer and second-in-command before a bunch of enlisted men." And he said, "I know. I know. I'm sorry." After that he was as pleasant as anybody in this world could be.

Q: From the things I've heard about him and read about him, it was not his personality to apologize for anything he might say.

Adm. W.: Very, very unusual for him to apologize.

Q: Would you think that he was an ambitious man?

Adm. W.: Exceedingly ambitious. Absolutely. And that I think was the underlying reason for his attitude. His extreme desire to have the ship always be in the right place at the right time and doing what it should be doing was, of course, the motivation for his taking over the ship - that is, the handling of the ship - from the officer of the deck, thereby preventing the officers of the deck from getting the proper experience in handling the ship themselves, which they all needed and which was shown to be a very severe lack in their training after he left the ship.

Q: How long did you serve with Admiral Turner?

Adm. W.: I served with him for about nine months, as near as I can remember. He was detached and sent back to the Navy Department, again in war plans' section, and he was there, as a matter of fact when Pearl Harbor was bombed. He knew Admiral Nomura, the Japanese Ambassador, very well, and from what his wife told my wife, I gather that they did everything they could to sort of alert Admiral Turner to the fact that something curious was in the offing, but of course they didn't actually inform him of what was going to happen. Admiral Turner probably had better knowledge of the situation between Japan and the United States at that time than any other naval officer. My duties on the Astoria and the activities of the fleet were perfectly normal. I mean, we had no problems on the ship and we had no activities in the fleet other than what I have mentioned that really stand out as worthy of description. In other words, we had a good ship, we performed our duties successfully, which consisted mostly of training, and there was not a great deal to describe about that period. There never is about a Navy ship that's well run carrying out its function successfully.

Q: How would you describe the atmosphere in the fleet at that time?

Adm. W.: The atmosphere in the fleet at that time was quite normal. We used to get a good many messages about preparing against sabotage which, to my way of thinking, was quite misplaced. In other words, the possibility of sabotage on a Navy ship in commission, I think is very slight. The danger, which I think all of us felt, was from the outside. In other words, from the Japanese. But we never seemed to get any orders relating to that, except that I do remember that toward the latter part of my cruise on the Astoria we had orders that the fleet should not anchor off Honolulu any more, because there was a feeling that it might be dangerous from the point of view of an attack by submarines. So, generally speaking, the fleet anchored at La Haina, which was farther away from Honolulu of course, and was much more easily protected — that is, the anchorage was much more easily protected than the anchorage off Honolulu.

Q: The fear was of attack from submarines, not air?

Adm. W.: Submarines, yes. There were hardly any people in the fleet that anticipated attack by air, except possibly some of the high commanders, like Admiral Richardson, who was the commander-in-chief at that time. He was tremendously exercised about the safety of the fleet, as it was well known that the entire American fleet - that is, the ships from the East Coast, the scouting fleet, and the ships from the West Coast, the battle force - were all combined and operating off the Hawaiian Islands. Admiral Richardson was terribly concerned about having so many ships out in that area. As a matter of fact, we knew Admiral and Mrs. Richardson quite well, and in the spring of the year - of the following year - that would be 1941, Admiral Richardson went to Washington and pled with President Roosevelt to return most of the ships to the east and west coasts, because he felt they were too much exposed in Honolulu. For reasons of his own, which will probably never be known, President Roosevelt declined to move the ships from Honolulu. He did send one division of battleships of the Idaho class to the East Coast, but the better part of the fleet remained right there at Honolulu.

Q: He went direct to the President?

Adm. W.: He went right to the President. So when Roosevelt informed Richardson that he would not withdraw the fleet, Richardson then asked to be relieved of his command, and he was relieved, and Kimmel was ordered as relief for Admiral Richardson. Kimmel, of course, had been President Roosevelt's personal aide, and he was far too junior, that is according to seniority, to be in command of the fleet, but because, I think, of his having been the President's aide, the President went way down the list and picked him up in order to send him out there as commander-in-chief. Before the Richardsons left, however, Mrs. Richardson, who was a great friend of my wife's, told my wife that she was very, very concerned, not only about the fleet as her husband was, but for their own safety in Honolulu. She felt that conditions there were such that anything might happen, and she didn't like the idea much of living there.

Q: By the Japanese?

Adm. W.: Yes.

Q: How long did Admiral Richardson stay on active duty?

Adm. W.: Well, I don't recall that, exactly. I think he went back and was a member of the General Board or something like that. The General Board was a board of very senior naval officers where most people who had held high commands...

Q: People they didn't know what to do with.

Adm. W.: Yes.

Q: Those are interesting comments.

Adm. W.: I think it was about in January or February, I can't remember exactly, I was selected captain and, as often happens in the Navy, when you get some very nice plum, why, the detail office seems to think that that's a good time to give you a job that is not so desirable, because these jobs have to be filled by somebody. So, soon after my selection for captain, I was ordered to command the Relief, the Navy's only hospital ship at that time, which was a very interesting job. We had only one Naval Academy graduate on board, the rest were merchant marine naval reserve officers. We had, of course, a very large medical staff headed by a Dr. Ross - Captain Ross - who was a delightful gentleman and whom I asked to mess with me in my cabin. He was the head of the medical department which, of course, constituted most of the ship. We also had 13 nurses on board, one of whom was the Chief Nurse, an older woman, who was very efficient, very reliable, very dependable, and she fortunately ran the nurses. The only difficulty we had about them was that one night one of the merchant marine naval reserve officers came on board slightly under the weather and tried to break into one of the nurses' rooms. But we got rid of him in short order, and after that everything was serene. The Relief was only there a few months...

Q: There is...?

Adm. W.: In Honolulu...before she was ordered back to the West Coast, and the story about that cruise is quite interesting in that I had one Saturday morning in May, I think it was, after I had completed inspecting the ship, I drove to my home and found that my wife had gone out somewhere, and so I took the children and we went down to the beach at Fort de Russy, a very nice little beach run by the Army, where they have a clubhouse.

Leaving the children on the beach, I swam out to the second raft and was lying there looking at the beautiful weather and the beautiful scenery and thinking, "Gee, this is too good to last," and after a few minutes I swam back again. collected the children and went back to our home. When I arrived, my wife, who had come home in the meantime, said, "There's been an officer trying to get you for the last hour or so." I said, "Who was it?" and she said, "Well, it was your executive officer." The Relief was secured to a buoy and we had telephone lines, and so I called him up and asked him what he wanted and he said, "I can't tell you over the phone." So, I said, well then come on down and have lunch with us, and he said he would. In about half an hour he arrived and I said, "Now, what's the story?" He said, "Well, I can't tell you with these people around," so I chased the family out and he said, "We have secret orders, and we're not allowed to open them until we're at sea, but we have to sail as soon as possible." So, we had lunch and I told my wife I was going back to the ship with my executive officer, and she said, "Isn't it rather unusual to go back on Saturday?" I said, "Yes, but I can't tell you why I'm going back either." We both left and went back on board and made preparations for getting under way, which we did shortly thereafter, got out to sea and opened our orders, and they said, "Proceed to San Diego," which was rather a surprise inasmuch as we had been due for a Navy yard overhaul at Mare Island, but we proceeded to San Diego.

Q: What was secret about it?

Adm. W.: I'll tell you after a while. In due time, of course, we arrived in San Diego and my orders had said that upon arrival in San Diego I should report to the commandant of the 11th Naval District, which I did. He told me to go back to my ship and figure out exactly how long it would take me to arrive in Panama, and that I should plan my arrival there after dark. So I went back to the ship and the navigator and I figured it out, making allowances for the fact that the ship was really due for Navy yard overhaul and we weren't in very good form for making high speed or anything like that. So I went back and reported to the Admiral and he said, "Well, now you're to leave immediately, today, for Panama." I said, "What's all the rush?" And he said, "That's not for you to know," but we sailed that evening about 10 o'clock...

Q: Excuse me, but did you have any patients on board?

Adm. W.: We had some patients who were to be transferred to the hospital at Mare Island, and we unloaded those at San Diego.

Q: When you left you had no patients aboard?

Adm. W.: No. We proceeded out of harbor and the next morning we noticed a Japanese ship flying the Japanese flag on the western horizon, and that ship kept within sight of us the entire way to Panama. She was following us, I mean, tracking us. We arrived in Panama in due time and I had orders to proceed to transit the Canal and, again, the orders were secret, not to be opened until I got out into the Atlantic. I had to transit the Canal that night, the reason being that the Navy was trying to keep the passage of this ship through the Panama Canal secret. That was the reason, of course, for doing it at night, all of which, to me, was very absurd because the Relief was painted white with a green stripe and red crosses on it, which certainly could be seen going through the canal, and I couldn't really see whether we went through the canal day or night made much difference.

Q: If they had wanted to see it, it was quite apparent.

Adm. W.: There it was. At any rate, we proceeded through the canal and, sure enough, just before daylight next morning, we passed out into the Atlantic and opened the orders.

Q: Did the Japanese ship go through the canal, too?

Adm. W.: No, we didn't see it again after arriving at Panama. And, to my great surprise, it said to proceed to the Norfolk Navy yard. So we proceeded to the Norfolk Navy yard. All this puzzled me no end. I couldn't figure out any of it, so I went over to see a member of the staff of the Commander, Base Force, under whom we were operating, and I asked him what was going on, what was all this about. He told me a story which I have yet to discover anybody else knowing anything about, although I think it was absolutely true. It seems that during one of the conferences between Admiral King and the British, arrangements had been made for the United States and Britain to take over Iceland, the Azores, and Dakar. This was all, as you realize, before the declaration of war and by that time, Iceland had already been taken over by the Americans, as you may remember.

Q: I don't remember. Already?

Adm. W.: Yes, by the time this officer was telling me that. The British had chickened out on the other two objectives, that is the Azores and Dakar.

Q: Would they have been owned by France then?

Adm. W.: No. The Azores are Portuguese, but Dakar was French, held by, you know, the French that were in with the Germans. But this staff officer told me that the original purpose of having the <u>Relief</u> transit the canal in all this rush and everything was that it was anticipated that there would be terrific losses at Dakar and the <u>Relief</u> was to stand by a convenient distance, say, may be 20 miles or something like that, west of Dakar to receive the wounded at the time the attack on Dakar was to take place. I've never heard that from anybody else, but I'm sure it was true because this officer was later one of the commanders of some of these assault operations in the fleet, and a very reliable chap. I had known him for years.

Q: What was his position in Norfolk?

Adm. W.: He was on the staff of the Commander, Base Force...

Q: I mean was he in a position where he would have obviously known, had the information?

Adm. W.: Oh, yes. You see because the admiral in command of the Base Force was in Washington at that time, and this was his senior officer.

Q: Oh, this was the man acting. Well, who was he, do you remember?

Adm. W.: Dan Barbey, a Captain at that time. He was later in command of some of these assault operations in the South Pacific.

Well, at any rate, shortly after we arrived in Norfolk I got orders to...

Q: Before you go on, I do think perhaps a vignette of history that is not recorded.

Adm. W.: Yes. Like the case of the landing of the activities of the landing up in Vladivostok.

Well, as I say, shortly after we arrived I got my orders to report to Holy Cross College in Worcester, to organize and run an NROTC unit. An interesting side light on that transfer was that the man who relieved me was Commander Mackey Lewis, class of 1915, whom I had known for years and was very fond of, and in the course of the transfer I said to Lewis in connection with the turnover, "You know we have to go through all this rigamarole about signing papers, inspection, and so on, but the thing you really ought to know is that you've got a navigator that can't navigate. That's the only thing that really matters." And he said, "Oh, gee, I'm glad you told me that. I will certainly make sure that we don't leave anything to him."

Q: Had you done all the navigating?

Adm. W.: I had discovered that on the way across the Pacific and did all the navigating myself.

Q: That must have given you awfully long hours.

Adm. W.: Yes, but the strange thing was that after being detached and going to Holy Cross College to take over my new duties, I don't think I'd been there more than a few weeks before I picked up the newspaper and read where the <u>Relief</u> had gone aground off Cape Hatteras. He hadn't followed my advice, evidently.

Q: I'm interested in a hospital ship. Are they quiet in the places where the patients are?

Adm. W.: Oh, yes.

Q: How do they make them quiet?

Adm. W.: How do you mean "quiet"?

Q: Are the patients aware they're on a ship?

Adm. W.: Oh, yes.

Q: Do you hear the noise and the beat of the engines?

Adm. W.: Well, yes, it's just like being on any ship. As a matter of fact, it's kind of rythmic. It's not anything that is disturbing at all. It's sort of relaxing.

Q: I wonder if it was specially insulated because of being a hospital ship.

Adm. W.: No. I think they had a stabilizer on board, but we never used it.

Q: Did you have good weather most of the time?

Adm. W.: Yes, as far as I can remember. I mean, normal weather. No storms or anything like that.

Q: How long hours would you have to stand, if you had no navigator?

Adm. W.: Not very long. It meant, for instance, getting up earlier in the morning and catching - and getting star sights, and also taking sights in the evening, and at mid-day.

Q: Did you do that yourself?

Adm. W.: Oh, yes. As soon as I found out he couldn't navigate, why, I wasn't taking any chances.

Q: Did he attempt to learn?

Adm. W.: Yes, he went through the motions, and he told me - his name was Martinson, I still remember - that he had been captain of an oil tanker, but I never believed that. He would have wrecked too many oil tankers.

Q: How would you write a fitness report on a man like that?

Adm. W.: I found that rather difficult, but I just put down what was true, and the strange thing was that it didn't seem to bother him much because, years later, even after I came out here about 16 years ago, and soon after that I had a message from him. He apparently saw in the papers that I was out here and he wanted to come and see me, but I managed to escape that.

Q: At some point, I want to discuss fitness reports with you. Maybe when we get to the Mobile and the various facets ~~of commandin~~g of the commanding office.

Adm. W.: I think that's one of the most important duties that a naval officer has. I always took that very seriously. Well, the experience at Holy Cross was interesting in that, to begin with, I had been really very distressed when I got these orders because of course, we all realized, I think, that we would soon be at war with Japan. I thought among other things that I would not care much for the President of the college. I anticipated that he would be an older man that wouldn't understand anything about the Navy, and that we would be at swordpoints most of the time. Instead of which, to my great surprise and delight, I found that the president of the college was a younger man than I was and one of the most delightful people I've ever met anywhere.

Q: Is that a Catholic school?

Adm. W.: A Catholic school, although I'm not a Catholic, and he said to me that I could put the naval ROTC headquarters any place I wanted to, but that they had just built a new building there and he'd like to show me that and see whether I wanted to put the headquarters there, which I did. He said, among other things, that he - they - had already received a 4-inch gun and I could put that anywhere I wanted to, except on the altar of the chapel. So, I put it in a kind of an auditorium right under the altar in the chapel, where we had our winter drill. That proceeded quite normally except that I found considerable difficulty getting enough people - enough freshmen - who were qualified to enter the naval ROTC units. Many of them had physical difficulties and many of them were scholastically below par, which was a great surprise to me as ~~I had always~~, being from the South, I had always heard that the New England schools were tops, but that wasn't the case. So I had to go through practically all of the freshman class before I could get 110 acceptable candidates for the naval ROTC unit.

Q: It was voluntary?

Adm. W.: Voluntary, yes. At any rate, everything progressed quite normally until the end of the first year, the end of the first academic year, which was in June of the following year, and I said to the President of the college that at the Naval Academy we always had a little ceremony at the end of the academic year and that the student who had the best record was permitted to present the colors to the young lady of his choice, etc, etc. ~~and that we had supper and that kind of thing~~. He said, oh, yes, he was all for it. And he said, now who do you want to have? And I said, "Well, we ought to have the commandant of the district, and Admiral Couverias, who was retired but also President of Worcester Tech, and I named a number of other people. And he said, "Aren't you going to have Senator Walsh?" Senator Walsh at that time was the Chairman of the Senate Naval Affairs Committee. And I said, "Why should I invited Senator Walsh?" who incidentally, of course, was the senator from

Massachusetts and lived only a short distance from Worcester. And he said, "Well, he's the one who had you ordered here, so I think maybe you ought to have him." Well, this answered a question that had been in my mind for sometime about why I had been ordered there, because not being a Catholic I couldn't possibly conceive of any reason why I should be sent there. Then I remembered that when I had been on duty in Washington the time before I went to sea, my wife and I had gone to a garden party on the Potomac given by the Wilkinson captain who, at that time, was liaison officer to the Congress - liaison between the Navy Department and Congress. It was a lovely party, in the spring, and held out of doors, and it so happened, as it often does at parties, that I got - found myself - talking to Senator Walsh, just the two of us. There was nobody else nearby and we stood and talked there for, I guess, half an hour. I don't know why. It just happened accidentally. He had remembered that and apparently he had been trying for years to get a naval ROTC unit at Holy Cross, which was his alma mater, and when 27 new naval ROTC units were authorized by the Congress the previous year, he asked to have me sent there.

Q: One never knows what contacts are going to affect one's future life. You didn't say whether you did invite him and he did come.

Adm. W.: We did invite him and he did come and the party was a great success. But by that time, I was getting restless about going to sea.

Q: I want to interrupt you, because during this time some things were happening in the Pacific and I wanted to ask you how you felt on December the 7th 1941 at Holy Cross.

Adm. W.: On December the 7th 1941, which was a Sunday, of course, my wife and I were reading and listening to the radio. At 2.30 p.m., which was 8.00 a.m. Honolulu time, the program was interrupted by an announcement that the Japs had just bombed Pearl Harbor, and I said to my wife, "This means war. This is war. Fortunately I know that they couldn't have done too terribly much damage because there was an order in the fleet when I was there that not more than one division of ships could be in Pearl Harbor at one time. So they can't have gotten more than about three of our battleships." But it was a terrible thing and I just think it's awful that it should have happened.

It so happened that a few days after that I was invited to the launching of a destroyer at the Boston Navy yard, which was about 40 miles away. After the launching there was the usual reception at the Officers' Club and, as I was walking from the launching platform to the Officers' Club, the captain of the Yard, whose name I can't recall at the moment but whom I had known for many years, was walking alongside of me and we, of course, were talking about Pearl Harbor, and he told me what had really happened. He was among the few people in the Navy outside of Honolulu who knew the whole story, because as captain of the Yard, all of the Navy divers at that Navy yard were under his command, and, of course, as soon as the bombing took place, why, the Navy divers from all the Navy yards were collected and sent to Honolulu as quickly as possible in order to raise these ships. So, under the strictest secrecy, he told me the whole story, all the ships that had been sunk, which I could scarcely believe, and when we arrived at the Officers' Club my wife, who had been walking with somebody else, looked at me, and said, "What on earth has happened to you?" And I said, "Nothing that I know of," because of course I couldn't say anything. She said, "You're as white as a sheet." I wasn't conscious of it.

Q: What had happened to the fleet order that had permitted this?

Adm. W.: It had been changed. The order that not more than three ships should be in there at one time had been issued by Admiral Richardson, and Admiral Kimmel had changed it, so that most of the fleet was there.

Q: There are so many unexplained things still about that period of time.

Adm. W.: Yes. It really is amazing. Well, as I say, I was getting more and more anxious to get to sea, and I learned that the USS Mobile...

Q: Before we get to the Mobile, where were you - or did you know ever about the sinking of the Astoria?

Adm. W.: Oh, yes, but that was later.

Q: Yes, but where were you when you read about that?

Adm. W.: I think I was there. Yes, I'd forgotten that. I was - I think I was in Worcester at that time.

Q: I know that it was at Savo Island. I don't have my dates, but I...

Adm. W.: I think it was while I was in Worcester. And that might be interesting, too, because my niece who had visited us in Honolulu while I was still aboard the <u>Astoria</u> had met and had married one of the officers on board the <u>Astoria</u>, and she was still in Honolulu when the bombing took place. Her husband, of course, was on the Astoria, and as soon as we heard of the sinking of the <u>Astoria</u> and these other ships, I endeavored to find out from my friends in the Navy Department what the story was and, of course, to find out whether ~~this boy~~ her husband, Lt. Willman was still alive. ~~Willman~~. It was very difficult, of course. The secrecy was terrific, but I did eventually find out that he was wounded but he was still alive.

Q: I was wondering what the reaction was to know that a ship of which you could not help but be fond, had been sunk by the Japs.

Adm. W.: Oh, it was a terrible feeling, naturally. A sort of a personal feeling. Some part of your life gone. But the amazing thing which I heard about later on - about ~~this boy~~ Lt. Willman's being recovered was that he was the antiaircraft control officer and he was stationed in the foremast where he had charge of all of his antiaircraft guns. He had communication with all of his antiaircraft guns, but during the course of the battle, these communications were shot away, and his orders - the organizational orders - provided that when you lost communication you should go down to each gun emplacement and take charge from there. Well, he had gone down. He'd left his station on the foremast, and was walking along the main deck, the order having already been given to abandon ship, when a shell must have passed close by because he was knocked out completely, and the wardroom mess attendant Fernandez who is now in charge of the kitchen up at the Admiral Nimitz Club in San Francisco, saw Lieutenant Willman lying on the deck, wrapped him in a life preserver, and threw him overboard. When he got in the water, he apparently came to, the shock, I suppose, of the cold water, and soon thereafter a destroyer came by and picked him up, and that destroyer was commanded by one of his best friends. So he has pulled through, but he is now retired.

Q: Would that be a place to talk about Ghormley and his part in the action?

Adm. W.: I suppose it could be. Admiral Ghormley, whom I had known as a captain in Constantinople in command of a destroyer, was in command of the four cruisers which had been sunk at Savo Island, but he had really nominal command, since the orders were really issued by Admiral Turner. In other words, these four ships were actually under the orders of Admiral Turner at the time when they were sunk, but Admiral Ghormley was in over-all command, and so he got the blame and was ordered to shore and, I don't think, ever got another command. Too bad, because Admiral Ghormley was a very, very fine, conscientious officer. But those things happen, you know.

Q: And who replaced Ghormley?

Adm. W.: Admiral Ghormley was replaced by Admiral Halsey, and Admiral Halsey, with whom I had served in World War I, was one of the most popular officers in the Navy. Everybody loved him. He had been detached from command of the South Pacific because of having picked up a skin disease which was very prevalent in the South Pacific. It topped even malaria. The story told is that after the sinking of those four cruisers, the morale of the fleet, particularly in the South Pacific, was very, very low. Admiral Nimitz learned that Admiral Halsey had recovered sufficiently so that he could be sent back to duty, so he had Admiral Halsey ordered back in command of the South Pacific forces. The story is that just as soon as the word spread around the fleet that Halsey was back, the esprit de corps, the morale, rose 50 per cent immediately.

Q: Marvelous characteristic of leadership to have that result, isn't it?

Adm. W.: Terrific. I remember when he was detached from the destroyer that I was on during World War I, he'd only been in command a few months, why, every man on the ship manned the rails and some of them with tears in their eyes when he left.

I was his executive officer on the destroyer Benham, at that time in World War I.

Q: I don't think when we talked about the Benham that you told me about his being there.

Adm. W.: Well, it's so difficult to remember all these things.

Q: Certainly, and when you get the manuscript back, do make yourself a note and include it because I would have - well, I'll ask you now and then you can pick it out and put it in, as to what he was like then when he was...

Adm. W.: Well, he was a perfectly marvelous character. He just exuded good nature, good feeling. Apparently he never disliked anybody. I remember the fitness reports he made out, he gave the highest marks of any person I've ever seen. He gave me one which read that "this is the finest officer that ever served with me," or something like that, which was all very nice but it was a little bit overrated, I think. But he gave everybody good marks.

Q: I don't think when people get good marks that it means that they're then going to turn around and do a bad job, do you?

Adm. W.: No, I don't think so, either. But everybody liked him. Hardly five minutes would go by without his breaking into a smile. He was a wonderful character.

Q: He must have had a tremendous sense of confidence.

Adm. W.: Oh, he did. Now the amazing thing is that people can be so different and universally loved. Now, you take Admiral Nimitz, whom I have known for years. He was a very serious character, but everybody loved Admiral Nimitz. Completely different from Admiral Halsey, but everybody admired him. He was so fair and such a human sort of a person. Yet their characters were completely different. Halsey was the finest example of an extrovert I've ever known, and I would say that Admiral Nimitz was somewhat of an introvert, but the best kind of introvert, if you know what I mean.

Q: Did you sense when you were on the Benham that Halsey had these characteristics of leadership that he later typified so well?

Adm. W.: I sensed that he was universally liked. Of course, I was only a lieutenant then and I didn't know enough to appreciate the value of the qualities of leadership as much then as I did later.

Q: He was a captain?

Adm. W.: He was a commander.

Q: And that was when his crew lined the...

Adm. W.: Yes. He was the best shiphandler I've ever seen. He would put the destroyer alongside of a dock and, honestly, I think you could have put an egg in between the ship and the dock and it wouldn't have broken. It was beautiful. It was a work of art to see him handle the ship.

Q: We want to cover Admiral Halsey and the torpedo boats. When would that be an appropriate time?

Adm. W.: That should have been back in the days when I was in the <u>Benham</u>.

Q: Well, then, this follows along, doesn't it, because... Admiral Van Duers told me that I should ask you about your experience with Halsey and the torpedo boats.

Adm. W.: Well, that was it. Admiral Halsey was one of a group of "makee learn" skippers, we used to call them. There were about 18 destroyers that were sent over to ~~Kingstown~~ Queenstown, Ireland right after we entered ~~the war~~ World War I, and they were the newest ones, of course. Then they sent the older ones but the Navy Department realized that they didn't have nearly enough destroyers, so they started building new ones furiously. They built one I remember, the <u>Ward</u>, I suppose sort of a special case, in 30 days.

Q: What Navy yard?

Adm. W.: I don't know.

Q: I was wondering was it civilian or Navy.

Adm. W.: I don't really know, but they were turning them out as fast as possible and, of course, the problem then became getting crews for them and skippers, so we always carried at least one extra skipper, whom we called the "makee learn" skipper, and he would ride around on the ship with no responsibilities or duties for anywhere from a few weeks to a month or six weeks, and learn the job, and then he would take over command and the regular skipper would be sent home for a new destroyer. And they did the same thing with the crews, so that we always had about 15 or 20 new men on the ship, which we could manage to train without any difficulty. They weren't extra men. They would take 15 or 20 away and send us 20 others you know. That is how we were able to fill the crews of all these new ships. Of course, some of these ships weren't even finished till after the war. I could have gone home and been ordered to a new destroyer, but every time one of the senior officers was detached, why, I went up one step higher and so about two years after I graduated from the Naval Academy I was exec of a destroyer, operating in the War Zone, which I thought was much more fun than being in a Navy yard putting a new one in commission.

Q: Well, how did that relate to the torpedo boats?

Adm. W.: There were no torpedo boats. They were all destroyers. They were torpedoboat-destroyers. Torpedo boats went out a long time ago. I saw a few torpedo boats when I was a midshipman at the Naval Academy, but as you probably know, torpedo boats originally started out being quite small, and the idea was that they'd run in under cover of darkness and fire their torpedoes and then escape. And destroyers - the proper term, of course, is torpedoboat-destroyer, you see, because destroyers, the large ones, were supposed to sink the torpedo boats.

Q: Then they came back in World War II very prominently.

Adm. W.: Torpedo boats? Oh, well, those werent' torpedo boats, they were patrol boats.

Q: What Kennedy...

Adm. W.: Yes, they were patrol boats.

Q: I thought they were called torpedo boats.

Adm. W.: No, not really, no. They weren't torpedo boats.

Q: One time later I have heard and read, Admiral Halsey was hospitalized for some reason other than a physical condition. At the time of Pearl Harbor that Spruance took over, just before then?

Adm. W.: But they had two teams, you know, in Pearl Harbor.

Q: But I thought he'd had so much pressure down in the South Pacific that he had to be hospitalized for a short period of time.

Adm. W.: No, I don't think so. He only had a skin disease. ~~It never came to my attention.~~

Q: Now, we're almost up to the time, I guess, when you were going to start telling me about the Mobile.

Adm. W.: The story about the Mobile began a few years earlier than this, in that back about 1935 I was on duty in the Navy Department as Atlantic communication officer and, while there, a letter from the President passed over my desk informing all the senior officers in the Navy Department that five new cruisers were going to be built under the President's NRA program. The thought passed through my mind that it was a strange thing that, although Mobile was a port and on account of that I had first learned about the Navy when the ships used to come in to Mobile at Mardi Gras time and on the 4th of July, as far as I knew no Navy ship had ever been named the Mobile, whereas countless ships had been named for places out in the Middle West, a thousand miles or more from salt water. So I wrote a letter to a former high-school classmate of mine in the Chamber of Commerce in Mobile and suggested that steps be taken to have one of the new ships named the Mobile. I immediately had a reply saying that he and all of the members of the Chamber of Commerce thought this was a marvelous idea and asked me how to go about it. I told him that, in my opinion, the proper way was to write a letter to the Secretary of the Navy, to both of our senators, and to our Congressman, making that suggestion, which they did. Time passed, so that about six years later - I was on duty in Honolulu when I got a letter from this same man saying that inasmuch as I had been the one who suggested it, he thought that I would like to know that they had received word that one of the new cruisers was to be named the Mobile, and down at the bottom, he said, "By the way, Julian, do you have any idea who'd make a good skipper for this ship?" I certainly did, as a matter of fact I'd thought of that a long time before. So, I asked my friends in the Navy Department to keep me informed about the progress of the building of the Mobile, which was done, and I knew that she

was about ready to be commissioned about the time that I
thought I was due to leave Worcester. So I went to the Navy
Department and made my request in person, but I got nowhere
because it was wartime and everybody was far too busy to
listen to anything like that, except to just give me a cursory
answer, so I went back to Holy Cross very much crestfallen.
Only a short while later, Admiral Cluverius who was retired and
was serving as President of Worcester Tech and was a great friend
of mine, told me that he had been down to the Boston Navy yard
to attend a launching or commissioning or something, and while
there he had heard that the new commanding officer of the
Mobile had been ordered. Well, that bothered me even more,
because of course I thought that meant that somebody else
had been ordered to the Mobile, which I up to that time considered was my ship. I think that Admiral Cluverius really
knew who had been ordered but he just wasn't saying. In any
case, about two weeks later I got my orders to the command of
the Mobile. In the meantime, my wife said that I wasn't fit
to live with during those two weeks. But I went to Newport
News Shipbuilding yard in Newport News and commenced to organize
the crew. I was fortunate in having a number of enlisted men
and some of the officers who had just concluded their
survivors' leave. They had been survivors of the San Francisco
and several other ships whose names I can't remember, but
they were really veterans of the war already. So, in a matter
of about a month we organized a crew and
the ship was then towed over - to Norfolk Navy yard where we
had the commissioning ceremony. After that we spent another

month or so "shaking down," as it's called in the Navy, in the Chesapeake Bay. We were somewhat handicapped in that the new battleship Iowa was also shaking down at the same time and in that constricted space available for ships of our draft to operate, we frequently got in each other's hair but we managed to iron that out. Then we had a few other exercises, short-range battle practice and activities of that sort, after which we went to Portland, Maine, outside of which we conducted target practice with our long-range guns. When that was over, after a few days in Boston, the Mobile was ordered to the West Coast. We proceeded through the Panama Canal...

Q: Before you leave the East Coast, were there any interesting incidents that happened while you were in the ship yard?

Adm. W.: Nothing that I can remember, except of a personal nature. Many of the friends that I had made while at Holy Cross came down on board ship to see me, and we had receptions on board and things of that kind.

Q: Were any other ships being commissioned or launched while you were there?

Adm. W.: No, not that I can remember. Nothing outstanding, I mean. There were a number of ships there undergoing repairs.

Q: Where was the incident with the Yorktown?

Adm. W.: Oh, yes. I'd forgotten to tell you about the Yorktown. While at the Newport News shipbuilding yard before being commissioned, we had the pleasure of watching the launching of the carrier Yorktown, during which a very amusing incident occurred, in that the commanding officer of the previous Yorktown which had been sunk, Captain Buckmaster, had been detailed to make the address from the launching platform where a number of notables were gathered, including Mrs. Franklin D. Roosevelt, who was the sponsor. It was explained to me afterwards that it was rather difficult on a ship as large as the Yorktown to determine exactly when the launching gear was going to let go so that the ship would actually slide down the ways. Buckmaster got very wound up in his address, and the ship actually started down the ways before he finished and before Mrs. Roosevelt was aware of it. I was standing fairly close to them and I saw the supervisor of shipbuilding reach over and grab Mrs. Roosevelt by the arm and tell her to break the bottle then, which she did after running alongside of the ship on the platform for several steps she finally succeeded in breaking the bottle.

Q: Probably the only person who ever chased a new ship down the ways.

Adm. W.: After that we all went over to the Officers' Club and had a very nice luncheon, at which Mrs. Roosevelt was the guest of honor and we were all very much impressed with her grace and warmth throughout this occasion. The way she greeted everybody, she was really a first lady in more ways than one.

Q: Did she speak?

Adm. W.: No.

Q: Have you said what kind of a ship the Mobile was?

Adm. W.: No. The Mobile was a 10,000-ton light cruiser. She had 12 6-inch guns in 4 turrets and 8 5.8 - 5-inch - guns mounted in four turrets, two in each mount plus additional 40mm. and 20mm A.A. guns. She was equipped with all the very latest radar. I counted up and I think that there were altogether 13 radars on the ship when she went into commission, which was really astounding to me because when I had left the fleet in Pearl Harbor in 1941, I remember that the first radar which was considered very secret in those days and which people only referred to as a bedspring was being installed on one of the cruisers in the Navy yard. In three years, the progress of the development of radar had just been unbelievable. In fact, I later learned that they were turning them out so fast that the principal difficulty was in teaching technicians to be able to operate them and repair them, not so much in actually producing the radars but in being able to keep them in condition. We had surface radar, we had two antiaircraft radar on the mast, and a number of smaller radars for use in control of the antiaircraft batteries, which were most useful during the Japanese air attacks and operated very successfully. We had a crew of 1,200 men. The number of men in the crew provided for the maintenance of the antiaircraft watch at sea at all times. In other words, the antiaircraft guns were manned round the clock, which was one reason that we had such a large crew. And we had over 100 officers, of whom I think probably only about 25 or 30 were Naval Academy men. The rest were all Reserve, but they were a superb group. I think I was probably one of the most fortunate men in the Navy because my crew never gave me any concern whatsoever. They were always doing their job when they were supposed to. They were always willing, and although I had a few cases that came to the mast, they soon found out that I meant business when it came to giving out punishments of any kind and they decided it wasn't a good idea to appear at the mast any more. I'm very devoted to that crew. I still hear from some of them, and I consider I was very blessed in having the kind of crew, both officers and men, that I had.

Q: I imagine they returned that in like fashion.

Adm. W.: Well, they did. I think they were very appreciative. I remember one man whose father wrote back and said that his son had told him not to worry because he had a good skipper.

Q: I don't think he said quite that. You told that differently at lunch. Now you tell me exactly what he said.

Adm. W: Well, he said he had the best skipper in the Navy so he was perfectly all right and for his father not to worry about him.

After leaving Boston, we went to Panama where I picked up a Carrier and three or four other ships - destroyers - which were placed under my command because I was the senior officer in the group, and we proceeded to San Diego, where the group was disbanded. In those days, we had the plan that whenever a group of ships was organized they were designated as a task group. For instance, two carriers might be known as Task Group 50.1 If there were two or three cruisers in the group that would be known as 50.2. If there were 8 or 10 destroyers in the group, that would be known as 50.3. When that group joined another group, which might be called, say, Task Group 51, then the two task groups together would be known as a task force, and that could be given any number the senior officer decided to use. Usually, the numbers of the task force would correspond with the number of the fleet. For instance, the Seventh Fleet task Force would be known as seventy, and the task group would be known as 70.1 and 70.2, and so forth and so on.

After leaving San Diego, the <u>Mobile</u> proceeded to Mare Island Navy yard to have some adjustments made on our turbines, which were done in a few days, but this also provided some shore leave and recreation for the officers and men, which was very welcome at that time before we started out for the Pacific and after our long cruise round from the Atlantic. After we completed that we went on to Honolulu, where I reported to...

Q: Did you proceed independently?

Adm. W.: We proceeded independently from San Francisco to Honolulu.

Q: When did you arrive in Honolulu?

Adm. W.: Let me see, I think - I don't have the exact date, unfortunately. You know we weren't allowed to keep log books of what we did. I would say it must have been in April some time, or May. It may have been May. We were commissioned on the 24th of March and I think - in May, it must have been May. And one of the first things that happened was that Admiral Nimitz came on board to inspect and he gave us a very fine report that the ship was in fine condition and in a state of readiness. I was reminded at that time of the fact that when I had last seen him in Washington about 1938, when I was in his bureau at the Navy Department, I went to say good-bye to him and told him that, "The next time I see you, Admiral, you will be commander-in-chief of the fleet." He was.

Q: Do you think this might be an appropriate time for you to tell me about your various experiences with Admiral Nimitz? I know that you knew him quite well.

Adm. W.: I just can't remember too much about where we were together before, but I always seem to have known Admiral Nimitz and I remember particularly when we arrived in Washington for duty - oh, I think it must have been about 1929, that he and Mrs. Nimitz very kindly came to call on us, and we kept up with them...

Q: What was his rank then, his grade?

Adm. W.: He was either commander or captain. I'm not sure. But he was one of the very senior officers. We always liked him and admired him. He was the kind of person that easily drew you to him. He was not a particularly outgoing person, but he was so sincere and you felt when you talked with him that you were absolutely talking to a very wonderful character who was going to be heard from later on, as of course we all did.

Q: Do you have any particular anecdotes of your relationships with him?

Adm. W.: No, I don't. I don't think Admiral Nimitz was the kind of a person that you had anecdotes about, except possibly when I come to tell you about being his house guest at Guam later on when I was with Lord Fraser. That might be the time to mention that.

Q: Did he remember you when he came to inspect...?

Adm. W.: Oh, yes.

Q: How did he treat you?

Adm. W.: Like a friend. Yes, indeed. I can tell you right here that I got him to write in my Mobile guest book, which he wrote some very nice words in.

Q: Do you have it handy?

Adm. W.: Yes. Do you want to see it?

Q: I think you ought to read it. Now, is this when he made the inspection?

Adm. W.: This is when he made the inspection, and I see by the date hereon that my recollection of the date when we first arrived in Honolulu was way off, because this is dated July the 27th 1943, which was my birthday, and Admiral Nimitz wrote: "C.W. Nimitz, Admiral, USN, CinCPac, congratulates Captain Wheeler on his birthday. His fine ship and smart crew and wishes him, ship and crew best of luck in the coming engagements."

The Mobile and the Yorktown, an aircraft carrier, were among the first ships of what was to become the Central Pacific Force to arrive in Honolulu. At that time, some of the ships were engaged in Alaska, where they had just participated in an Alaskan naval campaign, but they soon after arrived in Honolulu and together we all formed the basis of the Central Pacific Force.

Q: That was a new force, wasn't it?

Adm. W.: That was a new force which was organized to proceed across the Central Pacific and eventually overcome Japan. As some may know, there had been considerable argument about how this Pacific campaign would be waged. General MacArthur had believed in proceeding from the southern islands up through the Philippines, and thence, to Japan. But the Navy Department thinking was that we should proceed directly across the Pacific and attack Japan in that way. A compromise was eventually reached and General MacArthur was given command of what was called the Southwest Pacific, which had some - it was composed mostly of Army troops but also some Navy ships. As the Central Pacific Force moved westward and the Southwest Pacific Force moved northward, they eventually converged in

Philippines and from there on, of course, the plan was to assault Japan, but this wasn't necessary because of the atomic bomb.

Q: How much were the officers who participated in the Central Pacific Force aware of the strategy involved, or that it was something new, that it had never been tried before?

Adm. W.: We were all aware of it. We weren't aware of the talks that had precipitated it. We knew that General MacArthur was a very powerful character in the military hierarchy, and Admiral Nimitz was likewise in the naval high command, and neither one of these officers could be shunted aside. I mean, it was realized, I think, that both of them had to be given a high command. Therefore the Pacific was divided into these two parts. In other words, it would never have worked to place Admiral Nimitz over MacArthur, or MacArthur over Admiral Nimitz, so they had to be given different areas. Of course, MacArthur originally had his headquarters in Brisbane, Australia, and then he and his staff worked up from there to the eastern end of New Guinea and westward along New Guinea, and up through the islands from there to the Philippines. But the Central Pacific Force began with the bombing of Marcus, which was the Mobile's baptism of fire. As a matter of fact, there was no resistance offered from Marcus, so it was really more of a training exercise than anything else.

Q: How many ships were involved in that action?

Adm. W.: I think there were only about six or eight. It was

a very small action. The Yorktown and the Mobile - there may have been another cruiser, but if so I don't remember it - and five or six destroyers. All we did was to bombard Marcus. We made a number of hits, of course, on the island but there was no retaliation. With a larger task force, later on, we bombarded Wake with much the same result. I mean that we could see the damage that we caused due to the fires that were caused when the bombs hit - both aircraft bombs and ship bombs, ship shells - landed ashore and set warehouses and oil storage depots and things like that on fire. We could easily see that. But there was no response.

Q: Was that in the nature of a training exercise as well?

Adm. W.: No. I think that was a business exercise. We really meant business- I think we did a good deal of harm there, too.

Q: Who was the commanding officer at the Wake Island action? By that time was that Admiral   ?

Adm. W.: It may easily have been. He was in command of a number of those operations, but I don't remember who was in command of that one?

Q: The senior ship would have been the Yorktown?

Adm. W.: Yes. It would have been the flagship.

Q: And her commanding officer at that time was?

Adm. W.: Oh, it was Jocko Clark. They had a very interesting command setup in that war which had never been tried before. Due to the evolution of the carrier task force, in that the carriers were always at center of the formation, on a circle about two miles beyond the carriers were - if they were there - the battleships. There weren't always battleships there. About three miles out beyond that circle was another circle on the circumference of which would be stationed the cruisers. And then about five miles beyond that circle would be a circle on which would be stationed the destroyers. The center, of course, of the whole operation was the carrier, and the battleships, cruisers, and destroyers were largely of a defensive nature. In other words, the purpose of those was to prevent enemy aircraft from penetrating the screen and bombing the decks of the carrier, which were very vulnerable. The simplest way of maneuvering the task force was from the carrier, because everything pivoted on that, as you can well see. Therefore, it soon developed that the Admiral in command would select the carrier as his flagship and run the entire operation from there. Even if the Admiral in command of the Carrier Task Group was junior to the Admiral in command of the battleships, the carrier Admiral would be in charge of the Task Group operations. And another interesting feature was that when the war began, we didn't have enough aviator admirals really to man the fleet and conduct a war of this kind, so many younger officers were promoted to the temporary rank of admiral in order that they would have the rank to exercise this command. That, of course, was something entirely new to the Navy, because up to that time the senior officer present had always been in command, but you can see how awkward it would have been if the senior officer present were in a battleship on one of these outer circles, whereas the whole operation was being controlled from the carrier. As a matter of fact, they carried that even to the extent of some occasions when Admiral Spruance, who would be in command of the operation, would be flying his flag in a battleship, and an admiral much junior to him flying his flag on the carrier would give the orders for the task group. It was most unusual, but it worked. It worked beautifully.

Q: Did you ride in the same place usually in this screen? Your ship?

Adm. W.: Well, it all depended on - no, I mean I was always riding with the cruisers, but I might be sometimes on the right flank and sometimes on the left flank, sometimes ahead and sometimes in rear.

Q: It depended on what the operation was and they had a complete organization for that particular setup?

Adm. W.: Oh, yes. They'd have complete plans for each setup.

Q: I was trying to picture in my mind exactly where you were.

Adm. W.: As a matter of fact, even that didn't make much difference because when you're in the van on one course, if they reversed order you'd be in the rear. It didn't matter. You just went round and round. After the operation on Wake, we next made a bombing raid with a larger carrier task group down on the Gilberts, which include Tarawa and Makin. That was a softening-up raid to - well, it was primarily really in order to enable the carriers - the Air Intelligence people to make photographs of the fortifications and emplacements at Tarawa, which they did, and of course based on that, later on the plans for the assault on Tarawa were made. That was our next operation, as I remember, the assault on Tarawa. Admiral Hill was in command of that operation, which consisted of his flagship, which I think was the New Mexico but I'm not sure, and of course there were numbers of transports loaded with Marines, and there were several cruisers. By that time I think two other cruisers which were the - just like the Mobile, I mean the same class as the Mobile, had joined up - the Birmingham and - well, there were two cruisers and I'll think of the other one's name in a moment. That was organized into Cruiser Division 13, commanded by Rear Admiral du Bose, and the night before...

Q: I have the Santa Fe, the Mobile...

Adm. W.: The Santa Fe. It was the Santa Fe and the Birmingham. The Biloxi didn't report until later. The night before we went in...

Q: Now, this is the actual invasion of Tarawa?

Adm. W.: This is the actual invasion. Before we went in, we escorted these transports close along the shore line, and just before landing, about an hour or so before, we began the bombardment, which was later determined to have been too late. The bombardment should have been begun much earlier, but that mistake was corrected on the occasion of the assault at

Kwajalein. The result of that was, of course, that the Japs who were holed up in caves and kind of emplacements that were built out of coconut palm trees and which were quite secure against bombardment, they just sat back in their emplacements and not many of them were too much damaged, I mean by the bombardment.

Q: You mean you didn't have long enough to bombard?

Adm. W.: We didn't have long enough. We didn't bombard long enough. So that when the landing actually took place there were terrific losses of life among our Marines, which was further complicated by the fact the British had apparently not recorded - the British from whom we got the data regarding the plans in connection with the invasion - had not properly recorded the rise and fall of the tide.

Q: Why did we get that from the British?

Adm. W.: Because they owned it before. They were there before. They were there before the Japs took it over.

Q: Oh, before World War I. The Japs took it.

Adm. W.: Yes.

Q: So that was awfully old data, then.

Adm. W.: Awfully old. And some of these ships went aground before they were able to land and they were just sitting ducks, and the men, particularly the Marines, had to wade ashore, and these Japanese troops by the thousand were lined up there on the beach and they just mowed ~~them~~ *our troops* down. I remember at one point in the assault when I heard the Marine commander - of course, we heard everything over our radio, I mean it was heard on the radio throughout the fleet - that ~~this Marine~~ *Col. Aho* commander reported that the situation was in doubt. In other words, whether they could make that landing or not was problematical. I remember also that the Marine corpses, and Japanese also, were floating by the ship in great numbers. It was a terrible sight. The only way you could distinguish between the Marines and the Japanese was that the Japanese wore wrapped leggings and we wore - our Marines wore - the regular leggings, don't you know. But they were all face down and we just saw these hundreds of bodies ~~flying~~ *floating* by, some of them would catch in the various parts of the ship as they went by, in the scuppers and things like those. It was a ghastly sight.

Q: How close were you to the island?

Adm. W.: We were, oh, I should say a matter of about six miles.

Q: And the bodies were floating out that far?

Adm. W.: That far. Sometimes we went in closer. At one stage, I received an order from the task force commander, that was Admiral Hill, to go in closer and deliver twenty minutes of gunfire on strong point on one of the atolls there, which was being held by the Japanese, and we went in to within a few miles of this point, and let fly with our whole main battery, and we had rapid-fire guns. We could see from the bridge when the shells started to fall on this Japanese strong point. First, it was just a lot of rubbish, you know, and smoke and that sort of thing, and then we could see these Japanese bodies whirling around in the air in the most grotesque looking fashion. After the 20 minutes of gunfire, there was no more resistance and our Marines walked right up and took it.

Q: Could you see them from...?

Adm. W.: Oh, yes.

Q: How did you feel? I can't imagine one's personal reaction to this kind of horror.

Adm. W.: Well, I think at that time you're so engrossed in the idea of winning that you kind of felt sorry that all this was happening, but your mind was focused on the end, the necessity to win this battle because with all this loss of life, why, think of what it would have been if we hadn't won it.

Q: Oh, yes. I didn't mean necessarily how you felt about the gunfire hitting the Japanese emplacements, but the horror of what was happening to our Marines.

Adm. W.: Oh, yes. That was ghastly. It was awfully hard to take. And then, of course, all the time there were Japanese submarines operating in the areas, so we never knew when we might get a torpedo in our innards. As a matter of fact, one ship was torpedoed soon after that - the Liscom Bay, which incidentally, was commanded by Admiral Mullinix, who stood No. 1

in my class. But of course eventually we won...

Q: What was the atmosphere aboard your ship? Was there fear, or...?

Adm. W.: Oh, no. I never saw any fear exhibited on my ship at all. I'll tell you an incident later on that will amuse you about how undisturbed they were about that when we were bombing another island. But we were glad when that was over. In those days we used to go back to Pearl Harbor.

Q: Did you see any particular acts of courage during the Tarawa...?

Adm. W.: Well, no. We couldn't because we were too far away from the landing. As a matter of fact, most of the time from our position, the atoll was in between us. The Marines landed on the inside. We were on the outside, of the atoll. No, we weren't able to see and, of course, there was no opportunity to display any courage on board ship because everybody was just doing his job without worrying about the consequences. But there were terrific acts of courage, of course, on the part of the men who were going ashore. You've read, you know, about how they'd pick up the bodies of the wounded and carry them back to these landing craft under fire, and that sort of thing.

Q: Wasn't Admiral Turner in over-all charge of the amphibious operations?

Adm. W.: Adm. Turner was in charge of the Northern (MAKIN) Attack Force, but Adm. Harry Hill was in charge of the Southern (TARAWA) Attack Force.

later.

Q: The basis really was the lack of proper intelligence, was it not?

Adm. W.: Well, lack of proper intelligence and also a lack of understanding. As I said, when we went in to Kwajalein, we bombed that area the day before, and when we went in there was practically nothing left. The place was just full of shell holes and most of the people had been routed out of their protective huts and things like that. So that many lives were saved by that preliminary bombing. Of course, one has to learn. I mean you can't ...

Q: A terrible lesson, but it was the first and many lessons that were learned there, weren't they?

Adm. W.: Many lessons. Well, now, let's see. Where do we go from there?

Q: You started to say that you went back to Pearl from Tarawa.

Adm. W. You see, in the early days we were close enough to Pearl to run back to refuel and replenish ammunition and provisions. Later on, we didn't. We'd captured another base, Majuro, which we went in to later. I should mention that along about this time, or may be before, my wife received a letter from the Secretary of the Navy appointing her as sponsor to launch the USS Putnam up here. (Pointing to a photo of the launching) I had written in some time previously and requested that she be assigned to launch one of the new ships because they were building them by the hundreds you know. So they selected her to christen the <u>Putnam</u> because her name was Putnam before she was married, and there was a Putnam in the Navy in the early days who died on a ice flow in the Arctic. He may have been a collateral connection. I don't think she's a direct descendant. At any rate, she got a great thrill out of that.

Our next big operation was the assault on Kwajalein, which was a much larger undertaking than the raid on Tarawa, and fortunately we were able to profit from some of the mistakes made in the Tarawa operation to avoid some loss of life at Kwajalein. The principal mistake made at Tarawa was the fact that bombing did not start soon enough, and this was corrected at Kwajalein by continuous bombing for almost 24 hours before the landing took place, and there was much less difficulty in securing a foothold and taking over control of the island. Soon after that...

Q: Could I ask you before that, in history, as I read it, several of the commanders did not want to go directly to Kwajalein after Tarawa. They thought that there should be some protective islands taken first. Nimitz thanked them for their advice, but said, no, we will go directly to Kwajalein anyway. I wondered how much of the strategy you were aware of.

Adm. W.: We were aware of the strategy called island-jumping -

that's not the exact term for it. We were conscious of that and were very much in favor of it because, of course, it saved a great many lives and once these islands were bypassed, they never gave us any trouble. The reason was, of course, that once they were behind the areas that we had overcome, the Japs had no way of supplying them. They tried to - and they did - send some supplies to some of the islands by Japanese submarines, but they weren't nearly large enough to carry enough supplies to make them dangerous in any way. So, once we had bypassed them, they were out of the war.

Q: Were the commanding officers of the ships ever brought together on the flagship and the strategy discussed, and purused so that you knew what your objective was?

Adm. W.: No. No, not in that way. Whenever we went to Pearl we were always invited to the commander-in-chief's conferences, Admiral Nimitz's conferences, in the war room, where all of these operations were discussed, but there was not much opportunity while the ships were at sea or at these outlying islands for things of that sort. Furthermore, the operations were so clearly planned, the operation orders were so clearly worded that there wasn't much chance for any misunderstanding. It was about this time that the two forces came into being - well, I guess it was later on, because I think our next - after the Kwajalein operation, Cruiser Division 13, and by that time we had been joined by the fourth ship in our division which was the Biloxi, we were ordered to participate in the landings at Empress Augusta Bay, which was down just north of Guadalcanal. The reason for that was that Cruiser Division 12 had been badly mauled in the fight with the Japanese off Empress Augusta Bay, and it had to undergo some repairs. So Cruiser Division 13 was detached and ordered down to join the South Pacific Force which, at that time, was under Admiral Halsey, and our function was to protect the landings at Empress Augusta Bay. That was the time when we really got our first baptism of fire. We stood up and down to the westward of Empress Augusta Bay, which is at the southwest end of Bougainville Island, which was to be occupied by American troops. Of course, this landing was being opposed by the Japanese. The greatest threat was from the Japanese planes based at Rabaul in the islands to the northward and, sure enough, during the first night of our presence there, we soon detected Japanese planes heading toward us on our radars. We had not previously had any night air attacks, and it was a weird experience to see these Japanese planes heading toward us on the radars, and then when they got within 8,000 feet, which was - 8,000 yards, I mean - which was the range at the Commander Cruiser Division 13 ordered us to open fire with our antiaircraft guns, we would open fire and, without having seen the planes by eye. If the shots were successful and we got hits, we would see a ball of fire suddenly appear in the sky and then this flaming mass, which, of course, was the plane, would drop to the water and burn on the water for some 15 or 20 minutes. It was a very exhilarating feeling, if I may say so, to see these planes that were trying to sink our ships come to their end.

Fortunately, the Mobile was not hit. We did have the misfortune to have two men in one of our turrets - in one of our anti-aircraft batteries - killed due to the fact that a piece of mechanism in the forward antiaircraft gun turret on the port side failed to operate and the turret trained too far to the left - killed two of the men on one of the smaller antiaircraft guns. But we didn't lose any men from enemy fire.

Q: How many planes did you see shot down?

Adm. W.: It must have been five or six. at that time.

Q: And then did the rest of them get through?

Adm. W.: One of them got through and fired a torpedo into the port bow of the Birmingham. I'm not sure which ship it was. They saw it coming but they couldn't avoid it. You see, these were torpedo planes and their object was to fly in low and get close enough to the ship so they could launch a torpedo. One of them got hit that way, but it wasn't serious. It didn't sink the ship. We had to go in to Purvis Bay near Guadalcanal and make some temporary repairs. Then we went back and joined the Central Pacific Force after this operation was over...

Q: And it was successful?

Adm. W.: It was successful, yes. The Marines took Empress Augusta Bay and held it and then they marched farther up and eventually took over all of Bougainville Island. Cruiser Division 12 had been repaired after that operation, so we joined the re-

Central Pacific Force and, according to my recollection, we rejoined our force at the island of Majuro which had been taken by our ships, and it was there that I had my famous walk with Admiral Spruance. The ships were all at anchor, and I had some reason, I've forgotten what, to go over and see the captain of the New Jersey, which was anchored a considerable distance from us. So I got in my little gig and proceeded to the New Jersey one morning, did my business with the captain of the New Jersey, Carl Holden, who was a friend of mine, and he looked at his watch and said, "Well, Julian, it's almost lunch time. Why don't you stay and have lunch with us?" Recognizing that it was some little distance to get back to my own ship, I said, "Why, yes. I think that's a fine idea." And in those days the admiral and captain of the ship messed together. This was done in order to cut down on the number of mess attendants and stewards and so on that were necessary to keep the admiral's and captain's mess going. So, we went up to the admiral's cabin and Admiral Spruance, whom I had known before, very kindly seated me on his left and we had a nice chat during lunch. He had his staff there also, so there must have been about 12 people at lunch, including his chief of staff, a Captain C.J. Moore, who was on his right. Towards the end of the luncheon, Admiral Spruance said, "Would you like to go and take a walk with me this afternoon?" I knew they had been building an air base - and airfield - at Majuro so I was anxious to see that, and also anxious to stretch my legs as I hadn't been ashore for four or five weeks, and so I said, "Well,

Admiral, I'd be delighted to go with you." Nobody else spoke up which seemed a little strange, but nevertheless he pointed to one lieutenant way down at the end of the table and said, "Lieutenant, aren't you going with me?" "Yes, Sir." He answered. So Ad. Spruance said, "Well, I'll meet both of you at the gangway at 1 o'clock." So, at 1 o'clock this lieutenant and I were at the gangway, the Admirals barge was at the foot of the gangway. The Admiral came out and we all embarked in the barge and landed, at one of the rickety landings that the Japs had left there before they had been run out, and we started walking. Well, it was hot, awfully hot. I hadn't been ashore for a long time and I wasn't accustomed to walking, and I got awfully tired, and very upset because, every few minutes, a jeep would pass by, and they'd see these four stars on Admiral Spruance's collar and ask him if he wouldn't like to have a lift. The Admiral said, "Oh, no, we're out for the exercise." And so they passed by. That happened three or four times, and I was getting more and more tired, and finally we got back to the landing. The Admiral's barge was there. It was about 5 o'clock. We'd walked for, oh, I guess, three and a half hours without a stop for anything. When we got back to the landing Carl Holden, the captain of the <u>New Jersey</u> and some of his staff and others that were sitting round there, they all gave me the horse laugh. I was obviously done in, you know.

Q: That's an awfully long walk.

Adm. W.: Well, they knew that, and that's the reason they hadn't volunteered. The devils didn't caution me about it, so they laughed, and I kind of fell into the boat, and we all went back to the <u>New Jersey</u> (~~Mobile~~?)

Q: Did Admiral Spruance do this daily?

Adm. W.: Every time he got the chance. He was in wonderful condition. He was very slender. My guess is that he probably weighed, oh, he was a fairly small man, I doubt if he weighed more than 135 or 140 pounds. He was in beautiful physical condition. I wasn't. He'd had more opportunities to go ashore than I had. Well, I got my boat and went back to the ship. It was about a 30-minute ride back to the ship. I was taken there, got alongside my gangway, and I couldn't get up. I was really quite worried, I thought, my word, what does this mean? So I called up to the officer of the deck and said he'd better send somebody down to help me, so he sent a couple of men down, and they helped me up. I sent for the doctor and said, "What's the matter with me, doctor? Am I going to die or something?" And he said, "Oh, no. There's nothing in the world the matter with you except that you've been de-salted - de-salinated." See, when I perspired I perspired all the salt out, and I couldn't move, my legs were absolutely stiff. It was very painful. So he said, "Oh, we'll give you some salt pills and you'll be all right." So I said, "Give me a lot of them right away, won't you?" And he said, "Oh, no, we can't do that. I'll have to give them to you gradually," which he did, and in a few hours I was all right. Of course, the walk with Admiral Spruance was really fabulous because he told me a great deal about the forthcoming operations, and he's a very delightful gentleman. He's a wonderful man. I'm very devoted to Admiral Spruance. He sent me an autographed copy of his book. It was frightening.

Somewhere along about this time, we came to the Mobile's first birthday, and I had the ship's baker bake a 500-pound cake. We put it out on one of the mess tables and invited everybody to come and participate. You should have seen the cake after they'd finished with it. There was hardly anything left. We also had the experience of "Crossing the Line" and making real sailors out of pollywogs. Then, to get down to more serious business, we...Oh, I forgot to mention also while on board the New Jersey, I had the pleasure of meeting ex-Governor Stassen.

Q: When you went to see Admiral Spruance?

Adm. W.: Well, I really went to see Carl Holden, the captain, but I had luncheon with Admiral Spruance. Stassen was on Spruance's staff, and he seemed like an awfully nice chap. I mean he didn't act a bit the way he has since that time, you know, he has been running for president every election year, kind of ridiculous. But I was quite taken with him at that time. I think our next operation was a raid on Saipan, and for that raid I received and, I suppose, to the captains of the other cruisers and carriers that took part, also received the commendation medal because it seems that the raid was known to the Japanese before we made it. Most of these raids and assaults were kept pretty well secret, but this one was made against considerable opposition. We had a charmed life on the <u>Mobile</u>. I mean, I never lost a man to enemy action the whole time I was on her, but some of the others did. We shot down a number of Japanese planes.

Q: Was that a night raid again?

Adm. W.: No, that was a daytime raid. Now we're getting up close to the first Battle of the Philippine Sea. That occurred on my wedding anniversary - my wife and I were married on the 20th of June 1944. That was the occasion where the Task Force No. - the Fifth Fleet under Admiral Spruance was ordered to protect the American landings at Saipan, so the entire Central Pacific Force, was mobilized to protect these landings at Saipan. I suppose we must have kept about 150 miles west of Saipan. In other words, we were operating north and south about 150 miles west of Saipan, in order to guard against any interruption by the Japanese while our landing operations were going on. And it was one night during operation when an American shore-based plane sighted a Japanese fleet some 500 miles to the west of Saipan, obviously heading toward Saipan to prevent us from securing the safety of the landing.

So as soon as that report was received, we headed west at about 25 knots - the whole fleet headed west - and we were all fired with enthusiasm with the idea that we would engage the Japanese fleet. We had never had a surface engagement. You see, up to this time it had all been aircraft. Well, about 8 p.m. the first night, I don't know how long we'd been traveling, all day, I think, and then 8 p.m. that night after we got the orders to head west toward this fleet, why, Admiral Spruance gave the order to reverse course. And I could just almost hear the sighs from the lower deck because everybody, you know, was crying "Let me at 'em." But we turned back, of course, and I wondered about that, until I started to think about some of the lessons I had learned at the Naval War College, and I realized exactly why Admiral Spruance had done that. And that was because the prime objective of the Task Force 58, Fifth Fleet, was to protect the landings in Saipan. Our mission was not to destroy the Japanese fleet, and if he had gone after that fleet and another Japanese fleet had come down from the north, which they might easily have done because at that time they had Okinawa and all these places, why, they could have easily gotten in between us and Saipan and prevented the landings from taking place, which was the primary object of the Japanese. So Adm. Spruance was carrying out his orders to protect the landings at Saipan.

Q: I wonder if it was hard for him to make that decision.

Adm. W: I bet it was. That afternoon - I guess it was a little bit too difficult for him to allow the Japs to get away unpunished - so about 3 o'clock that afternoon, he launched

Wheeler #4 - 285A

the planes of our task force to go after the Japanese fleet. They did and they sank most of the carriers and some of the other ships. Then, the problem was our planes had gone out so far that they couldn't get back before dark, and night flying in those days was in its very early stages. So it was a question if and how many of these fellows were going to get back on board the carriers safely. Well, they didn't come in, they didn't get back till well after dark. It must have been 10 or 11 at night, and Admiral Spruance did, I think, a very wonderful thing. Although he knew there were Japanese planes flying around there, he ordered all the ships to turn on their lights. Of course, we always steamed darkened. And even had the carriers turn on their searchlights pointing straight up so as to guide these fellows in. They came in. Of course, with all this light they had a better chance of landing, but it wasn't like daytime because they couldn't see the water. The great difficulty was that some of the first of these planes cracked up on the flight decks and they couldn't allow others to land till they cleared those off. They threw them overboard as fast as they could. By that time, some of these planes were running out of gas, and some of them landed right in the water and the destroyers were permitted to stop and pick them up because they had shallow draft, but the cruisers weren't. I remember passing these fellows by. It was one of the hardest things I ever had to do. To pass right by him - it must have been 50 feet from me on the bridge - and one of them called out, "Hey, save me." But we had to go right on by. Most of them, though, were picked up and...

Q: Was he still in his plane or had he gotten out of his plane and was in the water?

Adm. W.: He was in ~~one of these boats~~ a rubber life raft. You know, they all had these inflatable rubber boats.

Q: Why couldn't the cruisers stop?

Adm. W.: They had too much draft. They'd have been endangered by submarines.

Q: You didn't have the facility to stop and start as quickly as the destroyers?

Adm. W.: No, and even stopping for a moment would increase the danger because our draft was about twice that of a destroyer.

Q: And a lot more space for a submarine to hit.

Adm. W.: That's right. Terrible as it seems for one man to lose his life, it's a whole lot better than having a ship sunk with 1,200 of them. But we went back the next day, and he spread all the ships out on the scouting line, and we ~~went~~ Cruised up and down that same area two or three times. We picked up quite a few, too, still in their little boats, rubber boats. I don't know how many men were lost, but it was a surprisingly small number.

Q: Was that called the First Battle of the Philippine Sea?

Adm. W.: First Battle of the Philippine Sea, yes. 20th of June 1944. I'll always remember that.

Q: You were nearing the end of your tour out there, too, weren't you?

Adm. W.: Yes, that's true. Now, let me see, what else happened after that. I'm not sure just when this incident took place, but I remember we were bombarding one of these islands called Wotje. We had gone in pretty close so our shellfire would be much more effective, and we were getting a lot of opposition from the Japanese shore batteries. Shells from the Japanese shore batteries were falling some on one side of the ship, and some on the other side of the ship. In other words, they were straddling us.

Q: Were you headed this way or broadside to this?

Adm. W.: Broadside.

Q: You were parallel to the island?

Adm. W.: Yes. They were hitting all around us. Any one of them could have hit the bridge at any moment.

Q: And where were you?

Adm. W.: Oh, we were all standing on the open bridge. We always had flag signals paralleled by radio signals. In other words, the flagship would make a signal, speed 15 or speed 20, or ships right, or column right, or something like that, it would go up on the flagships yardarm, and we'd get the same thing by radio from what we called the CIC (Combat Information Center), and we had a talker on the bridge to relay these messages by radio from the CIC, which is way down in the lower part of the ship. In between times that these signals would come through, like "open fire," "cease fire," or something like that, the talker would keep the people on the bridge informed about the progress of the World Series. A man in the CIC had a radio tuned to the World Series, so you'd see a shell hit the water beyond the ship, you know, with a big splash and the next time the shell would fall short of the ship. This boy on the telephone would say, "Craig is at the bat. Oh, he walked him," and the next thing would be, "Jones is at the bat," then another shell would go over our heads, and then he'd say, "What do you know, he struck out." There was more concern with that, you see. I mean, there was more concern about the World Series. You just can't imagine that sort of thing, now, can you?

Q: I thought you were going to tell me the incident about whether they were afraid or not.

Adm. W.: That's right. They just didn't seem to have a fearful bone in their bodies.

Q: You know, I think they must have known that if you were the skipper you weren't going to let anything happen to them.

Adm. W.: I wish I'd known that.

Q: You'd have been a lot happier.

Adm. W.: Yes. They were completely fearless. Amazing. Of course, there were a lot more engagements. We went to...

Q: You told me the ship was engaged in 27 incidents.

Adm. W.: Yes, well, they are all shown on the Commission personal on the wall which my executive officer gave me when I was detached. I think one of the last things we did was to bomb Iwo Jima on the 4th of July 1944, and that was the first bombing of Iwo Jima. Later on, it was captured - assaulted and captured, but this was the first. We just ran by and fired on it. I frankly don't remember whether the fire was returned or not. Nothing much happened. I mean, it was an operation, that's all. Then we were down and we participated in an operation off New Guinea also, off Biak. That is where MacArthur was - well, he wasn't at Biak, he was at Hollandia, but that's where his headquarters were at that time. All we did was some night bombing, and we were more or less protecting that area. I mean, safeguarding the area, the northern New Guinea area. Nothing of any consequence happened there. We just patrolled up and down.

Q: Did you ever go ashore on any of the islands that you had bombed?

Adm. W.: Yes. Well, not that we'd bombed, no. I don't think I ever did. Let me see. No, I didn't go ashore at Marcus or Wake, Tarawa. I went over to see somebody after the Kwajalein operation, but that was on board ship. I didn't go ashore at

Kwajalein. I stopped ~~was ashore~~ at Kwajalein when I was detached, that's right. I was ashore there on the way home.

Q: Could you see the damage that had taken place?

Adm. W.: No, not there, because - no, I don't recall any damage. Yet, I suppose there was damage. I had gone to lunch there with the commanding officer, Captain Wyatt, but I don't remember seeing any of the damage there.

Q: We were going to save several things to talk about when we came to the Mobile, and some of them relate to the citation that you received - the Legion of Merit for your services.

Adm. W.: On board the Mobile. Well, that I received when I went back to Washington.

Q: I just wanted to read some of the things that it said because it reads for "exceptionally meritorious conduct in the performance of outstanding services to the government of the United States as commanding officer of the USS Mobile operating against enemy Japanese forces in the Central and South Pacific area from September 1, 1943 to June 23, 1944, Displaying brilliant leadership and distinctive professional ability, Captain Wheeler maintained his ship at the highest point of efficiency at all times, thereby contributing to the combat readiness of his gallant command during numerous engagements and campaigns throughout this important period. The superb seamanship and aggressive fighting spirit were vital factors in the success of his vessel as an extremely effective unit of our fleet."

Adm. W.: Thank you.

Q: I'm sure it was well deserved, which must have been satisfying, and brings up some of the questions that we had said we were going to leave until this period of your career. I wanted you to talk something on leadership, which I know you have some ideas about.

Adm. W.: My ideas of leadership are very simple. I believe in loyalty up, and loyalty down. In other words, I think that every naval officer should be loyal to his superior and should also be loyal to his juniors. Now, I was reminded as you read that citation from the Mobile, that I made a point when that citation was given to me by the Acting Secretary of the Navy in Washington, D.C., of announcing that I was sorry that my crew had not been able to participate in that because I don't feel that that Legion of Merit was given to me alone. I think it was given to me and the crew of the Mobile without whom I couldn't have functioned nearly as effectively as we did, and I feel that that is a necessity in any matter of leadership, you've got to make the men feel that you are on their side and you are thinking about them all the way. I think the men did feel that way. I remember one time when we came back to Southern California, before the Kwajalein operation, we were ordered back to Long Beach to participate in a rehearsal of the Kwajalein operation, which was held out in the islands off Santa Barbara. Fortunately, we got there just before Christmas - just after Christmas, I guess - and the Navy regulations require that drills should be held - at least they used to, I don't know whether they still do or not - morning and afternoon, at 10 a.m. and 14:00 they call it for the gunnery department in *printing* drills and loading drills, and so forth and so on. The executive officer came up to me when we arrived in Los Angeles and he said, "Captain, what do you want me to do about drills?" Well, we were in port in Los Angeles for four or five days, and I said, "Forget 'em. Arrange it so that the minimum number of people that we have to have will be on board all the time, and let the rest of them go for two days so that everybody will get two days ashore while we're here, because, in the first place, if you have the drill nobody's mind would be on it. The boys are here for a short time. They've been out in the Pacific for six or eight months or so, and we are going right back out again. We're going to have some tough times. I want you to arrange it so that they can have all the time they can get ashore." Well, you know, after that, I think those men if I'd said to them, "Look, we're going to put wheels on the Mobile and roll her up ashore some place here," I think they would have said, "When do we start, Captain?" I mean, those sort of things, they're nothing. They don't amount to anything, but the men just think it's wonderful.

Q: It is such a wonderful position as commanding officer to be able to make decisions that mean so much.

Adm. W.: Oh, yes, It's perfectly wonderful. I've covered this already, but I do remember when we came back in the Relief that time, I told you about it earlier, and the commandant of the 11th Naval District told me - let's see, we got in there in the morning, and the commandant, 11th Naval District, told me that we'd have to leave that night at 10 o'clock for Panama. Some of the men had wives in Los Angeles and other places nearby there, some had them in San Diego, and the executive officer said, "What do we do, Captain, about giving the men leave?" And I said, "Let them have shore leave until 8 p.m." and he said, "Well, some of them want to fly to Los Angeles," you see we were in San Diego. So I said, "Well, that's their own business. All that I am interested in is that they get back by 8 o'clock." And you know every one of them did, but one man, and he followed us all the way out in a shore boat.

Q: That made you feel good.

Adm. W.: Well, if you treat people right and they'll treat you right. They'll do anything for you. You've got to know what you're doing and you've got to trust your men, and they will always live up to it, in my opinion. I never found otherwise on board ship. I never had an unhappy ship.

Q: What guidance did you get from your commanding officer? When you were out in the <u>Mobile</u>? Did you get any guidance about ...

Adm. W.: You mean from the basic command?

Q: Yes.

Adm. W.: Oh, no. They never participated in anything like that. The basic commander - unless something goes wrong - leaves the running of the ship entirely to the Captain. He wouldn't dare - as a matter of fact, on most large ships, you know, there are two bridges. There is a flag bridge and a captain's bridge. The Admiral hoists the signals from the flag bridge, and the ship's signalman reads the flags and answers them on the ship's bridge.

Q: The guidance you received from your seniors, then, was in the nature of leadership when you described Admiral Nimitz, Admiral Halsey, Admiral Spruance...

Adm. W.: It was mostly contact, and I might say, that it is - I mean you copy - not copy, that's not the word, but you use them as an example.

Q: You said when we get to the Mobile, ask me about giving orders and forgetting it.

Adm. W.: Oh, yes. Well, that was at the time of the turnover that it came to mind. My relief came on board, a Captain Miller, and in those days, you know, they didn't necessarily send a ship into port to get a new captain. If the fleet was operating at sea, or some ship was operating at sea, why, the Navy would send the new captain out by aircraft to the nearest base, and then we would he put on a destroyer smaller ship, and send him out and transfer him by breeches buoy. So that's the way Captain Miller came on board.

Q: Where were you?

Adm. W.: We weren't too far from Kwajalein because I flew in to Kwajalein. We were out to the westward of Kwajalein. I can't remember the exact place, but that was where I told you, you remember, that Jocko Clark flew me off his carrier to Kwajalein and I took a plane from there back East.

Q: Why don't you repeat that, because that's getting close to the end of your tour, isn't it?

Adm. W.: Miller came on board and he was on board for four or five days and during that time I was busy trying to tell him about the standing orders and the campaigns we were engaged in, and about the various officers on the ship, who were the best ones, and who were the most experienced, and things like that. Most of this we did - the turnover took place in what is called the captain's sea cabin. You see, I had two cabins, one on the bridge, and one on the main deck, which I spent little time in. We were at sea, of course, so I was talking to him in the sea cabin. Of course, we could hear everything that went on on the bridge, the orders, and the signals, and everything like that, and I had trained my officer of the deck so I had absolute confidence in him. I mean, I would go to sleep at night and I'd just sleep like a top. Nothing ever bothered me. I didn't know if I'd always wake up in the morning if the ship were torpedoed, but that was all in the day's work. This fellow was so worried, this man, Miller, he was so worried. He'd say, "Captain, I've just heard an order to go ships' right, don't you think we ought to go up on the bridge and watch this maneuver?" I'd say, "No, there's no occasion to go up on the bridge. I have absolute confidence in the officer of the deck. Let's go on with what we're doing." Well, he would be twitching the whole time. I always wondered what happened after I left because - well, as far as I know, it went all right, but he was a nervous type, you know. He just couldn't let anybody else do anything without his being there. That's what I was talking about.

Well, in any case to get back to the wind-up in the Mobile.

Q: Before you leave the Mobile, I want to ask you - we just quickly touched on fitness reports. Do you have any further comment?

Adm. W.: Well, I think fitness reports are one of the most responsible jobs that any officer has to do, I mean commanding officer. It really shapes the future of the Navy, and I'm afraid that a good many officers don't always have that same attitude because the marks are so high. I mean, the tendency is to give higher grades, I think, than are really necessary, which really forces other people to do it. In other words, if one officer marks very strictly and gives even a correct evaluation, another officer might give one of his juniors a much higher mark when the man is not really up to it. So it's a very difficult thing to do, but I think after you've been in the service a long time and you have seen a lot of reports, you get more experienced and you know how to read in between the lines and give a correct report. But my attitude is that it's a very serious business and I think one should be awfully careful and awfully conscientious about how you give fitness reports.

Q: Did you have time to do that, to take care of your paper work when you were out in the Pacific?

Adm. W.: Well, the executive officer does most of it. He always sends the captain a preliminary report. In other words, he marks in very light pencil what he thinks the people are worth, what marks he thinks they should get. Then the captain can erase that, or give higher or lower marks if he sees fit. The reason for that is that in the case of the very young officers, the captain doesn't have much contact with them. Now, for instance, I just learned the other day that this man who is - I think it was the head of the court on inquiry out there when the collision took place, you know, between the American destroyer...

Q: The Evans and the Melbourne?

Adm. W.: Yes. The senior member of that court of inquiry, Admiral King, was an ensign on my ship. I'd even forgotten him, you see. I didn't know - I mean, I hardly knew all of them, by name. There were too many.

Q: Always we think of ourselves as being the "good guys," which we are. Did you ever see any occasions of cruelty on the part of Americans to Japanese? Did you ever have any situations? The only Japanese that you saw were the dead ones at Tarawa.

Adm. W.: That's right.

Q: I remember we used to say that the only good Jap was a dead Jap.

Adm. W.: Yes, and yet, you know, I've got a Japanese gardener that I'm very fond of. I don't think they're all - of course, this boy was born in this country.

Q: It's 20 years later, anyway. The world has changed.

Adm. W.: But they did do some awfully cruel things. There's no question about that. Of course, we never had the occasion to do it, but I've talked to other people who passed Japs on rafts and things in the Pacific and the Japs didn't want to be picked up, because they had been told that they would be killed if they were picked up by Americans. So they struggled not to be picked up.

I was just going to tell you that after I had turned over to Captain Miller, why, I left the ship by one of these sea chairs that they used to have in those days, and was taken by destroyer to the Yorktown, Jocko's ship...

Wheeler #4 - 299

Q: Did you hate to go?

Adm. W.: Oh, yes. It was a wonderful experience in command of that ship. It was just out of this world.

Q: I'm sure your crew hated to have you leave.

Adm. W.: They were awfully nice. There have been two reunions since then, and we're going to have another one next year.

Q: How many of your crew would be involved?

Adm. W.: We hope to have between 50 and 100. Before it was on the 4th of July 1966, that was the first one, and it was in Mobile. I've never been so hot in all my life.

Q: That's why you left Mobile, as I remember.

Adm. W.: Then I was flown to Kwajalein from the deck of the Yorktown, and then on the way back - well, I went to Carmel for a leave with my family months - and I had a hernia operation while there. My doctor had come to me about six months before that, after an annual exam - you have to have them every year, you know, in the service - and he told me he was going to send me ashore to a hospital to have this hernia taken care of. I knew this doctor very well. He'd asked to come to my ship, and I made arrangements for him to be ordered to the ship. So he came up a few days after the examination - I think it was in January of that year - and said, "Captain, I'm going to have to send you to the hospital." And I said, "You get off this bridge, Bill. You know I'm not going to any hospital, not while I have command of this ship." He said he had to send me, and I said, "Go on with you. Get down off the bridge. I've heard enough of that." He went, you know. So he came back a few days later and I knew what he was up to, and I said, "Well, Bill, what's the story on this?" "Well," he said, "you know you've got a hernia." Well, I knew I had the hernia. It had been bothering me for some time. But, you know, on board ship a captain can - he sits on the bridge most of the time, so it wasn't that I was standing or anything like that. So, I said, "I'll make a deal with you, Bill. If you let me alone, I'll agree to go to the hsopital as soon as my orders come in the regular course of events to be transferred." After I got back, you see, from that cruise I went to Carmel with my wife and children and made contact with the Oak Knoll Hospital, and I went up there and had this hernia out. And a very funny thing happened there because I'd been in the hospital only a few hours when I looked up at the door and the Chief Nurse, who had been with me on the <u>Relief</u>, came in and she was flanked by two of the prettiest girls I've almost ever seen, one blonde and one brunette, one on each side. She came in and she said, "Captain, I'm sorry to see you here in the hospital, but I want you to be well taken care of. This girl is the night nurse and this girl is the day nurse." And, boy, my wife said that they just ruined me. I wasn't fit to live with after I got back, they shaved me and fed me and everything.

Q: How long were you in the hospital? Did you say a month?

Adm. W.: Oh, no. About ten days.

Wheeler #4 - 301

Q: And how long was it before you returned to duty?

Adm. W.: I went back to active duty pretty soon after that. I got this, I think it was about the end of my leave. That didn't count in my 30 days leave. But I remember the doctor told me afterwards, when I left, he said, "Now, you're not to pick up anything for at least 30 days, even if you have to go off and leave your suitcase" he knew I was going to join the British fleet, "at the airport, don't pick up a thing for a month." Well, I'll tell you later on what happened about that when we come to the rest of the trip.

After a month's leave with my family in Carmel, California, I reported to Washington, D.C. for indoctrination before joining the British fleet at Colombo, Ceylon. In Washington, D.C. I was called by Fleet Admiral King for a conference prior to leaving to join the British fleet. Admiral King told me that there were three things that he wanted the British fleet to do prior to joining up with the American fleet. One, was to bomb the Japanese oil installations at Palembang on the island of Sumatra in the East Indies. Another, was to capture the western terminus of the Japanese railway across the Japanese-held part of the Malay Peninsula. And the third one, I've forgotten.

Q: That must have been an impressive ceremony with Admiral King.

Adm. W.: It was. It was just a meeting between Admiral King and myself, in which he gave me instructions as to what he wanted the British to do out in the Far East. It seems that some time before this the British and Americans had had a conference, and the British were very anxious to have their fleet join up with ours in the Pacific. Admiral King, it appears, was very opposed to this because he felt that since the British ships were, in general, short-legged - that is to say that they had been accustomed to operating from many different bases scattered all over the world - they didn't have the fuel capacity to remain at sea for long periods, that ours did. And furthermore, by that time, the American fleet had developed a very high skill in fueling, re-provisioning, and re-ammunitioning at sea, which the British had no experience in at all. Therefore, he felt that the British fleet would be more of a handicap to the American fleet than it would a help, because we would always have to be supplying it...

Q: Would we have had to take over the logistics end of it?

Adm. W.: We'd pretty much have to take over the logistics end of it. Furthermore, the British didn't hold any bases in the Pacific, anyhow, so that most of the supplies would have to come from the United States. That is true. But the British were insistent and they, of course, could foresee the end of the war, the war was pretty much over in Europe. In fact, they had determined not to allow any of their fleet to leave home waters until Germany had been defeated.

Soon after my conference with Admiral King, I made arrangements with the transportation officer at the Navy

Department to leave for Colombo, Ceylon, where I was to join up with the British commander-in-chief and British fleet. The transportation officer told me that Washington was about half way from Colombo, either way, and gave me a choice of whether I wanted to go east or west. Well, having spent most of the war in the Pacific, I thought I'd like to go east, so I did. I went by Navy plane as far as Port Lyautey in North Africa, hence Casablanca where I joined up with the Army transport service. Before going to bed at Port Lyautey the day that we arrived, I was informed that a plane would take me to Casablanca the next morning at 4 o'clock. I noticed during the war that the aviators were famous for their early hours. I was there, nevertheless, at 4 o'clock and waited around about an hour, which was customary, and finally was told that they were waiting for another gentleman who was going on the same flight. But he never showed up, so I was flown to Casablanca and arrived before noon pretty well exhausted after my long flight from Washington, so I took a nap in the hotel, having been informed that I wouldn't be able to leave until the next day, and that afternnon I went downstairs to the lobby and was looking around for a place where I could get a cocktail, when I saw another gentleman apparently doing the same thing. He came up to me and spoke to me and said, "Are you looking for some Scotch?" I said, yes, and he said, "So am I," but we both noted that there was nothing there but Vermouths and brandies and other European kinds of drinks, so he said, "Wait a minute. I've got a bottle of Scotch and I'll send for it." So he sent up to his room, and in a few moments two of his secretaires came down, and it turned out that the gentleman who I had spoken to me was Ambassador Nabuco, who was on his way to be Brazilian ambassador to the Vatican from Brazil. We all sat down at a table and killed this pinch bottle Haig and Haig before dinner. By that time we were feeling no pain and I said, "Well, you know, I've been looking around here to try to find something to get my wife for a Christmas present." And Ambassador Nabuco said, " Don't bother about that. I've got just the thing for her. I've got ten pairs of nylon hose which my girl friend gave me in Rio just before I left because, she said, "You know, in Italy with ten pair of nylon hose you can have any girl you want." Is said, "Under the circumstances, Ambassador, I couldn't possibly accept any of those nylons." "Oh, yes," he said, "I'm going to give you two pair of them." So, he did, and we parted company, very good friends, and the next day I went out on an Army plane and discovered to my great grief that those Army people didn't know the difference between an Army captain and a Navy captain, because they put me in with all the shave-tails, and I had a very uncomfortable trip. But we finally got to Algiers and were waiting, as usual, for the take-off when I saw a very attractive young girl laden with baggage standing near me. So, forgetting the warning which my doctor had given me previously, I offered to help, and between the two of us we got our baggage on the plane, and she told me that she had come from Brazil, also, and that she was Senora So-and-so, and to my great surprise - to show you what a small world it is - she had known my wife when they were both girls in Chefoo, China. Isn't that funny? So, we went on to - well, she had only a short flight before she made connection with her plane for Paris, she was going to Paris to do war work. She was French and she felt it was her duty. But, I flew on to Cairo, and eventually to Karachi, where I was held up for a day or so waiting for a British plane to take me to Colombo. En route from Cairo to Karachi, we developed a faulty engine, and had to land at some place in Persia, the name of which I have forgotten, but I do remember that it was the hottest place I've ever been in in my whole life. At Karachi, after spending the night - in an American officers' club, the British furnished a plane to take me to Colombo, where I reported to the chief of staff of the British Pacific Fleet. The commander-in-chief had recently left Colombo for a conference in London and, as a matter of fact, he was detached upon arrival in London. A new commander-in-chief by the name of Sir Bruce Fraser was ordered to command the British Pacific Fleet and he arrived after a week or two. In the meantime, I had made contact with Lord Mountbatten, who had his headquarters at Kandy. He was in command of the Southeast Asia Command and was really like a caged lion because he's an enormous man, full of activity, and very anxious to achieve results, but he had not been able to get sufficient support from the British at home to launch any attack in Burma, which was his objective, or to take the western terminus of the Japanese railway on the Malay Peninsula, which was one of the points that Admiral King made when he talked with me in Washington. I did, however, have a very pleasant day with him. He was living in the King's Pavilion with the other members of his staff, and he invited me to luncheon with him and his staff. He questioned me at length during luncheon about the activities of the fleet, and after that was over, he took me out into the King's garden and walked me up and down for another hour or so, questioning me further. As some of his staff referred to it later, he was picking my brains and, believe you me, I felt picked when it was all over. But he's a delightful person, ~~whom I later met after I retired in San Francisco~~, and while talking with him, he asked me to serve as an honorary member of his staff which I accepted very promptly. Later, after retiring I had the pleasure of presenting my wife to him in San Francisco.

Immediately upon Sir Bruce Fraser's arrival, he invited me to dinner and disclosed his plans for the future. He said he wanted me to go to Honolulu and make arrangements with Admiral Nimitz for him and some of the members of his staff to confer with Admiral Nimitz about the movements of the British Pacific fleet, which was then on its way from England, although some ships had already arrived in the dockyard in Ceylon. He asked me how soon I could leave, and I said, "Would tomorrow be time enough?" He said, yes, so it was arranged that I would leave for Perth, Australia, early the next morning. I then unveiled to him Admiral King's plan for him ~~to bomb - for him~~ and his fleet to bomb - Palembang in Sumatra, Dutch East Indies on the way. He seemed very reluctant to do this because, he said, he didn't want to arrive with his fleet in the Pacific in a damaged condition, as his fleet was just then going to join the American fleet in Pacific waters. I argued with him pleasantly for some time and finally told him that I thought that Admiral King didn't care if the fleet was damaged, if necessary, but he wanted those oil wells in Palembang put out of commission. So, he finally, reluctantly agreed to do so, and ~~a few months after that, I read - a few months after the fleet had arrived,~~ the British fleet had arrived in Australia - I read with great enthusiasm an intelligence report that the oilfields at Palembang had been put out of commission and were not able to be used again thereafter.

Q: That must have taken a great deal of forcefulness in your part, to argue with this man.

Adm. W.: It did, because he - I had only met him, don't you know.

Q: And you were a captain.

Adm. W.: I was a captain and he was a four-star admiral, but I knew what Admiral King wanted and I stuck to it, and they didn't have much damage. They had some, but it wasn't much. But he didn't want to do it. The next morning about 5 a.m. I left in a British Liberator - a British plane, which was a converted American Liberator plane - with a very limited amount of luggage, and flew over what was then called the longest non-stop flight in the world from Colombo to Perth, Australia. The plane was fairly well loaded and we had an uneventful trip, but it was a long and tedious trip.

Q: Almost all over water, wasn't it?

Adm. W.: Almost all over water. The reason for it was, of course, that the intervening islands were Japanese-held. From Perth,

I took a plane around the south coast of Australia to Sydney. Everywhere we stopped, I was put on the first plane which left after that because I was traveling with priority 1. I was also traveling with a terrible cold, so it was one time when I wasn't so anxious to be sent ahead so rapidly. I went to see a Naval Medical Officer in Sydney and he gave me something which made me feel better, so I went on to Brisbane, Australia, and, incidentally, had one of the roughest airplane trips I've ever had between Sydney and Brisbane, for no reason, except that it was very windy and a stormy trip. At Brisbane, I got a Pan American chartered plane for Honolulu, where I arrived without incident, except that we had several stops along the way - I've forgotten the names of the places where we stopped, but we did have a few stops.

Admiral Nimitz was most kind and helpful in regard to the arrangements which were speedily made for Admiral Fraser and his staff to confer with Admiral Nimitz and his staff. So they all arrived in a week or so and the conference was held, and Admiral Fraser was about ready to take off for Sydney to rejoin his command.

Q: You participated in the conference, I presume?

Adm. W.: Yes, some of them. During the time that this meeting was going on - I mean during the period that I was in Honolulu, I learned that my wife was in the hospital with asthma and, inasmuch as it was almost Christmas time and there wasn't much scheduled back in Sydney when we returned, I asked Admiral Fraser if I might have a few days to fly back to the United States and see my wife, which he very kindly granted permission for me to do. Planes were leaving Honolulu at that time about every hour on the hour, and so it was no problem to fly back to see her, which I did, and found that she was much better. So I returned to Honolulu a few days later and learned that on his way back to Sydney, Admiral Fraser had been invited by General MacArthur to witness the landings at Lingayen Gulf - the American landings at Lingayen Gulf - and he had, of course, accepted that invitation, and had gone to one of our battleships, from which he watched these landings. The strange thing to me, a rather fortunate thing, was that I didn't go with him because while witnessing these landings, the American battleship that he was on was struck by a kamikaze and one of his staff officers on the opposite wing of the bridge was killed.

Q: That would have been you, probably?

Adm. W.: I've often wondered which end of the bridge I would have been on. That visit to the West Coast really may have saved my life. Well, we all arrived back in Sydney in due time and began our operations. As Senior American Liaison Officer, I had about 200 officers and 400 enlisted men serving under me in the British fleet. They were mostly concerned with communications, because the British, when they joined up with our vessels, undertook to use our signals entirely, our signals and codes entirely. This was exactly the reverse of what happened in World War I when I was at Queenstown in a destroyer and we used the British communications entirely. It was among my duties - to detail - these young officers and men throughout the various ships of the British fleet and provide them with the necessary codes and ciphers and so forth and so on, all the communication material. The British fleet operated with our fleet - with the Central Pacific Fleet, I might say - far to the north of Australia, but Sir Bruce Fraser (afterwards Lord Fraser), maintained his headquarters in Sydney in the same manner that Admiral Nimitz maintained his headquarters, first, in Honolulu, and then in Guam. So I had an apartment and lived in Sydney for about a year under very pleasant circumstances. The Admiral and his staff met every morning to discuss the situation and, of course, I always met with them. I had my own staff in Sydney and my own offices and was in complete touch with all of the British fleet operations throughout, as Admiral Fraser ordered in the very beginning that I should be shown all dispatches coming and going, so I had complete knowledge of everything that was going on. I would take frequent trips up to Manus, which was in the Admiralty Islands, where we had a base and from which I could deal more effectively with my own officers that were with the British fleet.

Q: Did you help plan the operations with the British planners?

Adm. W.: No. The operations were planned by the American Naval Headquarters.

Q: All back in Pearl?

Adm. W.: All back in Pearl, yes.

Q: And your job was just to work with them?

Adm. W.: Work with them and any contact that we had with the Americans was through me.

Q: And you saw if there was need for interpretation or anything of that sort?

Adm. W. Any subjects that came up in the conference dealing with Americans was always referred to me. It was a very pleasant assignment. Admiral Fraser was a bachelor, and he was certainly a delightful character, one of these people that you like on first sight. No frills about him at all, very down to earth, but very sincere, very likeable. He had been in command in the battle in the North Sea off the North Cape when the Bismarck was sunk, and was afterwards made Lord of North Cape.

Q: I always picture the Pacific action being entirely an American show, and I...

Adm. W.: It pretty much was.

Q: ...and I was wondering which engagements the British fleet participated in?

Adm. W. They participated in the Okinawa operation, and in some of the others. They were not nearly as active as our fleet because they didn't have the staying qualities, you see.

Q: Well, they didn't have much out there, did they?

Adm. W.: Oh, they had about five battleships, eight or ten cruisers, and about twenty destroyers. They had a sizable fleet.

Q: Would they be working in their own units, or would they be assigned to...

Adm. W.: They worked in their own ~~home~~ units. They would be given a part of the operation to participate in, and it usually was not the most important part, because Admiral Nimitz, I think, had more confidence in his own ships.

Q: Were they helpful?

Adm. W.: Oh, yes. Oh, yes.

Q: They did really make a contribution?

Adm. W.: Oh, yes, they made quite a contribution. They had carriers that had a great advantage over ours. Their carriers had steel decks, and ours did not. Ours had wooden decks.

Q: What was that advantage?

Adm. W.: Well, ~~then~~ *when* the kamikaze flyers landed on the *carrier* decks, ~~why~~, ours were out of commission and roaring fires took place, but in the case of the British, they just slid off, you see. The Americans I think felt that those decks were too heavy, but they've been building steel decks ever since. All of our carriers now have steel decks.

Q: We learned that from the British, then, I presume?

Adm. W.: We learned that from the British. You can learn something from everybody if you have enough intelligence.

Q: Of course, if you have an open mind. You may not be smart enough to figure it out yourself, but you're smart enough to learn from somebody else.

I guess being two nationalities, there would have been problems arise from time to time?

Adm. W.: We had no problems at all. I had the unique experience of serving with the British in World War I. When I was on the Benham, we were under the command - of course we had our own U.S. commanding officer - but the over-all commander was Sir Louis Bailey, who had his headquarters on shore at Queenstown. We operated with the British and, of course, when we went ashore we saw all of them at the various hotels and golf courses and tennis clubs and things like that.

Q: Do you think that had anything to do with your assignment to this job?

Adm. W.: I don't think so, but....

Q: Do you know how you were selected?

Adm. W.: No, I don't know that.

Q: It was quite a prestigious assignment.

Adm. W.: Yes, it was, and it led to some very, very interesting things.

Q: I was going to ask about personalities. You mentioned Admiral Fraser. Were there any other interesting personalities on the staff?

Adm. W.: Yes. There was the chief of staff, who was a commodore. He was a very interesting person, a rather unapproachable person. I don't know that he did anything outstanding, but he was a good consultant, a good man to run a staff. He became an admiral after that, but I don't think he ever did anything outstanding. Oh, he had one very interesting character there who was in command of the British Carrier Task Force, Philip Vian. He was one of the heroes of the British Mediterranean battles with the Germans before we came into the war, and he was a real rough character. He never trimmed his eyebrows or the hair out of his ears or out of his nose. He looked like something - well, almost like a hippie today. But he was a real fine person. Now, let me see if there was anybody else there. No, they were all pretty regulation type fellows. Rawlings was the task force commander. He was a vice admiral and he commanded the seaborne end of the task force, you know, like Spruance and Halsey did. He was with the ships at sea. Nichols, the skipper of HMS Duke of York, was an interesting unusual character, but nothing - that's the trouble about naval officers, they're all pretty much according to type, don't you think?

Q: Oh, I - yes, the majority, but there's a great bunch in the middle are somewhat similar, but at either end there are the people who are different. That's true in life.

Adm. W.: Oh, I think it is, very much so.

Q: There's the great average, and a few outstanding ones, and a few bad ones.

Adm. W.: I liked them all. They were all awfully good to me and we never had any problems.

Q: I have to comment again, Admiral, that your career is fantastic, in that we say you're a catalyst for interesting things, but also because of your own personality, it seems to me you've gone through every and all of the varied phases of your career with having beautiful, fine personnel relations with everyone.

Adm. W.: I was very lucky, I think. Of course, I think I was also very lucky in the choice of my parents. I think they brought me up right.

Q: That, of course, is basic to all of us, but at the same time you had these good experiences because you were the kind of person that causes them to happen.

Adm. W.: I also have the faculty, without meaning to, of picking up an accent very quickly. For instance, I remember just before leaving Sydney - I'd been there, by that time, almost a year - I was at a cocktail party given by the - it may have been the editor of the Sydney Morning Herald, at any rate he was there with his wife, and his wife was an American. And, of course, you know the uniform is quite different. We have stars and they have little curlecues - of course, we were all in uniform - but apparently she wasn't looking at my uniform while I was talking with her, but by that time I had acquired a good British accent and I said to her, "Admiral Fraser's never been to the United States and I do hope he'll come sometime." She looked at me and she said, "Captain, have you ever been to the United States?"

Q: May be you have the facility of protective coloration.

Adm. W.: I don't know what it was, but I was quite surprised at that.

Q: I do want to mention your achievement in this particular job. You were awarded the Bronze Star medal, which reads that "for meritorious achievement as senior United States naval liaison officer serving with the British Pacific Fleet from October 1944 to September 1945, maintaining contact with the commander-in-chief of the United States Pacific and Pacific Ocean areas, Captain Wheeler assisted and advised the commander-in-chief, British Pacific Fleet, in all matters pertaining to the United States Pacific Fleet ensuring the coordination of joint operations and procedures, in order to bring maximum power to bear against the Japanese. His devotion to duty was in keeping with the highest tradition of the United States naval service."

Adm. W.: And I also got one from the British, you know.

Q: No, I didn't know that. I think you should read that. Do you mind reading it. I think that would be appropriate.

Adm. W.: No, it wouldn't be. I'd be too bashful.

Q: Is this the stationery of ~~George, King~~ King George?

Adm. W.: Well, it came in a kind of a roll, don't you know.

Q: But the name of George?

Adm. W.: George, Rex Imperator.

Q: George VI, by the Grace of God, of Great Britain, Ireland, and the British Dominions beyond the seas, King, Defender of the Faith, Emperor of India, and Sovereign of the Most Excellent Order of the British Empire. To Captain Charles Julian Wheeler, United States Navy. Greetings. Whereas we have thought fit to nominate and appoint you to be an honorary commander of the military division of our said Most Excellent Order of the British Empire, we do by these presents grant unto you the dignity of an honorary commander of our said order, and hereby authorize you to have, hold, and enjoy the said dignity and rank of an honorary commander of our aforesaid order together with all and singular the privileges thereunto belonging or appertaining. Given at our court at St. James under our sign, manual and seal of our said order, this 7th day of October 1946 in the tenth year of our reign, by the Sovereign's command, Signed Mary R, Grandmaster. And down in the lefthand corner, it says "Grant of the dignity of an honorary commander of the military division of the Order of the British Empire to Captain Charles Julian Wheeler, U.S.N.."

Adm. W.: That's kind of flowery, isn't it?

Q: Very Flowery. Very nice.

Adm. W.: Perhaps I should mention the occasion in which I might have lost my life. My duties as senior U. S. Naval Liaison officer required me to make frequent trips to Manus in the Admiral Islands and I had planned one in particular, which for some reason, I cancelled at the last minute. Several days later, Admiral Fraser and his staff including myself attended the funeral of all the officers and crew of this plane who had been killed, as that plane had struck a telegraph wire while taking off from the airport at Sydney.

Wheeler #5 - 319

Interview #5 with Rear Admiral C. Julian Wheeler, U.S. Navy
(Retired)

Date: 27 September 1969

By: Etta Belle Kitchen

Adm. W.: An amusing incident occurred at one of the staff conferences in British fleet headquarters, which I mentioned previously. On one occasion Admiral Fraser invited the Duke of Gloucester to attend a meeting. The Duke of Gloucester was at that time serving as governor of New South Wales, and he was invited merely as a compliment to attend one of these meetings. Admiral Fraser mentioned, however, that this would create somewhat of a contretemps because the rule in Britain is that the Army can have mustaches or beards and the Navy can have beards but no mustaches. So, inasmuch as the Duke of Gloucester was an honorary Army officer he wore a mustache and all of the other officers at the conference would be clean-shaven, which would make him out of order, and he supposed that that would be all right, inasmuch as he was the duke, but it did present a little problem.

Q: Did they let him come in?

Adm. W.: They let him come in. They received him, of course, very graciously.

Q: That was the Duke of Gloucetser?

Adm. W.: The Duke of Gloucester, who was the governor of New South Wales. While serving as senior U.S. naval liaison officer, in the Admiralty I made many trips up in the islands, principally Manus, where we had a naval base, for the purpose of interviewing and redistributing the other liaison officers serving throughout the British fleet who were under my command. I also had three or four such officers serving with me on board the Duke of York but, inasmuch as I had a complete headquarters of my own and a clerical staff, these visits and the operations concerned presented no problem. I did have the opportunity of meeting the Duke and Duchess of Gloucester at a reception given by the Lord Mayor of Sydney and found them to be a very gracious couple. I knew the governor and Lady Wakehurst much better. I must correct myself because I'm reminded now that the Duke of Gloucester was the Governor General of all Australia although his headquarters were in Sydney, whereas Lord and Lady Wakehurst, who were also in Sydney, were much better friends of mine. Lord Wakehurst was the governor of New South Wales.

The year passed fairly quickly with routine operations, but the really exciting part of my tour with Admiral Fraser began when he planned to embark upon his flagship the Duke of York and proceed to Guam to deliver to Admiral Nimitz the Knight Grand Cross of the Order of the Bath. ~~Correction, that was Admiral Nimitz to whom he was going to deliver the Knight Grand Cross of the Order of the Bath.~~

Q: Say that again, you went to Guam with Lord Fraser...

Adm. W.: Yes, to give the Knight Grand Cross of the Order of the Bath to Admiral Nimitz. After all the plans were made,

Admiral Fraser received an urgent message from the Admiralty in London which made him defer his departure, but he ordered the flagship, the Duke of York, to continue as planned and he would join her at Manus in the Admiralty Islands. I proceeded on the Duke of York, occupying the chief of staff's cabin, where I was very comfortably provided for, and in a few days Admiral Fraser rejoined the Duke of York by plane in Manus. We then proceeded to Guam, where official calls were duly exchanged between Admiral Nimitz and Admiral Fraser, and on that same afternoon we were entertained at Admiral Nimitz' headquarters with a delightful cocktail party...

Q: This was at his quarters, not his office?

Adm. W.: Yes.

Q: What were they like? Describe his headquarters on Guam to me.

Adm. W.: Well, they were very delightful quarters, similar I would say to a ranch type house, with a large living room, a good-sized dining room, several bedrooms, expansive porches with binoculars, through which one could see the surrounding islands, and I noted particularly that the binoculars were of Japanese make, so I assumed that they had been left there by the Japanese when they were driven out. After the cocktail party, we were entertained at dinner and provided with quarters to spend the night.

Q: All of the island was men? No women there at all?

Adm. W.: No women at all except of course the natives. After dinner, Admiral Nimitz turned on his phonograph and - I think it was before the days of hi-fi- and played many records for all of us, which were his favorites.

Q: Do you remember what they were?

Adm. W.: No. He gave Admiral Fraser and each member of his staff, including me, a record - mine was "Gaite Pariesienne" - and I asked him to sign it, which he did and I have since given it to my daughter, Mrs. Richard Little. He also gave each of us a sport shirt to wear during the evening so it would seem a more informal gathering.

Q: Were the records classical?

Adm. W.: Yes, classical.

Q: Had it been one of his own records that he gave you?

Adm. W.: Oh, yes, one of his own collection. The next morning we returned on board the Duke of York and proceeded with the ceremony of the presentation of the Knight Grand Cross of the Order of the Bath to Admiral Nimitz. Admiral Fraser had consulted me about whom he should invite to the ceremony and I recommended that he also invite senior Air Force commander, General Spaatz, a 4-star general, to the ceremony, which he very graciously did. The ceremony was held on the quarterdeck of the Duke of York, where a platform had been erected, and Admiral Fraser placed over Adm. Nimitz's head the Knight Grand Cross of the Order of the Bath, which extends across one shoulder with a long ribbon which passes both in back and front of the body and winds up with a medallion at the end of the ribbon - a most diamonds, and sapphires. The whole thing was really very spectacular. If Adm. Nimitz were an Englishman, he would be addressed as Sir Chester. The British bluejackets and Marines were lined up on each side of the quarterdeck, both Admiral Fraser and Admiral Nimitz made appropriate speeches, after which the time-honored custom of "splicing the mainbrace" was held. To those who are not familiar with that, it means giving every body on board ship a free drink of rum. The custom on board British Navy ships is that every man on board is also entitled to a tot of rum with his noon meal.

Q: How much is that?

Adm. W.: It's quite a sizable amount, about a half a pint. It depends, of course, upon the rank of the person who is getting it. The ones who are very junior get a smaller amount, and the more senior get a larger amount. The more junior ones have to have theirs mixed with water, which makes it grog, rather than rum, and the men who choose not to take their ration of rum get credit of, I think, sixpence a day for the rum that they did not consume. I attended one of the regular ceremonies of dispensing the rum on the Duke of York, and it's quite picturesque. The "Bosun" goes to the place on board the main deck from which the rum is hoisted from the storeroom below, where it is kept, and it is poured into a big circular drum, which looks like a barrel. It has brass bands, and across the front of it is written, "The King, God bless him." The mess cook in charge of each mess comes up and gives the "Bo'sun" the number of people in his mess, and it is then measured out so that each man gets his allotted portion, and those who get the grog have their portion mixed with water. I digress somewhat now, but the ceremony of the presentation of the Knight Grand Cross of the Order of the Bath being over, the American dignitaries left the ship and we on the <u>Duke of York</u> all went about our usual affairs.

Q: Everybody was in full dress white?

Adm. W.: Everybody was in full dress white with decorations and everything. It was a very, very beautiful affair.

Q: Was this after the close of the war?

Adm. W.: No. This was in the latter part of August 1945, and that evening, of course, it became the turn of the British Admiral to entertain Admiral Nimitz and his staff, which he did most appropriately on his flagship in the admiral's cabin. As a member of Admiral Fraser's staff, I was privileged to be a member of his mess, and, as a matter of fact, it was our custom every evening after dinner when port was being passed around, as is the British custom on board every British Man of War, to toast the King. I was the first to toast the King. It was my privilege to toast the King, and we did that sitting down, which is most unusual because it is the only group of people in the world that is privileged to toast the King sitting down, a custom which has come down through the ages, through at least many hundreds of years, I imagine because in the old days the space between the deck and the deck above was so short that it did not permit a man to rise all the way. In any case, after I toasted the King and after everybody had drunk to that, Admiral Fraser would toast the President of the United States and we would all drink to that. This same custom was, of course, carried out that same evening, and the cabin was very colorful with all the British and American uniforms - a very striking occasion. The cabin of a British ship really sparkles more than the cabin of one of our ships because the British go in for such beautiful polished woods, which for some reason that I never could understand, they never altered at all during the war. In our ships during the war, when we stripped ship, we took off everything we could dispense with in the way of wood to prevent troops being killed by flying splinters.

Q: Or for fire.

Adm. W.: Or for fire. In fact, in some ships they even scraped the paint from the walls. But the British never did that. So this was a very sparkling occasion. After the dinner was over, I was talking with another British officer and, all of a sudden, we heard a commotion and saw a British junior officer carrying a dispatch which indicated that the Japanese had offered to surrender. This, of course, was the most exciting news of the war and there were great goings-on on the ship. Admiral Fraser got on the loudspeaker system and informed the ship and everybody gathered in groups and talked about it.

Q: Do you remember what Admiral Nimitz looked like when he saw the news?

Adm. W.: Admiral Nimitz had left the ship. This took place

after Admiral Nimitz and his party had left the ship.

Q: That same night?

Adm. W.: The same night. Admiral Fraser had been intending to leave the next morning for Sydney, where his headquarters were located, but in view of this exciting message, he decided to delay his departure to await events, which was a wise decision because very soon He got instructions from the British Admiralty that in the event of a surrender, he would be the one to sign the instrument of surrender for the British Empire.

Q: By the way, by this time, had anyone heard of, or did you know about the dropping of the atomic bomb?

Adm. W.: Oh, yes.

Q: You knew that had happened?

Adm. W.: Yes.

Q: So this wasn't really entirely unexpected, was it?

Adm. W.: It was hoped for. It wasn't quite as big a surprise as if we hadn't known about the bomb. The bomb, of course, was the instigating medium which brought this about.. So, the next day or so we stayed in Guam awaiting developments, and finally Admiral Fraser ordered the Duke of York to join the American fleet, which was then operating off the coast of Japan. As it will probably be recalled, there was some delay between this first offer of surrender and the final agreement upon the terms of the surrender. In fact, there was a time there when it seemed as though there might not be a final agreement. Admiral Halsey, who was in command of the Third Fleet, then operating off the coast of Japan, took that occasion to give the Japs another treatment by bombing the Japanese mainland, and that seemed to have the desired effect, because in a very short time after that the final agreement was made, and within a few days we made plans to enter Tokyo Bay. But before doing so, I recall that the commander of the Third Fleet, that is, Admiral Halsey, decided to take a picture of the massed airplanes which all of the carriers sent up for the occasion, and that was unsuccessful because it covered so much territory that he couldn't encompass all of the planes in the picture. Then he tried to take a picture of the entire fleet, which was also far short of expectations because that fleet, which was the most powerful fleet that ever has been before or since assembled in the history of the world, was just too big to get in a photograph. It was just simply fantastic the size of it.

Q: And where were you then?

Adm. W.: I was on the Duke of York.

Q: Were you still in Guam, or were you proceeding...?

Adm. W: Oh, I said the Duke of York joined the Third Fleet.

Q: And went up to Tokyo?

Adm. W.: We went up to join the fleet. The fleet was operating off of the Japanese coast, you see. It was ~~going~~ operating up and down the Japanese coast... off the entrance to Tokyo Bay.

Q: And you, unaccompanied, went up...?

Adm. W.: We went up singly, but joined the Third Fleet as a unit of that fleet.

Q: At Tokyo?

Adm. W.: Still off the Japanese coast.

Q: Could you see - was the fleet so big, could you see it all?

Adm. W.: Couldn't begin to see it all. During these operations off the coast of Japan, Admiral Fraser took occasion to go over on board ~~the~~ - Admiral Halsey's flagship, and present him with a decoration, which was a lesser order of the Order of the Bath. I can't exactly remember what the name of the order was. It was the same order but one degree below that of Admiral Nimitz. And Admiral Fraser made that transfer from the Duke of York at sea to the Missouri, which was Admiral Halsey's flagship, also at sea.

Q: By high line?

Adm. W. High line, except that we had perfected that method of transfer to the point where, although the high line was used, a very comfortable chair was attached to the high line so that the - Admiral Fraser - was able to make the transfer very comfortably seated in a chair attached to the high line.

Q: Did you go, too?

Adm. W.: Yes. The night before entering Tokyo Bay, the entire American fleet and also the Duke of York anchored in Sagami Wan, which is a bay just off the entrance of Yokohama, and it was the most awe-inspiring sight to see this tremendous fleet of carriers, battleships, cruisers, destroyers, submarines, every conceivable kind of ship.

Q: Transports?

Adm. W.: There were no transports there.

Q: All fighting ships?

Adm. W.: All fighting ships. And in the distance, one could see Mount Fujiyama. The weather was magnificent and, although when we first anchored, there were no people in sight on the beaches, we noticed after we had been there a few hours, during which I imagine the Japanese who lived nearby had decided that we were not going to harm them, all came out and went in swimming. The next morning, arrangements having been completed, we entered Tokyo Bay, and it was most interesting on the way in to note that each of the guns of the shore batteries was marked with a white flag hanging from the muzzle, so that we could see what kind of a bombardment we would have been subjected to if we had attempted to enter there without preliminary arrangements having been made for the peace treaty. After arrival in Tokyo Bay, I can't remember whether it was that morning, or probably the next, the surrender ceremonies took place on board the Missouri, and, of course, I accompanied Admiral Fraser to the Missouri for the surrender, which took place on the quarterdeck of the battleship Missouri. The quarterdeck of the Missouri is the forward forecastle deck, instead of the after part of the ship, as is often the case, and one interesting feature of the arrangements was that the flag of Commodore Perry which he flew when he first entered Japan one hundred years ago to open Japan to foreigners, was framed and hanging from one of the bulkheads of the Missouri. There was a table with a green baize cloth in the middle of the quarterdeck on which the signing was to take place. The American officers were lined up fore and aft from the captain's cabin to No. 2 turret, in a fore and aft line. The foreign officers, including representatives of all the allied governments, were lined up athwartships from the Admiral's cabin to the starboard side of the ship. The ceremony opened with the arrival of General MacArthur, who came in a destroyer, which went alongside the port side of the Missouri, and from the destroyer he was hoisted up to the main deck of the Missouri, where he was met by Admiral Nimitz and Admiral Halsey and the captain of the Missouri, and they all went in to the Admiral's cabin until the ceremony was actually ready to proceed.

The Japanese came on board over the starboard gangway, of course, wearing frock coats and pin-stripe trousers and top hats, and they all lined up forward of the gangway extending athwartships from the gangway to the midship line of the ship.

Q: Were there no military uniforms on the Japanese?

Adm. W.: No military uniforms at all. None of them was in uniform. The striking thing was that the American officers all wore khaki and not even neck ties. In other words, for us, it was another work day. But for the Japanese it was a ceremony of great importance. The actual ceremony was begun by the chief Japanese delegate - signing the instrument of surrender - after which General MacArthur made a very moving speech and then signed for the Allies, and the other Allied representatives signed. General MacArthur was followed by Admiral Nimitz, and after that the Allied representatives signed in numerical order - I mean, in alphabetical order of the first letter of the name of their country.

That afternoon, Admiral Fraser invited Admiral Nimitz and all of the high-ranking officers in the American fleet on board the <u>Duke of York</u> for what the British called "A musical sunset," and that is a very colorful ceremony in which flags are displayed and music is played by the ship's band and orchestra, and it takes place exactly at the moment that the colors are lowered. It was a very moving sight, because here was all this pomp and ceremony going on in the presence of the entire allied fleet which was anchored in Tokyo Bay.

Q: Can you remember how you felt that day?

Adm. W.: I had chills running up and down my spine. One interesting incident was that while on board the <u>Missouri</u> I noticed people running around with canceled postal stamps on letters, and not to be outdone, I decided to get some letters stamped, which I believe are called cachets, and marked September the 2nd, 1945 - wait a minute, USS Missouri, September 2nd, 1945, Tokyo Bay.

Q: Who canceled those stamps?

Adm. W.: The Post Office.

Q: The Post Office on the Missouri?

Adm. W.: The Post Office on the Missouri. After getting back to the Duke of York, I went to the Post Office and asked them if they had any stamps, cancellation of their stamps, and they said, no, but they thought it was a fine idea. I showed them the cachets that I had and they said, we'll make a stamp. So they proceeded to make a stamp which reads, "Japanese formal surrender, Duke of York, September 2nd, 1945, Tokyo Bay." So I proceeded to have some of my cachets stamped with their stamp also, and I suspect that these stamps will one of these days become very valuable, because I don't think there are any others like that. If so, there are probably very few.

Q: I would not think very many. Probably fewer on the Duke of York even than the Missouri.

Adm. W.: Yes, well, I mean, my point was that my letters were stamped with both American and British Cancellation stamps.

Q: Oh, you had both on the same letters?

Adm. W.: I had both on the same one.

Q: Oh, I see. May be you're the only one that has it.

Adm. W.: One of these days they'll be very valuable.

Well, after the surrender was over, the next day, Admiral Nimitz...

Q: Do you remember what the weather was like on that day?

Adm. W.: Beautiful weather. After the surrender, the next day, Admiral Fraser, I should say, and some of his staff and I took a destroyer and landed at Yokohama. From there we took a ride around the city, which was in terrible condition due to the bombing, and many of the people were in rags and looked very poorly fed.

Q: Did they make any reaction to you?

Adm. W.: Their reaction was - they were completely indifferent to us. They didn't show any hatred, they didn't show any friendliness. They were completely - it was as though we weren't there. Then I took a boat and went to the Japanese Navy yard Yokasuka. On the way I stopped at the Japanese battleship <u>Haruna</u>, which I went on board because I was particularly interested in this ship because she had been the one that Admiral Bristol and I had been entertained in during the Japanese coronation naval review. At that time, it was the flagship of the Japanese fleet. I wanted to see what change had taken place and, believe you me, there was a terrific change. One shell had gone down through the smoke stack and done considerable damage and other damage to the superstructure, but my objective was to go down to the cabin in which we had had dinner, Admiral Bristol and myself and the other foreign fleet commanders and their aides had had dinner with the commander of the Japanese Imperial Fleet. It was a very saddening sight because the center table was filled with specimens of Japanese clothing which some American inspectors - naval inspectors - who had gone on board before I did, had brought up from the store rooms to examine to see what kind of clothing Japanese sailors were furnished.

Q: Why was that particular thing saddening?

Adm. W.: Well, it was saddening because the last time I had seen it, it had been set for this magnificent dinner.

Q: Nothing about the clothing itself?

Adm. W.: Oh, no.

Q: It was just the contrast.

Adm. W.: Yes, just the contrast.

Q: I thought you meant there was some specific incident.

Adm. W.: After the activities at...

Q: Excuse me, what did you find at the Navy yard?

Adm. W.: The Navy yard was interesting in that from all that I could visualize, the entire activity of the Navy yard was concentrated on building these midget submarines, which were being built in the dry docks, which of course had been constructed for larger ships. These dry docks had dozens of these little miniature submarines in the construction stage, and the impression it gave one was that the Japanese had just about given up winning the war from the standpoint of, ~~at that stafe~~, real offensive operations, but they seemed to have the idea that as the American fleet came closer in shore they could send these midget submarines out and sink ~~the~~ our ships. There were no large ships in dry dock at all.

Q: Had the ship yard been damaged by bombing?

Adm. W.: It didn't show much evidence of damage. I noticed that there was evidence that the personnel had left in a great hurry. The equipment was on the drawing boards that the draftsmen used and was left just as though the people had gone out to lunch. We went to the naval officers' club which was quite a comfortable little club. One incident I remember was that I saw two large Japanese vases and I say vases purposely because they were quite large and I'm sure they cost more than $20, and a music box, one of the oldtime music boxes, and I happen to remember those, I don't know why because I didn't stay there very long, but we went on our way and eventually returned to the ship. I had some business with Admiral Halsey...

Q: Excuse me, on the way going and coming, did you see any bomb damage?

Adm. W.: Only this ship...

Q: Only on the ship. Nothing in the terrain or the...?

Adm. W.: I saw tremendous bomb damage on my expedition through the city. There was hardly a building standing in many sections.. But as I was saying about these things that I noticed, I did have to go back to the Missouri a day or so before we sailed because I knew that Admiral Fraser was going to Hong Kong to take the surrender there of the Japanese in Hong Kong, and in view of the fact that we had a number of Americans on board, including myself, and although it seems rather far-fetched now, there was a feeling at that time, as indicated by the papers and magazines that we got from the United States, that all foreigners should leave China, and I wanted to bring to the attention of Admiral Halsey the fact that if the Duke of York went in to Hong Kong there would be five or six Americans, including myself, on board, and I didn't want us to go there if we were later going to be criticized as having a part in the surrender of Hong Kong and giving the impression that we were a party to the British holding Hong Kong.

So when I went on board the Missouri I was met at the gangway by Mick Carney, who was Admiral Halsey's chief of staff and a classmate of mine...

Q: Where was the Missouri? Tied up or out in the stream?

Adm. W.: Out in the stream. I said to Mick that I'd come to see Admiral Halsey, and he said, "Well just come on to his cabin and sit down. He'll be with you in a few minutes." So

I went into his cabin and sat down, and I was amazed to see the two Japanese vases and the music box that I had seen in the Japanese naval officers' club. It struck me as very peculiar, because I remembered having seen a dispatch from the Commander, Third Fleet, namely, Admiral Halsey, cautioning everybody about looting, taking anything from the Japanese on shore. So, jokingly, when Carney came in again for something, I said, "Hey, Mick, what about these things here? Don't they belong in the Japanese naval club?" He said, "Oh, yes. The Admiral's taking those back. He's going to give them to the Naval Academy Museum." Well, I suppose it was mean of me but when I went to my fiftieth reunion at the Naval Academy in 1964, I checked all around and those articles were not to be found in the Naval Academy Museum.

We arrived in Hong Kong...

Q: Admiral Halsey said, go ahead, and go, obviously.

Adm. W.: Oh, I forgot to say that Admiral Halsey said, it won't make any difference at all, go right ahead, think nothing of it. So my staff and I went on in to Hong Kong with the Duke of York...

Q: So you really saw two Japanese surrenders, didn't you?

Adm. W.: I was not actually present at the final signing of the Japanese surrender in Hong Kong. I suppose Admiral Fraser thought that it was a British-Japanese affair and had nothing to do with America, and so I was not invited to the actual signing of the thing, but I saw the camps that the Japanese were put in, which, incidentally, had been the camps which the Allied soldiers had formerly been put in. I also went out to the Stanley prison camp, which was most interesting. The Stanley prison camp had been built by the British just before World War II to update their prison arrangements for malefactors in Hong Kong. As a matter of fact, it was completed just in time apparently so that when the Japanese took over Hong Kong, they immediately interned all the foreigners and put them in it. I talked to many of the foreigners who had not yet even been released. You see, I was one of the first Americans in Hong Kong after the Japanese surrender in Tokyo.

Q: Were there people still in this prison camp?

Adm. W.: There were people still in those prison camps, allied prisoners. Arrangements had not yet been made for their release, and they told me about the horrible conditions in which they lived. They had been made to fabricate all of the cooking utensils that they had - they had great big pots made there, in which they made their soups so-called. They got very, very poor rations. Some of these people had lost 50 or more pounds. Some of them were just skin and bones. I remember looking at some of the cells where the foreigners had been put by the Japanese because the Japanese had discovered that they had radios, secret radios, and they were sentenced to be beheaded, and in one cell, I remember, there was writing on the wall and a calendar had been fabricated up there, and on it it said "the number of days left before I am to be beheaded". And you could see where the prisoner had crossed off each one until the last.

You could see the place where the British had hanged criminals. It was all very, very upsetting. Then I went up to the Peak and I was surprised at what I found up there, because looking at the Peak, which is the high spot of Hong Kong, you know, from which you can see Hong Kong Harbor and it's a beautiful sight, particularly at night with all the lights blinking there. I couldn't see where there had been much damage from the deck of the <u>Duke of York</u>, I could see no damage whatsoever to the houses on the Peak, so I concluded that probably they'd been taken over by the Japanese officers. I got up there and I found that there was only one house up there that was really in proper condition, and that was the one that was occupied by the Japanese military commander. The rest of them had had the most extraordinary things happen to them. The Chinese had cut out all of the wood around the window sills, they had cut out the wooden floors, and they had taken out the staircases, and you'll never guess why.

Q: To burn for wood?

Adm. W.: It seems that before the war - you know, the Japanese use charcoal for cooking their food, the Chinese, and the Japanese, too - the Orientals, I might say, use charcoal - and most of the charcoal, it seems, had come from the East Indies, places like Borneo, or the wood had come from there and then the Chinese had made it into charcoal. That was all stopped during the war. These things happen which one doesn't realize. When the war cuts off communications, why, all kinds of things happen. So, the Chinese were desperate for wood, and they went up and just took the wood out of these homes and made charcoal out of it.

Well, from there, we went on down to the Philippines...

Q: I was going to ask you who took you through the Stanley prison camp?

Adm. W.: They had a man there, the man who was in charge, an Englishman.

Q: Did the man who had had an official job there before take you through?

Adm. W.: I think he did, yes. Did I tell you that?

Q: No, you hadn't told it. Your wife told it. That the man was very upset because they had destroyed the place where he used to do his hanging.

Adm. W.: Yes, that's right. This place had a hole in the floor and they could take this thing out in order to let the man drop. But the Japanese had floored that all over, so that there was no drop for the man who was being hanged to drop through. Because the Japanese beheaded everyone, you see.

Q: So it was the hangman who showed you around?

Adm. W.: That's correct. After leaving Hong Kong, we went to Manila, the purpose being for Admiral Fraser to visit some of the British prisoners who had been held there by the Japanese during the war. Just like all the other prisoners, they were emaciated, many of them in hospital beds suffering from various illnesses and wounds, and so forth. They'd been very badly treated. One interesting incident of the trip was that during the war the Japanese had sunk many cargo ships throughout Manila Bay and they were connected together with chains so as to prevent the harbor being used again until they were all removed. Well, our navigator did a very good job in getting us in - getting the Duke of York in - but as we were about to leave, we got one of those chains hooked round one of the propellers of the Duke of York. Fortunately, by sending divers down the Duke of York was able to get the chains released and so we were able to leave.

Q: Did you see any American prisoners there?

Adm. W.: No, because they'd all been released by that time. The British prisoners had been released, too, but they were in this camp awaiting repatriation.

After leaving Manila, we went to Sydney and, while there, I had the pleasure and honor of presenting the Legion of Merit to Vice Admiral Vyan aboard his flagship, HMS Indomitable, a carrier which had been participating in British fleet operations in the Central Pacific. I think I've already described Admiral Vian, have I not?

Q: Yes, you did.

Adm. W.: Soon after that I realized that the show was over for my staff and me in Sydney, so I communicated this to Admiral Nimitz, who very graciously replied; "Write your own orders."

Q: How did you get in touch with him? By radio?

Adm. W.: By radio. So I wrote my own orders to return to the United States and, on the way, was granted 30 days' leave upon arrival. Admiral Fraser very kindly gave me his plane for my personal use to proceed to Manus, an American naval base, where I connected up with the American airlines for the United States. This obviated a difficulty which is of interest, I suppose, in that immediately after the war, President Truman issued an order that all lend-lease should cease, which meant that there would be no further interchange of services or supplies without payment, you see. And this was brought to my attention. The British were very embarrassed about it because they said that they would have to charge the U.S. Government at that point for my travel from Sydney to the American naval base, which seemed kind of silly in view of the fact that I'd made the trip a dozen or more times, but this was all because of Truman's order. Then Admiral Fraser came through with his very gracious offer to lend me his own private plane so that there would be no charge.

At Manus I remember an amusing incident. By the time I got there, the Magic Carpet operations had already begun in that all combat - practically all combat ships were being used to get the people back home as soon as possible. This, in my opinion, being one of the great mistakes that were made after World War II. In other words, we disarmed far too quickly and were therefore unable to offer any opposition to the Russian demands at the end of World War II. While I was in Manus, the Commodore Boak

Commanding Officer of the base there, with whom I was staying as his guest while waiting for a plane to the United States, told me that he had just received a message from an American carrier commanded by Admiral Dan Gallery, a well-known character in the Navy, which he quoted to me. It seems that among other naval personnel at Manus there were quite a number of nurses, so the commanding officer of the naval base had wired to Admiral Gallery and asked if he could take 12 American nurses on his next Magic Carpet trip back to the States. And the reply came back while I was there, from Captain Gallery to the commander of the naval base, which said, "Referring to your despatch about the nurses. Can do, can do. Oh boy, oh boy."

Well, after getting back to the United States, I immediately got a plane from San Francisco to where my family was in Carmel, California.

So, I went to Carmel and awaited orders there for further duty, which finally came through, and they were to the effect that I was to proceed to Rio de Janeiro as the American head of the Brazilian Naval War College.

Q: That's an interesting title, isn't it?

Adm. W.: An interesting way those orders were worded. I always wondered about that. I'd never seen orders like that before. The American head of the Brazilian Naval War College. You see, there is a Brazilian director of the War College. In other words, the Brazilian War College had a staff of its own, but I was the American head.

Q: Why was that position necessary?

Adm. W.: Well, the reason they had such a job as that is that back in, I think it was about 1921 or 1922, the Brazilian government applied to the United States for a naval mission to assist them to train and operate their own navy. So arrangements were made, and the first naval mission was sent composed of a captain - it may have been an admiral, I'm not sure. There must have been 10 or 15 officers who were ordered there, and they had the unique distinction of being paid both by the American government and the Brazilian government, which carried through and, as far as I know, is still going on. There was a chief of mission, the American head of the War College; there was a gunnery officer, an aviation officer, an engineering officer, a navigation officer, and so on, who were to impart their knowledge to the Brazilian Navy in order to help them operate their ships...

Q: I presume they had a counterpart in each department?

Adm. W.: Oh, yes. Well, they have in the Brazilian Navy just as we have, a department of ordnance and gunnery, a department of engineering, a department of aviation, and so forth.

Q: So they send an American to help and to guide and to train in each of the departments. So there was a need then for a head of the American group.

Adm. W.: That's right. As I say, they have this War College and I was not only a graduate of our naval War College but had served on the staff at the Naval War College in Newport.

We drove east as far as my home in Mobile, Alabama, where we visited family. Since it was only a short time after the war, the Moore MacCormick Lines had not reinstated their service to South America, so we sailed, about the middle of February, on a Brazilian ship, which was quite an experience because the food was different, the accommodations were poor, and it was a slow ship, but we got there safely, and on 23rd February 1946 I reported as the American head of the Brazilian Naval War College.

Q: Did you ever wonder if you would arrive safely?

Adm. W.: No. It wasn't that bad. It was a good-sized ship, but we never did lose confidence.

Q: Were they good sailors?

Wheeler #5 - 346

Adm. W.: They were good sailors, but we just didn't feel that we were - well, I mean,, we didn't feel the same way we would on an American ship.

Q: This was a transport anyway, wasn't it?

Adm. W.: No, it wasn't a transport. It was a regular commercial passenger ship.

Q: That's what I mean. It wasn't a military ship.

Adm. W.: Oh, no.

Q: The people running the ship were like the merchant marine.

Adm. W.: Yes. Brazilian merchant marine. In Rio I reported as the American head of the Brazilian Naval War College, which is located - or was at that time - in the Ministerio da Marinha, in other words, the Brazilian Navy Department, where the other members of the mission were also located. We had perquisites there. For instance, I had a Brazilian car and chauffeur furnished me. Through the courtesy of the American Army mission there, we had mail service, we also had commissary, and post exchange privileges.

Q: Where did you live?

Adm. W.: We lived in an apartment in what they call Bota Fogo, which is on the Bay and it had one of the most beautiful views that I can ever remember. It overlooked what they call the Pao d'Azucar, but in English it's called the Sugarloaf. It's a kind of a tabletop mountain and it's just on the other side of the Bay, and I remember coming into that apartment when I'd come home from the office in the afternoon, and looking through that great big window in our living room, I'd just look at that and wonder if it were really so. It was one of the most magnificent views I've ever seen in my life. It was there to admire every day. But we lived in this apartment house, where the chief of mission also lived, that was Rear Admiral Lovett, and my associations with the Brazilians were most pleasant. The Brazilians were very courteous and most of them very easy to get along with. There were about 120 or 130 Brazilian officers on the staff, and there were about, I should say, 80 to 100 students in the War College, which met daily, and my function was to plan the war games they participated in, and then to be present at the critique and point out mistakes that they made or other ways that they could have done the same operation.

Q: Who was their enemy?

Adm. W.: Well, usually, it's Argentina, or some South American country. They never would name their enemies, it was usually red, or green, or blue, or something like that. There was no national feeling shown - but you could tell that there was great rivalry between the Argentine and Brazilian navies. They had at that time six destroyer escorts which we had given to them, and they had a number of old battleships...

Q: Where had they gotten those?

Adm. W.: So far back that I don't even know, but I suspect they probably bought them in England, They stayed in port most of the time.
They had a training ship, they had a training school for Brazilian naval officers, they had a sailing ship as a training ship, which sometimes would come to the United States, and then they had a naval academy, which we visited. I was taken around pretty much through all their naval stations. Then they used to have a great many social functions. There was a beautiful naval club on the outskirts of Rio, where they had many social gatherings. Then there was also a naval club - a town club - down in Rio, which was very attractive. The work was usual. There's nothing much to comment on about that. Everything sort of ran according to schedule. One of my problems was that quite a few of our plans that we used, for instance, at the Naval War College are secret, are confidential, and I would have to be especially careful not to divulge anything of a confidential or secret nature because of course that would have been treason.

Q: You had to make up the games, in other words?

Adm. W.: Well, not entirely, but a good deal of them. I passed on them. I was in consultation with the President of the War College. We'd go over them together and talk them out and be there while they were being conducted, read the papers and correct the papers. I didn't speak any Portuguese at all when I went to Rio. I had taken a year of Spanish at the Naval Academy and I had a little Spanish in high school, so I wasn't completely unfamiliar with the language. Portuguese is quite a good deal like Spanish. As a matter of fact, the Portuguese are quite sensitive about it because they are accustomed to people who speak Spanish coming down there and speaking Spanish to them, and they don't like it. My wife was one of the guilty members, having lived in Spain for six years, and they accused her of speaking Spanish the whole two years that we were down there and laughed about it. But, of course, if you can speak good Spanish you can get along anywhere where Portuguese is spoken. I had forgotten most of my Spanish so I had a Portuguese teacher, one who had taught many Americans who had been attached to the naval mission and to the War College. I made considerable headway because I was able to spend a good deal of time on it. My job being principally an advisory one left me some time to myself, which I spent on this. I remember when the President of Brazil, Dutra, came to the opening of the War College - the first War College Course opened I think it was in March, because all of their seasons are reversed, you see, and they opened the War College in March and, of course, I wasn't at all fluent in Portuguese at that time. So I wrote out what I wanted to say in English and got my Brazilian aide - I had an aide also - to translate it into Portuguese, which he did, and I memorized it. When it came my turn at the opening exercises of the War College and knowing how proud the Portuguese are of their own language, it flattered them to have me speak to them in Portuguese, so I gave my address in Portuguese, and I could see President Dutra looking at me in a very intense manner as much as to

say, "How in the heck did this fellow learn that this fast."
I was very pleased that I had gotten away with it up to that
point, but I was a little chagrined after the exercises were
over when the President sent his aide over to me and said,
"The President would like to speak to you." So I went over
and spoke to him but not in fluent Portuguese, and I think he
got on to it.

Q: Oh, but that again was such a gracious, tactful, intelligent,
understanding - sensitive, is the word - thing to do. All
people like...

Adm. W.: Oh, yes, they're very flattered by that. President
Dutra was a very agreeable person. He was a man of few words
but he was affable and friendly. The poor man died while we
were there.

I think I mentioned before, but I don't know whether
it was recorded...No, before that, I must speak of Admiral
Halsey's visit to Rio. Of course, at that time, you know,
Rio was the capital. It no longer is. The capital is now
called Brazilia and it's way in the interior. About the only
way you can get there is by plane. But everything was going
full swing in Rio at that time because it was the capital,
and Admiral Halsey, my old friend, came down on an official
visit, and he was very cordially received, wined and dined
and in every way entertained. We met him at the airport, and
then we went to a fabulous stay luncheon party given for him in the

banqueting hall on the top floor of the Ministerio. I can't begin to tell you how large it is, but I'm sure it must be 200 or 300 feet long and at least 50 or 60 feet wide, and it was just filled with people. There was one great big long table and I remember down the center of the table was a centerpiece of orchids, the most fabulous thing I've ever seen. Of course, I wasn't growing orchids in those days so I really I don't suppose appreciated them, except the beauty of them. They were on slabs about 18 inches wide and about three feet long, and each one was put next to the other to make a continuous center piece all the way down. And I remember when the party was over, I was among the last to leave because of the fact that we were sort of hosts, I mean to say we were among the hosts, the waiters came up and handed me one of these plaques of orchids which I took home to my wife.

The next important visitor was General Eisenhower. He was invited down on an official visit because - and I hadn't known this until I got to Brazil - the Brazilians had a detachment of troops in Italy who fought with the Americans and, of course, under the command technically, of General Eisenhower, although I don't know that General Eisenhower, well, he may have seen them, as far as that goes, but, at any rate, these troops were under American command. So the Brazilian government wanted to pay respects to General Eisenhower because he had been the commander of their troops. And they really turned out the guard. I remember my wife and I met Ike and Mamie at the airport and, really, he's one of the friendliest people. He gives you his hand and you feel you're known this fellow all my life."

Q: You'd never seen him before, had you?

Adm. W.: Yes, I'd seen him. Oh, of course, there were ruffles and flourishes, and he went around to all the different places, and was widely entertained. There was a big dinner and ball for him at the Embassy, but the most outstanding event of all was the ball at Itamarity. Itamarity is one of the old houses dating back to the days when Brazil was an empire. It was then the State Department, but it had been prepared for this event in a manner which I have never seen before and hardly ever expect to see again. I've been to the White House many times, and I think it's very lovely and very well done in the American fashion, but it will never equal Itamarity. Itamarity built in the old-world grandeur, the furnishings are just perfectly fabulous, the architecture is such that I don't think it could ever be duplicated - it may have been added on to, I don't know, but the thing that I remember particularly was this long sort of lake which extended from the rear end of the building, it must have been about 40 feet wide, and it must have been, I should say, 400 or 500 feet long or maybe longer even, and on each side of it the building extended part of the way from the main building at one end. And then the rest of it was beautifully planted with all kinds of trees, plane trees, oh I wish I could remember the names of them, palms and plants of all kinds, and the whole thing was magnificently lighted. And that night there were tables on each side almost end to end, extending all the way down, just groaning with the most delicious food, sea foods, turkeys, roasts, ham, salads everything that you could possibly think of, and some of this was also inside. I mean, the whole affair was like fairyland, you could hardly ever believe that such a thing could exist in this world. It was really perfectly beautiful. Well, that was Ike, and as I think I mentioned before - I don't know whether it was recorded or not - about this opera singer Bidu Sayao sang at the head of this lake. There were many, many people we knew there by that time, because this didn't happen until I think it was about a year after we'd been there, and we were dancing and there was plenty to drink.

The next visitor was Mr. Truman, the President of the U.S., himself, who came down for a conference with the heads of the South American states, and they formulated a constitution for the Organization of American States, the OAS which has, in a sense, superseded the Pan American Union. We saw him arrive and we also went to a reception for him at the American Embassy, which was very magnificent. Mr. Pawley was the ambassador at that time and they tell a funny story about him. When he first arrived in Rio, he and the various cabinet ministers exchanged calls. In Brazil they have a custom of offering a visitor, even in a person's office, a small cup of coffee, which they call a "cafe zinho." For instance, if you went to call on somebody at 10 o'clock in the morning - well, to begin with, they serve those cafe zinhos whether they have a caller or not, twice in the morning and twice in the afternoon, and then in between if anybody comes to call, it's served again. The person who's being called on, the Brazilian, you see, just presses the button and a man comes in with a white coat and a tray and there's "cafe zinho" on it. So, they tell the story about Mr. Rawley, our Ambassador, after he had made a lot of these calls and he'd drunk about six cups of coffee, and he said to the cabinet minister he was visiting, "Mr. Minister, don't you find that drinking so much coffee keeps you awake?" And the old minister, who didn't have much to do anyhow, said, "Well, it helps."

I forgot to mention that among the people that we say - at Itamarin - were King Carol and Madame Lupescu. She really was one of the most beautiful women I've ever seen in my life. Her complexion was milk-white, and she had beautiful auburn hair, she was really - well, you could almost imagine a man deserting his throne for a women like that. She was really something. In the evening she usually wore black with emeralds, or white with pearls.

Q: Did you speak with her?

Adm. W.: Yes. I met her. We met her after that, too, at the French Embassy one time.

Q: Intelligent?

Adm W.: Very. But they tell a funny story about her. You know he wasn't married to her at that time, and they were living at the Copa Cabana Hotel in Rio. She was very worried because he wouldn't marry her, so she got quite ill at one time while we were there, and she said to him, "Oh, now Carol, you must marry me and make me an honest woman." So he did. And she immediately got well and outlived him with the title of Princess.

Q: Well, there are many ways to accomplish your purpose.

Adm. W.: Also, while I was in Rio I was invested with the British Order of Commander of the British Empire. The first time - I was invested with it twice, believe it or not - because while in Rio I got an invitation from the British Embassy asking my wife and me to come to attend this investiture. There were several others who were invested at the same time. This was for my services, of course, with the British Pacific Fleet. So we went, and they had a very nice little ceremony and when it came my turn the British Ambassador made a very nice little speech and he handed me a little piece of ribbon, and he said, "I'm sorry but because of the war and the impossibility of getting all the materials needed for fabrication, this is all we can give you at this time." We thought it was a funny thing to do, but that's all there was, so we went around and spoke to our friends who were at the Embassy cocktail party, then went on home. Let's see that was in 1947, I think, and about a year after we got back to the United States, I had retired, and I got a similar invitation from the - well, in each case, the invitations were from the palace in London. I could have gone to England and been invested by Queen Mary but I didn't want to. But later when I had the time and we were living in Worcester and I was with the State Mutual Life, I got a similar invitation from the

British Consul General in Boston and I went down to that affair, and they presented me with the actual decoration.

Q: Was this to replace the other one, or a second investitute?

Adm. W.: No, the same. I mean, it was the completion.

Q: A formal presentation of the whole ribbon and the symbol.

Adm. W.: While in Rio I had the pleasure of introducing my wife to Ambassador Nabuco who had just returned from Rome. I think in an earlier...

Q: The story about the man with the silk stockings?

Adm. W.: Yes, well, when we were in Rio, we had lunch together - I think he invited us, as a matter of fact, and I had the pleasure of introducing him to my wife and pointing out the girl to whom he had given the silk stockings, commiserating on it with him about what he may have lost in Rome as a result ...

Then there was another interesting occasion in Rio, that was the reception at the Argentine Embassy where we met and talked with famed Evita Peron. She was another fabulous blonde. Of course, she's dead now. That was also where we had dinner with Juan Trippe. Didn't I tell you about Juan Trippe in the previous recording?

Q: I don't believe so. The head of...

Adm. W.: Pan American Airways. Didn't I tell you about that?

Q: If you did, I don't recall it.

Adm. W.: Well, you're pretty good at recalling things. This harked back to 1934 or thereabouts when I was in charge of all the U.S. naval shore radio stations throughout the world, and we received a letter from Mr. Tripp asking for permission to establish some radio stations on the islands like Johnson's Island, Midway, Guam, Samoa, places like that, to aid him in setting up the first American airline across the Pacific. You see, at that time, there was no airline that ran beyond Honolulu. In this letter he said that he couldn't extend his airlines across the Pacific unless he was able to communicate with the island stops enroute, and he wanted to set up radio stations at these island places which we controlled in the Pacific. At that time — they've since been turned over to the Department of the Interior, which I think is a ridiculous thing, myself, but nevertheless — at that time they were all controlled by the Navy. For instance, at Guam we had a naval governor, at Samoa we had a naval governor. Now it's all civilian government under the Department of the Interior. So this letter came over to me, and it said that they'd like to have permission to do this. Well, I realized it was more of a legal matter than it was a communication matter, so I sent it over to the Judge Advocate General's office in the Navy Department and asked for their legal opinion. And a couple of days later, one of the lawyers came over and said to me, "Commander, we can give you any answer you like. We can find adequate reasons for denying this, or we can find adequate reasons for granting it. Which do you want us to do?"

Well, without consulting anybody else, I said, "Give them permission to do it."

Q: It certainly turned out to be advantageous to...

Adm. W.: It was the best thing in the world for the United States. As I couldn't do otherwise the lawyer a patriotic American. So took the letter back to the Judge Advocate General's Office, and it came back with an endorsement, and I forwarded it to Mr. Trippe. So, years later - that was in 1934 or 1935, and this was in 1948 - Admiral Powell, who's been a great friend of mine over the years, he was about the class of 1913, who was then in charge of Pan American Airways in Brazil, asked my wife and me to dinner at his house to meet Mr. Tripp, and we went, of course. After dinner, the ladies separated from the men as usual and I was sitting there on a sofa, sitting next to Mr. Tripp and we were having liqueurs, and I said, "Mr. Tripp, you're sitting next to the man who gave you permission to extend your airlines across the Pacific."

Q: I bet that surprised him.

Adm. W.: He certainly was surprised. Later on, I told that story to some friends of mine in San Francisco whose son is the passenger agent for all Pan American Airways in New York, and they told him that, and when we went to Europe three years ago, they really "turned out the guard." We were going Pan American Airways. They met us as soon as we got off the plane - We went United to New York, but we were going on Pan American across the ocean. They met us with a special car, they took us to the airport and took us out to get us all fixed up with our tickets, and took us to the Pan American Club, which is a very exclusive affair and gave us cocktails, and then we went on board the plane. Fortunately, we managed to get a sandwich or something before the plane took off, and we'd no sooner gotten seated on the plane - it was about 10 o'clock at night - than the bar boy came along with a cold bottle of champagne for us, and I said, "Thank you very much, but just kind of keep that for us." The amusing part of it was that, later on we took it ashore with us and used it for a dinner that our English hostess gave for us that night.

It was a pretty rough time in Brazil. The Commies were misbehaving and there were a lot of riots which, fortunately, we were able to keep out of. Our children went to the American school which is way out on the outskirts of Rio, but we always had good intelligence information about the riots pretty good intelligence. We always knew when there was going to be a riot, and I'd send my chauffeur out to get the children and bring them back before the riots started. There was a lot of Communist activity, but they did a thing which I thought we ought to have done in this country a long time ago. They outlawed the Communist Party completely and after that everything stopped for a while, but it started up again. Later,

Now, we come to the end. While there I received an invitation from the president of the State Mutual Life Assurance Company of Worcester, Massachusetts, asking me to join his staff. Not being an aviator and the war being over, I felt that that was about the time for me to call it quits, so I put in for voluntary retirement, and retired on the first day of April 1948. I was with this company for four years.. I don't know whether you want me to tell anything about that or not.

Q: Well, I would think maybe I ought to just bring you up to date here. You were with them for four years and then came to...? To California from Worcester?

Adm. W.: Yes. We came to California, and we got here in August of 1952. I was quite active in civic affairs. I've withdrawn from most of these things. The only thing I am now is the senior warden of a little church that we belong to, and I am the president of an investment club that meets once a month, about 30 gentlemen belong to that and we meet at the University Club in Palo Alto. When we first came here I was very active in school work and

I became the first president of the Town Hall Association of San Mateo County, which was very active and which, I like to think, had a good deal to do with stopping a number of undesirable laws which we were about to pass, among them there was a group that was trying to change over from - a number of the county offices from elective offices to appointed offices, like the tax collector, the tax assessor, the country clerk, and all the things like that, which really takes the government out of the hands of the people. Also, I think probably one of the greatest accomplishments was stopping the building of the rapid transit. Now, you'll think this is funny to hear me say that, but I'm not against rapid transit. I think it would be marvelous to have rapid transit all the way from San Jose to San Francisco and the air port, both ways, but - and of course we've got it anyway with the railroad, it's not as rapid, ~~it's four whee~~ls, not modernized - but this rapid transit law which they were trying to pass was going to saddle the taxpayers of this county with debt for many, many, many years, and it was so written that they had practically a free hand after the ~~thing~~ *law* had gone into effect that they'd have never been able to stop it. In other words, we were not so much against rapid transit as we were against the enabling act, which was full of flaws ~~and things like that~~.

Then I was the first president of the Naval Academy Alumni Association out here, which I organized, and I am still a member of the National Advisory ~~Commission~~ - Council - of the American Education League, which is a patriotic organization.

One of their projects and a very commendable one, in my opinion, is trying to rid the schools of these very slanted textbooks, many of which are just untrue. One of them that I read when I was ~~interested~~ taking an active part in the schools here said that the United Nations won the war. The United Nations wasn't founded until after the war was over. But they're slanted and they give the youngsters a completely false idea about the way our country was founded and been run and everything. This is a particularly bad area for drugs and for left-wing ideas and anti-patriotic ideas. It makes your blood boil sometimes when you see the things that are going on.

Q: Seeing this area, one wouldn't think...

Adm. W.: You'd think that people would be content, wouldn't you, just to let things remain as they are? It's a wonderful part of the world.

I was president of the Peninsula Retired Officers' Club, and I was President of the Peninsula Orchid Society, of which I'm still a member and a director, and was a member of the executive council of the Boy Scouts of America. So I've been pretty busy.

Q: You're still contributing to your country, Admiral.

Adm. W.: Well, I'm doing the best I can, but my years are beginning to catch up with me. I'm not quite as active as I was. I just get tired.

Q: Well, you don't appear to have your years catch up with you.

Adm. W.: Thank you so much.

Q: You certainly wear them beautifully.

Adm. W.: You're very kind.

Q: I hate to come to the end of our interview.

Adm. W.: I do, too. I didn't put in my decorations, I think they've got those.

Q: We have mentioned the Legion of Merit and the Bronze Star Medal. Then you have a letter of commendation with ribbon from the Commander-in-Chief of the Pacific Fleet, the Victory Medal, the destroyer class on the Benham, The Yangtze Service Medal, the American Defense Service Medal, the Fleet Asiatic-Pacific Campaign medal, the European, African, Middle East Campaign medal, and the World War II Victory medal.

Adm. W.: The Legion of Merit has a Bronze Star, I mean a bronze V, you know. That's called a combat V.

Q: I'm glad you mentioned it.

Adm. W.: And, of course, then, you got the Commendador of the Order of Naval Merit?

Q: No, what is that?

Adm. W.: That's Brazilian.

Q: That isn't listed in your biography. Would you say that name again?

Adm. W.: Commendador of the Order of Naval Merit. And you got this CBE, didn't you, Commander of the Order of the Bath (British Empire?). Well, I think that's the end.

Q: I do want to mention that you had published by Shipmate in May of 1946 an article called "Task Force 57"...

Adm. W.: That's the British...

Q.: That's British...And you had an article published by the Army-Navy Register in December of 1945 on the subject of the British fleet. Then you had another publication by the United States Naval Institute called, "We Had the British Where We Needed Them." So you have done some publishing, and I don't want to close without mentioning your beautiful orchids - orchid collection or growing, or how to say...

Adm. W.: It's a hobby, I suppose.

INDEX

for interviews with

REAR ADMIRAL CHARLES J. WHEELER, U. S. NAVY (RETIRED)

Achete, HMS, 17

Ackland, 135

Afrium Kara Hissar, Konia, 81, 121

Agra, Taj Mahal, 65-67

Alexandria, 67-68, 119

Alice Dollar, 50, 150

Amoy, 65, 144, 159, 175-177

Anatolia, 72, 85, 108-109, 111, 116

Ankara, 72-73, 81, 121

Armenians, 123-124

Army, 119-120, 158, 162, 303-304

Arnold, General Henry H., 120

Astoria, 223-226, 232, 247-249

Athens, 68, 119

Australia, 135

Azores, 238-239

Baguio, 158

Bailey, VADM Sir Louis, 10, 313

Bebec, 76-77

Belin, Ferdinand Lammot, 112

Benham, served on, 8-20, 25, 251-253, 313

Bey, Adnan and Mrs., 88

Biloxi, 270, 277

Birmingham, 270

Bismarck, 311

Black Sea, 73, 76, 106, 116-118

Bolsheviks, 36

Bosporus, 68, 76, 78-79, 82, 86, 94, 106

Bougainville Island, 278-279

Boxer Rebellion, 41, 159-160, 162

Brazil, as head of the Brazil Naval War College, 344-360

Brest, France, 9, 11, 13, 15, 17, 26

Bridge, 217

Brindisi, Italy, 134-135

Bristol, Admiral and Mrs. Mark Lambert, 69-71, 73-84, 87-91, 96-100, 104, 110, 112, 121, 123, 125-128, 131-132, 145-147, 151, 159, 161-162, 165-166, 168, 170, 175, 179, 187-188, 191-194, 333-334

British, 9-10, 13-14, 33, 42, 49-50, 57, 78, 107, 109, 118, 130, 135-136, 161, 238-239; Command of British Fleet, 301-303, 305-306, 309-314, 317-326, 337-338, 340-342

Brooklyn, 21

Bryan, CDR and Mrs. Hamilton V., 69-70, 104-105

Buckmaster, VADM Elliott, 259

Butler, General Smedley, 162

California, 143-144

Canton, 65, 150, 161

Carmel, California, 299-301

Carney, Admiral Robert B., 336-337

Casablanca, 303

Cassin, 8

Cecil, RADM Charles P., 135

Cetinje, 128

Chandler, RADM Lloyd H., 179

Chandler, RADM Theodore Edson, 179

Changsha, 48-49, 53-55, 59, 152

Chang Tso-lin, 150

Chengtu, 52-53

Chiang-Kai-Shek, 49, 150, 155-157, 189-190; and Madame, 134, 153-157

Childs, Richard Washburn, 110

China, 21, 41-65, 115, 122, 132, 144, 146-163, 171, 188-190, 217, 336

Chinese, 159-160, 339

Chungking, 48-49, 51-54, 59-60, 153

Churcher, Captain Maurice, (British Army) 118

Churchill, The Right Honorable Winston Spencer, 174

Churchill, Captain (British Army) 101

Clark, Admiral Joseph J. (Jocko) 267, 295, 298

Coast Guard, 214-216

Colombo, 303, 305

Communication officer, 213-215

Constantine, King of Greece, 106-108

Constantinople, 68-112, 115, 119-120, 123-124, 129, 131-134, 146-147, 194, 217, 248

Crane, 223

Craven, RADM T. T., 191-192; and Mrs., 191-193

Crimean War, 82

Curzon, Lord and Lady Edward Richard Assheton Penn, 112

Czechs, 35-36, 39

Dakar, 238-239

Daniels, Secretary Josephus, 21

Dardanelles, 68, 71, 106, 114, 118-119

Davao, 172-173

Decorations, 363-364

Delhi, 67

Dewey, Admiral George, 6-7

Dollar Line, 50, 150

DuBose, RADM L. T., 270

Duke of York, served on, 320-332, 336-337, 339, 341

Dulles, Allen, 75

Eisenhower, General Dwight D. and Mrs., 351-353

Empress Augusta Bay, 277-278

Evans, 297

Frazer, Admiral Sir Bruce, 193, 264, 306, 308-311, 314, 316, 319-326, 328, 330-331, 333, 336-340, 342

French, 32-33, 37, 42, 49, 78, 110, 130

Fuad, Prince and Princess Osman, 80, 88

Galapagos Islands, 24

Gallery, RADM Daniel V., 343

Gallipoli Campaign, 71, 118

Germany, 9-13, 126-127; Germans, 9, 49, 81, 160; submarines, 11, 13, 18

Ghormley, VADM Robert Lee, 120, 249-250

Gifu, 180-183

Gleaves, Admiral Albert, 22, 24-25, 40

Gold Star, 171

Greece, 125

Greeks, 75, 78, 86, 106-110, 114

Grew, Joseph Clark, 110

Guadalcanal, 120

Guadalcanal, 278-279

Guam, 170-172, 264, 310, 320-326, 357

Guantanamo, 71; Bay, 9

Halsey, Admiral William Frederick, 250-253, 255, 278, 294, 314, 327-328, 330, 335-337, 350

Hampton Roads, 9, 30

Hankow, 54

Haruna, HIJMS, 163-164, 168, 333-334

Hay, Camp John, 31-32, 158

Hellesport, 106

Henderson, 134-135

Hepburn, Admiral A. J., 74, 217

Hill, Admiral Harry W., 270, 272

Hirohito, 168-169

Holden, VADM Carl Frederick, 280-281, 283

Holland, 161

Holy Cross College, 240-241, 243-246

Homeric, 83

Hong Kong, 65, 161, 175, 336-337

Honolulu, 224-225, 232-233, 246, 248, 262, 265, 308-310

Howell, Captain Glenn Fletcher, 45, 52, 60-65, 68-70, 104

Huron, served on, 37-43, 150

Ichang, 45, 49, 59, 61

Idaho, 233

Iowa, 258

Ireland, 10, 238

Italians, 37, 42, 49, 78, 81, 110, 130

Ives, Consul General E. L., 119

Iwo Jima, 289

Jackson, Admiral Richard Harrison, 142, 144

Japan, 40, 170, 180-185, 222, 226, 231, 243, 248, 265-266, 326-327, 330, 333-335

Japanese, 33, 37, 40, 110, 157, 160, 162-163, 166-167, 169, 172-173, 181-186, 226, 237-238, 271-273, 277-278, 284-287, 298, 301-302; surrender and after, 333-338; prison camps, 338-341

Japanese Exclusion Act, 40, 184-185

Johnson Island, 225

Kemal, Mustapha, 71-73, 80-81, 85-88, 91, 108, 111, 118-119, 121, 129

Kiating, 52-53, 59

Kimmel, Admiral Husband Edward, 233, 247

King, Admiral Ernest J., 238, 297, 301-303, 305-307

Kinkaid, Admiral Thomas C., 74, 80, 119

Kung, Dr. H. H., 155

Kwajalein, 271, 275-277, 289-291, 295, 299

Lausanne, 109, 112-115; Treaty of, 87, 129-131

Leviathan, 26

Lewis, Captain James Mackey, 240

Lindberg, 19

Lingayen Gulf, 309

Lister Bay, 273

Long, Vice Admiral, 99

Lovett, RADM Benjamin Barnes C., 347

Luby, Captain J. M., 24

Lyautey, Port, 303.

MacArthur, General Douglas, 158, 173-174, 265-266, 289, 309, 330-331

MacLeish, 119

Magic Carpet operations, 342

Mahomed VI, 72-73, 84-87, 91, 95

Majuro, 275, 280

Malay Peninsula, 301, 305

Malaya, HMS, 85

Manila, 158, 160, 173, 340-341; Bay, 341

Manila Bay, Battle of; Spanish-American War, 6-7

Manus, 310, 319-321, 342-343

Marcus, 266-267, 289

Marines, 162, 171-172, 271-272

Marmora, Sea of, 76

Marquesas Islands, 25, 27

Marshall, General George C., 157-158

Matsu Island, 175-176

Mauretania, 83, 101

Mediterranean, ports, 119

Melbourne, 297

Melbourne, 135-138

Mejid, Abdul, 87-88

Merrill, Lt. Crd. (Tip) 96-98

Mesopotamia, 72, 116

Mexico, 148, 201

Midway, 27

Miles, Sherman, 75

Min River, 52, 59

Missouri, 7, 168, 283, 328-332, 336

Mobile, command of, 204-206, 208, 243, 247, 255-258, 260-262, 264-279, 282-299, 343

Mobile, Alabama, 1-2, 71, 82, 299

Moffett, Pierpont, 80

Monacacy, 43, 45, 162

Moore, RADM Charles J., 280

Morgenthau, Henry, Jr., 214

Moslems, 86-87, 92

Mountbatten, Admiral Viscount Louis Francis Albert Victor Nicholas, 305-306

Mullinnix, RADM Henry Maston, 273-274

Nabuco, Ambassador (Brazil) 304

Nagato, HIJMS, 166-168

Nakin, 269

Nanking, 54, 150, 188-190

Naval Academy, preparation and examination for, 1-3, midshipman at, 3-8, 96, 161, 244, 254, 260, 348

Naval War College, 220-222, 285

NC-4, 19

Nevada, 19, served on, 135-142

New Jersey, 280-283

New Mexico, 270

New Zealand, 135

Nimitz, Admiral Chester W., 144, 221-222, 250, 252, 263-266, 276-277, 294, 306, 308, 310, 312, 320-326, 328, 330-331, 341; Mrs. 263

Nimitz, Club, 249

Nomura, Admiral Kichisaburo, 231

Norfolk, Virginia, 9, 19, 238-240, 257

NROTC, at Holy Cross College, 240, 243-245

Oak Knoll Hospital, 300

Odessa, 116-118

Okinawa, 285, 311

Palembang, 306-307

Palestine, 72, 116

Palos, served on, 43-61, 63, 152-153, 162

Panama, 23, 25-26, 237-238, 258, 261, 293; Canal, 7

Panay, 162-163, 217

Paris; war ending celebration, 16-17

Pasha, Ismet, 111-112

Patmos, 81, 121

Pauley, Edwin W., 353-354

Pearl Harbor, 143, 144, 231, 255, 274-275; Day, 246-248

Peking, 41-42, 150-152, 161-162, 189

Pennsylvania, 217-218, 220-221

Philippines, 31-32, 158-159, 161, 170-175, 265-266, 340

Philippine Sea, first battle of, 284-286; second battle of, 74, 119

Pittsburgh, 147, 164, 191

Polish Village, 82-83

Portsmouth, New Hampshire, 20-21

Powell, RADM Paulus Prince, 358

President Garfield, 146

President Jefferson, 194

President Lincoln, 11

Princess Islands, 76

Putnam, 275-276

Queenstown, Ireland, 9-11, 13, 15, 17-18, 25-26

Quemoy Island, 175-176

Rabaul, 278

Ragusa, 134-135

Rangoon, 65, 67

Rawlings, RADM Norborne L., 314

Relief, 235-242, 292-293, 300

Retirement, 360-362

Rhodes Island, 81, 119

Richardson, Admiral J. O., 233-234, 247; Mrs., 234

Rickover, VADM Hyman G., 139-141

Robert Dollar Second, 50, 150

Rodgers, RADM William Ledyard, 21-22

Roosevelt, Mrs. F. D., 259

Roosevelt, President F. D., 165, 211, 214, 233-234

Rudio, Ortiz and family, 201

Rumbold, Sir and Lady Horace Anthony Claude, 112

Russians, 33, 36, 49, 76-77, 110, 116

Said, Port, 67-68

Saipan, 284-285

Saipan, 284-285

Samoa, 27-31, 171, 358

San Diego, 197-198, 200, 203, 236-237, 261-262

The Sand Pebbles, 57-58

San Francisco, 257

San Francisco, 7, 143, 146

Santa Fe, 270

Santee, 8, 18

Sarnoff, The Honorable David, 196

Savo Island, 249

Schley, 73

Scorpion, 78, 79, 104, 121-122, 134; cruise on, 125-128

Scutari, 80-81

Sevres, Treaty of, 72, 108-109, 130

Shanghai, 32-34, 42, 45, 48, 53-54, 59, 61-63, 146-147, 151, 153, 162, 176, 179, 190-191

Siberia, 36, 146-147

Sims, RADM William S., 10

Singapore, 65

Smyrna, 68, 72, 86, 108-109, 119

Soong, T. V., 155

South Dakota, served on, 20-37, 207-208

Spruance, Admiral Raymond Ames, 225, 269, 280-285a, 294, 314

Stassen, Harold (ex-Governor, Pennsylvania) 283

Strauss, Admiral Joseph, 64,

Stedman, Virginia, 96-98

Stevenson, Adlai, 119

Stimson, Henry Lewis, 159, 171, 173, 195

Sui Fu, 51-52

Sulu Islands, 172

Sumatra, 301, 306-307

Sun Yat Sen, 147, 155, 188-190

Sydney, 135, 308-310, 315, 320, 326, 341-342

Syria, 72, 116

Tahiti, 27

Tarawa, 269-276, 289, 298

Tarsus, 81, 121

Taylor, Congressman George Washington, 1-2

Tennessee, 21

Therapia, 104

Tientsin, 161-162

Tokyo, 161, 164-165, 168, 187; Bay, 163, 165, 327, 329-332

Treadwell, Consul General R. C., 119

Trippe, Juan Terry, 356-358

Truman, President Harry, 342, 353

Tsingtao, 160

Tung Ting Lake, 54, 59

Turkey, 68-82, 86-115, 123-124, 129-133, 145; Turks, 80, 82, 87, 93-95, 109-111, 114-115, 123-125, 132

Turner, Admiral Kelly, 228-231, 249, 274

Upham, RADM F. B., 21

Venice, 126, 131

Vian, RADM Sir Philip L., 314, 341

Vienna, 126-128

Virginia, 216

Vladivostok, 35-39, 147, 240

Wake, 267-269, 289

Wakehurst, Lord and Lady John de Vere Loder, 320

Walsh, David I., 244-245

Ward, 253

Washington, D. C., 10-11, 194-195, 233, 290, 301, 303, 305

Washington, Admiral and Mrs. Thomas, 144-146

Waters, command of, 199-200, 202-206, 213

Wellington, 135

Whangpoo River, 63

Wheeler, Mrs. Charles (Putnam) 144, 146, 176, 188, 193, 197-198, 215-216, 222, 226, 236, 275-276, 304, 309, 349, 355-356, 358-359

Wilson, President Woodrow, 6, 10

World War I, 9-18, 35-36, 160, 250-251, 253

World War II, 160, 163, 172, 174, 265-280, 284-311; surrender, 325-333; Pearl Harbor Day, 246-248

Wotje, 287

Wrangel, Baron and Baroness, 103

Wu Pei Fu, 150

Wyatt, Commodore Ben Harrison, 290

Yale-in-China University, 54, 56

Yale University, 54, 56

Yalta, 103-104

Yangtse River, 43-61, 150, 163

Yerba Buena Island, 144

Yokohama, 161, 165, 180, 183, 333-335

Yorktown, 258-259, 265, 267, 298-299

Yorktown, 9

Yuan Shih-Kai, 148

Zinnia, 14

The Presentation of the G.C.B. to Fleet Admiral C.W. Nimitz

and

An Account of the Japanese Surrender.

On the evening of July 30th I entertained the acting Governor of New South Wales and Lady Jordan, Commodore Evans-Lombe, Chief of Staff to Commander in Chief, British Pacific Fleet, and Captain A.D. Nicholl, Commanding Officer of HMS Duke of York, at dinner in my flat. Immediately thereafter, I took my guests to see the movie entitled "Fighting Lady". After the party broke up, I embarked with Captain Nicholl in HMS Duke of York, Flag Ship of the Commander in Chief, British Pacific Fleet.

At 0930, July 31, the HMS Duke of York got underway and stood out in Sydney Harbor enroute to Manus, Admiralty Islands. Except for being taken on various tours about the ship and being entertained in the wardroom, the voyage to Manus was uneventful and we arrived there at 0930, August 5th.

According to plan, Admiral Sir Bruce Fraser, Commander in Chief, British Pacific Fleet, was to arrive in Manus by plane from Sydney at the same time, but was delayed 24 hours on account of engine trouble. We, therefore, remained in Manus overnight and that evening Captain Nicholl and I dined on board the HMS Montclare as guests of Rear Admiral Douglas Fisher, the Commander British Fleet Train.

Admiral Sir Bruce Fraser, Commander Courage, the Communication Officer, Commander Carver, the Staff Officer Plans and Lieutenant Merry, the Admiral's Flag Lieutenant arrived in the forenoon and at 1600, August 6th, we got underway for Guam, the Advanced Headquarters of Fleet Admiral Nimitz, Commander in Chief, U.S. Pacific Fleet.

The primary purpose of this trip was to enable Admiral Fraser to present Fleet Admiral Nimitz with the Knight Grand Cross of the Order of Bath. As a member of Admiral Fraser's Staff, I occupied the spacious quarters normally assigned to the Captain of the Fleet, (who was then in Sydney), and I of course messed with Admiral Fraser, his Flag Lieutenant and Flag Secretary.

We arrived in Guam at 0930, August 9th, and Admiral Fraser, accompanied by the Flag Lieutenant and myself, immediately went ashore and called on Fleet Admiral Nimitz. Upon return to HMS Duke of York, Admiral Fraser had luncheon for the British Liaison Officers stationed in Guam.

At 1430 that afternoon Admiral Fraser and his staff had a meeting with Fleet Admiral Nimitz and his staff at the latter's Headquarters. At this meeting future plans for the activities of the British Pacific Fleet were discussed.

At 1800, Admiral Nimitz, Admiral Fraser, the Flag Lieutenant and I attended a cocktail party at Commander in Chief, Pacific Fleet's Wardroom Mess. At 1900 Fleet Admiral Nimitz gave a large formal dinner for Admiral Sir Bruce Fraser and his staff. Among the guests at this dinner were Admiral Spruance, Commander 5th Fleet, General Spaatz, Commanding the U.S. Strategic Air Forces, Vice Admiral Lockwood, Commander U.S. Submarines, Pacific Fleet, Vice Admiral Murray, Commanding Marianas Islands, etc. After dinner, Admiral Fraser, his Flag Lieutenant and I remained overnight as the house guests of Fleet Admiral Nimitz.

At 1100 on August 10th, Admiral Sir Bruce Fraser presented Fleet Admiral Nimitz with the Knight Grand Cross of the Order of Bath. This ceremony was conducted on the quarter deck of the HMS Duke of York, and in addition to the officers and crew of that ship, it was attended by the Senior U.S. Army, Navy and Marine Corp officers stationed at Guam, numbering about 50 in all. 100 enlisted men of the U.S. Army, Navy and Marine Corp were also present. The ceremony took place on a raised platform abaft the turret. It consisted of an address by Admiral Sir Bruce Fraser, a reply by Fleet Admiral Nimitz, the presentation of the G.C.B., the playing of the National Anthems and three cheers in honor of Fleet Admiral Nimitz, proposed by Admiral Fraser.

After the ceremony all the visiting officers were invited to the Admiral's cabin for refreshments and all the visiting enlisted men were served a tot of rum on the quarter deck. After the conclusion of the ceremonies, Admiral Fraser, Captain Nicholl, the Flag Lieutenant and I were the luncheon guests of Vice Admiral Lockwood at his Submarine Rest Camp, known as Camp Dealy. A delightful swim was enjoyed by all prior to the luncheon.

At 1930, Admiral Fraser entertained at dinner aboard his flagship in honor of Fleet Admiral Nimitz and about 12 other senior U.S. Army, Navy and Marine Corp officers stationed in Guam.

This party broke up about 2200. At about 2230, while Captain Nicholl and I were having a liqueur in my cabin, Commander Carver, the Staff Officer Plans, rushed in with a copy of a broadcast in which the Japanese agreed to surrender in accordance with the stipulation laid down in the Potsdan Declaration.

On August 11th, Admiral Fraser received instructions from the Admiralty to remain at Guam until further orders, instead of returning to Sydney as previously planned.

On August 12th, Admiral Fraser was appointed British Representative to receive the formal surrender of Japan, if and when that event should take place. That evening Admiral Fraser, Captain Nicholl, Lieutenant Merry and I attended an informal dinner at Fleet Admiral Nimitz's.

At 0930, August 13, the Commander in Chief, British Pacific Fleet, in HMS Duke of York sailed to join Task Group 38.5.

At 1030, August 14, Commander in Chief, British Pacific Fleet, reported by despatch to the Commander 3rd Fleet for duty.

At 0430, August 16, the Commander in Chief, British Pacific Fleet, in HMS Duke of York joined up with and took station with Task Force 38 as Task Group 38.5.

At 1000, Vice Admiral Sir Bernard Rawlings, Vice Admiral, 2nd in Command, accompanied by several members of his staff, came to call on Admiral Fraser. They transferred from Vice Admiral Rawlings flagship, HMS King George V, to a destroyer, thence to the Duke of York by a breeches bouy.

At 1430, Admiral Fraser, accompanied by his staff, transferred by destroyer to the USS Missouri where he called on Admiral Halsey, Commander Third Fleet. During the visit, Vice Admiral Rawlings arrived on board the USS Missouri from his flagship and made an address to Task Force 38. Following the address, Admiral Fraser invested Admiral Halsey with the Knight of the British Empire. This was done informally on the veranda deck of the USS Missouri, forward of the Captain's cabin.

On August 17, Admiral Fraser, accompanied by his staff, attended luncheon aboard the King George V, as the guests of Vice Admiral Rawlings.

At 1100 on August 19, Vice Admiral J.S. McCain, USN, Commander Task Force, accompanied by several members of his staff, called on Admiral Fraser.

At 1600, Admiral W. F. Halsey, Commander Third Fleet, accompanied by several members of his staff, returned Admiral Fraser's call.

On August 22, at the invitation of Rear Admiral A.W. Radford, USN, Commander Task Group 38.4, Admiral Fraser, Commander M. Hodges, Executive Officer of the Duke of York, Lieut. Merry and I had luncheon aboard Rear Admiral Radford's flagship the U.S.S. Yorktown. While aboard the Yorktown 106 planes were launched and recovered. These planes took part in the "Fly Past" of all the planes, about 1,000 in number, from Task Force 38, to be photographed.

On August 24, Rear Admiral R.B. Carney, USN, Chief of Staff to Commander Third Fleet, and several other members of Admiral Halsey's staff had luncheon with Admiral Fraser on board HMS Duke of York. Instructions were received about this time that the formal surrender would be postponed due to a typhoon over the Tokyo Area which interferred with the preliminary arrangements regarding the landing of planes, etc.

At 1600, August 25, Air Vice Marshall Isitt, representative of New Zealand at the formal surrender of Japan, reported on board.

At about 0630 on August 27, the Japanese destroyer Hatuzakura was sighted about 20 miles from Oshima, a large island outside the approach to Tokyo Bay. Admiral Halsey had arranged through General McArthur to have the Jap destroyer meet us at that time and place with pilots and interpreters to pilot us first to Sagami Wan, thence into Tokyo Bay. The Nicholas, an American destroyer met the Jap destroyer at about three miles beyond the fleet and the Japanese pilots and interpreters were transferred from the Jap to the American destroyer. There were thirteen pilots, six interpreters and two commissioners. All were searched and made to take baths on the American destroyer before being transferred to Admiral Halsey's Flagship, the USS Missouri.

The Japanese commissioners and some of the pilots who were naval officers wore swords which were confiscated after they reached the Missouri. Most of the Japs were quite subdued except for one of the commissioners who was quite fresh and who began smoking in the presence of the officers who were interviewing the Japanese on board the Missouri. Rear Admiral Carney, the Chief of Staff, removed the cigarette from the commissioner's mouth and informed him that smoking was not permitted during the interview. Admiral Halsey did not receive any of this party. After all the Japanese had been given a thorough going over on the Missouri, the pilots and interpreters were distributed among the other large ships of the fleet.

At 1100, our ship, the Duke of York, received her pilot and interpreter. The pilot was a Japanese Naval Officer in a tan uniform, and the interpreter was a very sorry looking civilian wearing shoddy clothes and a broken down panama hat. They were both very subdued and according to a petty officer who searched them, quite thin and undernourished looking.

After having successfully passed between the mine fields we anchored at Sagami Wan at 1337. Our anchorage was between the Island of Enoshima, a very picturesque island and tourist show place which I visited on my first trip to Japan in 1920, and Kamakura, another tourist spot, where the Diabutsu is located. At first no one could be seen on shore but after we had been anchored a little while and the people had evidently decided that we were not going to bombard them, they came out of their houses and a few went swimming on the beach, which surprised us as we had been told that the beach had been heavily planted with land mines.

Fuji Yama did not put in an appearance for some time, but eventually the clouds rolled away and it was a very majestic sight to see Fuji forming a background for the Allied Fleet, which pretty well covered Sagami Wan at the foot of Fuji. All precautions, including the manning of battle stations, darkening ship that night, etc., were taken but there was no indication of any kind of Japanese opposition, even by individuals.

On August 28th we remained at anchor at Sagami Wan all day. On August 29th, at 0700, we got underway and stood into Tokyo Bay. The leading ship in the formation was the USS Missouri, followed by the USS Iowa and then the HMS Duke of York. We were in the usual cruising formation with destroyers ahead and on each flank.

Shortly after getting underway a large Japanese submarine passed a few thousand yards on our starboard hand. It had been captured while attempting to run away by the American destroyer Blue, and about 20 Japanese officers and 179 Japanese sailors were lined up on deck. We learned later that this submarine is the largest in the world. It displaces 5000 tons and has a hanger accomodating four airplanes.

As we stood into Tokyo Bay we could see white flags flying from the shore batteries on each side of the Straits. The white flags, which were required under the terms of the surrender, marked the position of each shore battery. All of us who had been under the fire of Japanese shore batteries agreed that white flags were preferable to the white flashes from the guns as they were fired, to which we had become accustomed.

We were piloted into Tokyo Bay by the same pilot who brought us into Sagami Wan. He assured us that the mine fields shown on the chart in the parts of the channel through which we were passing were blown up the week before. We hoped he was right and he evidentially was as we arrived later without incident. Admiral Halsey, however, left nothing to chance and had had the channel carefully swept with our own mine sweepers before we ban our entry.

The most interesting part of the trip was that in which we passed Yokosuka Navy Yard. The navy yard itself was apparently deserted, as only one or two people could be seen walking along the shore line. It looked exactly like Sunday in peacetime in one of our navy yards. The principal object of interest was the "Nagato", a Japanese battleship which was heavily bombed during the recent strikes by the Third Fleet on the Tokyo Area. It was still afloat but was pretty badly battered looking. Her stacks were gone and her superstructure looked badly burned out.

While looking at this wreck I was reminded of my visit to Tokyo in 1928 when I was a member of the Commander in Chief, U.S. Asiatic Fleet's Staff. The occasion for this visit was the naval review in honor of the coronation of the Emperor Hirohito. During the visit Admiral Bristol and I dined on board the Nagato as the guests of the Japanese Commander in Chief of the combined fleets of which Nagato was the flagship.

Upon proceeding further up the bay a number of sunken and beached Japanese ships were observed. We could also see many of the damaged buildings in Yokohama which had been gutted in recent air raids.

At 1126 we anchored in Tokyo Bay, which marked the end of a long trek. For me, it began with the commissioning of the USS Mobile in Norfolk, Virginia, on March 24, 1943.

At 1400, August 29th, I watched Admiral Nimitz's plane land along side the USS South Dakota, which was anchored in the next berth to the Duke of York. Soon thereafter, he transferred from the plane, which was a PB2Y5, to his barge and thence to the USS South Dakota, where his five star flag was broken at the mast head.

At 0930 on August 30th, Admiral Fraser and I called on Fleet Admiral Nimitz aboard his flagship the USS South Dakota. Immediately after this call Admiral Fraser and I called on Admiral Halsey, Commander of the Third Fleet, on his flagship the USS Missouri.

At 1500 on August 30th, I called on Admiral R.K. Turner, Commander Amphibious Forces, U.S. Pacific Fleet, who was a guest of Fleet Admiral Nimitz aboard his flagship the South Dakota. After a long talk with Admiral Turner he invited me to dinner that evening. There were present at the dinner, Fleet Admiral Nimitz, Admiral Turner, Lieutenant General Geiger, U.S. Marine Corp, Rear Admiral J.J. Ballentine, Liaison Officer on the staff of General McArthur, and Rear Admiral Forrest Sherman, Deputy Chief of Staff to Fleet Admiral Nimitz. After dinner Admiral Nimitz, Admiral Sherman and I discussed matters relating to the British Pacific Fleet.

At 1500 on September 1st, I called on Fleet Admiral Nimitz and Rear Admiral Sherman for a further discussion of matters relating to the U.S. and British Pacific Fleets.

At 1700, Fleet Admiral Nimitz and Rear Admiral Sherman came on board the HMS Duke of York for a visit with Admiral Fraser. After which, they were introduced to the officers in the wardroom, gunroom and warrant officers mess.

Admiral Fraser and his party of eleven officers, including Air Vice Marshal L.M. Isitt, representative of New Zealand at the surrender ceremony, Lieutenant General Gaidner, British Army Liaison Officer on General McArthur's Staff, Captain Nicholl, the Commanding Officer of the HMS Duke of York, several other staff officers and I arrived on board the USS Missouri at 0820 on September 2nd. Many of the other U.S. and Allied officers had already arrived. We were shown to our places on the veranda deck of the Missouri, which is on the starboard side, forward of the Admiral's cabin.

General McArthur and his staff arrived at 0840 and were shown into the Admiral's cabin.

At 0855 the Japanese representatives who were lying off the ship in their boat were called along side. Among these representatives were Foreign Minister Shigemitsu, and 10 other representatives of the Japanese Government, Army and Navy. Shigemitsu has a wooden leg and had considerable difficulty negotiating the gangway and ship's ladders. They were conducted to the place reserved for them, just forward of the table where the signing was to take place, and made to stand there awaiting the arrival of General McArthur, Fleet Admiral Nimitz, etc., who were still in the Admiral's cabin. At exactly 0900, General McArthur, Fleet Admiral Nimitz and Admiral Halsey arrived on the opposite side of the table from the Japanese representatives, and General McArthur delivered a most appropriate and moving address. He then called upon the Japanese representatives to sign the surrender instrument, which they did. The Japanese Government representatives wore morning coats and top hats and looked exactly like undertakers. The Army and Navy representatives wore uniforms without swords. As the first Japanese representative stepped forward he laid on the table a document signed by the Emperor authorizing the representatives to sign on his behalf. After the Japanese had signed, General McArthur signed on behalf of all the Allied Powers. Standing behind General McArthur was General Wainwright, who had been captured at Corrigidor, and General Percival, British Army, who was captured at Singapore. General Wainwright was in such a weakened condition that he was obliged to hold on to General McArthur's chair occasionally. Among other guests present were several officers and men of the cruiser Houston, who had been taken as prisoners by the Japanese and released within the past few days. General McArthur was followed in the order named by representatives of the following Allied Powers:

    Fleet Admiral Nimitz for United States of America.
    General Hsu Yung Chang for China.
    Admiral Sir Bruce Fraser for the United Kingdom.
    Lieut. General Kuzma Nikolaevish Dereyanko for United
      Soviet Socialist Republic.
    General Sir Thomas Blamey for Australia.
    Colonel L. Moore Cosgrave for Canada.
    General LeClerc for France.
    Air Vice Marshal Isitt for New Zealand.
    Admiral Helfrich for United Kingdom of Netherlands.

Immediately after the signing General McArthur announced the proceedings closed and retired to the Admiral's cabin, followed by the other signatories. The Japanese left the ship. As the Japanese left the ship a fleet of 1400 carrier based aircraft from Task Force 38, which was still at sea, flew over the USS Missouri.

The complete lists of attending U.S. Flag Officers, Allied and Japanese representatives were as follows:

Maj. Gen. KEAN	Maj. Gen. VALDES	Maj. Gen. RYAN
Maj. Gen. WHITLOCK	Maj. Gen. SVERDROP	Maj. Gen. BERTRANDIAS
Maj. Gen. WILLOUGHBY	Maj. Gen. WURTSMITH	Maj. Gen. BYERS
Brig. Gen. CHAMBERS	Lt. Gen. GAIRDNER	Lt. Gen. WHITEHEAD
Maj. Gen. MARSHALL	Maj. Gen. SWING	Maj. Gen. FRINK
Maj. Gen. CHAMBERLIN	Maj. Gen. STIVERS	Maj. Gen. AKIN
Maj. Gen. CASEY	Maj. Gen. MARQUAT	General STILWELL
General KRUEGER	General HODGES	General SPAATZ
General KEENEY	Lt. Gen. EICHELBERGER	Lt. Gen. RICHARDSON
Lt. Gen. SUTHERLAND	Lt. Gen. STYER	Lt. Gen. GILES

U.S. NAVY

Fleet Admiral Chester W. Nimitz
Admiral Richmond K. Turner
Vice Admiral John S. McCain
Vice Admiral Frederick C. Sherman
Rear Admiral John F. Shafroth, Jr.
Rear Admiral Oscar C. Badger
Rear Admiral James C. Jones
Rear Admiral Lynde D. McCormick
Rear Admiral Lloyd J. Wiltse
Rear Admiral Robert B. Carney
Rear Admiral John J. Ballentine
Commodore Joel T. Boone, (MC)
Commodore Roland N. Smoot
Commodore John M. Higgens
Captain C. Julian Wheeler
Colonel Theodore J. Dayharsh, USA
Captain Edwin J. Layton
Captain Fitzhugh Lee
Captain Herbert I. Hoerner
Commander Howell A. Lamar

Admiral William F. Halsey, Jr
Vice Admiral John H. Towers
Vice Adm. Charles A. Lockwood, Jr.
Lieut. General Roy S. Geiger, USMC
Rear Admiral Donald B. Beary,
Rear Admiral Howard F. Kingman
Rear Admiral Wilder D. Baker
Rear Admiral Ingram C. Sowell
Rear Admiral Gerald F. Bogan
Rear Admiral Forrest P. Sherman
Commodore Oliver O. Kessing
Brig. General J.H. Fellows, USMC
Commodore Roger W. Simpson
Commodore Joseph C. Cronin
Captain Tom B. Hill
Captain Ralph E. Wilson
Captain John G. Cross
Captain Marion C. Cheek
Captain Arthur H. Taylor
Lieutenant Commander Kaufman

ALLIED REPRESENTATIVES

United States.
    Fleet Admiral Chester W. Nimitz.

Republic of China.
    Gen. Hsu Yung-Chang
    Vice Adm. Yang Hsuan Chang
    Lt. Gen. Chu Shih Ming
    Maj. Gen. Wang Chih
    Col. Li Sho Chang
    Col. Wang Pei Cheng

United Kingdom.
    Admiral Sir Bruce Fraser, KCB, KBE
    Captain, A.D. Nicholl, CBE, DSO
    Comdr. R.H. Courage, OBE, DSC
    Comdr. (S) A.P. Cartwright, SANF(V) Senior South African
                                                     Officer present.
    Surgeon Lieutenant G.R. Gayman, RCNVR, Senior Canadian
                                                       Officer present.
    Lieutenant V.C. Merry, RNVR
    Vice Adm. Sir H.B. Rawlings, KCB, OBE
    Commodore J.P.L. Reid, Chief Staff Officer
    Lieutenant G.E. Cook, RNVR
    Rear Adm. E.J.P. Brind, CB, CBE
    Lieutenant E.B. Ashmore, DSC

United Soviet Socialist Republic.
    Lt. Gen. Kuzma Nikolaevish Derevyanko
    Maj. Gen. Nikolai Vasilevich Voronov
    Rear Adm. Andrey Mitrofanovich Stetzenko
    Maj. Ivan Joseph Vorovsky
    Capt. Nikolai Michailovich Karamishev
    Lt. Nikolai Nikolaevich Tulinov

Commonwealth of Australia.
    Gen. Sir Thomas Blamey
    Lt. Gen. F.H. Berryman
    Rear Adm. George D. Moore
    Air Vice Marshal Jones
    Air Vice Marshal Bostick
    Commodore J.A. Collins
    Capt. J. Balfour

ALLIED REPRESENTATIVES (cont'd)

Dominion of Canada.
    Col. L. Moore Cosgrave

Republic of France.
    General LeClerc

Commonwealth of New Zealand.
    Air Vice Marshal Isitt, RNZAF
    Lt. J.D. Alfingham, RNZNR

United Kingdom of Netherlands.
    Admiral Helfrich
    Lt. Gen. L.H. Van Oyen
    Col. C. Giebel
    Comdr. A.A. Fresco

JAPANESE REPRESENTATIVES

Signers:
    Mr. Mamoru Shigemitsu, Foreign Minister
    General Yoshijiro Umezo, Chief of Staff, Japanese Army Headquarters

Delegates
    Katsuo Okazaki, Director General, Central Liaison Office
    Saburo Ihta, Director, Central Liaison Officer
    Shunichi, Kase, Director, Number One Government Information Bureau.

Army
    Lieutenant Gen. Shuichi Miyakazi, Representing Army General Headquarters
    Major General Yatsuji Nagai, Army Staff
    Colonel Kaziyi Sugita, Army Staff

Navy
    Rear Admiral Tadatoshi Tomoika, Representing Naval General Headquarters
    Rear Admiral Ichiro Yakayama, Navy Headquarters
    Captain Katsuo Chiba, Navy Headquarters.

When the surrender ceremony was over and after leaving the USS Missouri, Admiral Fraser celebrated the occasion by inviting Vice Admiral Rawlings, Commander of the British Carrier Task Force, his Chief of Staff, his own staff and the Captain of the Duke of York to his cabin.

In the afternoon, Admiral Fraser invited a larger group to what he called a "Musical Sunset". This was attended by Admiral Halsey and about 12 of his staff, Admiral Rawlings, a number of his staff, Rear Admiral Brind, several of his staff, and the Commanding Officers of all British ships present. The guests arrived on board about half an hour before sunset and proceeded to the Admiral's cabin for refreshments.

Prior to sunset flags of the leading Allied and British Dominions were hoisted to the yard arms on both masts. At sunset the band played the evening colors and all of the flags were hauled down simultaneously. It was a very colorful ceremony, quite unlike any in our navy, and we all enjoyed it very much. The band continued to play after colors and lent considerable gaity to the occasion. This marked the end of the surrender ceremonies as far as we are concerned.

On September 4th I accompanied Admiral Fraser to Yokohama in HMAS Warramunga. The Captain of this destroyer, Commander Clark, is a personal friend whom I met in Sydney, which made this trip especially pleasant.

The journey was only about 45 minutes; at the end of which time we went along side the same dock from which Doanda and I sailed in the Dollar Line Steamer, President Jackson, almost exactly 16 years ago.

Admiral Fraser and his party were intending to call on General McArthur and then to visit the British Embassy at Tokyo. I, therefore, invited the Captain of the Warramunga to go with me. We went first to General McArthur's Headquarters where I contacted Rear Admiral Ballentine, the U.S. Naval Liaison Officer on General McArthur's Staff. Arrangements were made there for a car to take us to Tokyo but Commander Clark did not want to get that far from his ship so we just rode around Yokohama.

The city of Yokohama is about 80 percent destroyed. Apparently it was done largely by fire bombs as there were no bomb craters visible. The dock area, with the exception of an escort carrier which was partially sunk along side the breakwater, was left undamaged. Undoubtedly this was so planned so that our own ships could make use of the docks, which they are doing in a big way.

With the exception of occasional concrete buildings scattered throughout the town, the whole place was laid almost completely flat. There was hardly a wooden building left standing. Although I realize that there must have been many people killed in these raids, I couldn't help wondering where the rest of the people lived, when it suddenly dawned on me that they must be living in the hovels constructed of rusted corrugated metal strips salvaged from burnt out buildings. The people were apparently well nourished but were wearing very shoddy clothes and dejected expressions. One thing I noticed in particular was that all the women were wearing trousers instead of kimonas which they used to wear.

On September 5th, Captain Nicholl of the Duke of York and I, together with a number of other officers visited the Japanese naval dock yard Yokosuka. We landed just forward of the USS Piedmont, a destroyer tender, which was flying the flag of Rear Admiral Badger who is in charge of the shore landing activities in the Tokyo area. We took a bus and proceded to the administration building to make our numbers with Admiral Badger but found that he had gone to luncheon. We succeeded, however, in getting the use of a jeep which took us to the dry dock area where we ate our picnic luncheon along side the big dry dock and in the shade of a big crane.

To our complete amazement we found the dry dock being used as a storage dump, the bottom of it being completely covered with old boilers, derricks, rolls of wire and junk of all description. There was about 18 inches of water in the bottom of the dock and therefore everything in the dock was being rapidly eaten up with rust.

After luncheon we made a tour of the shops surrounding the dry dock. This area of the dock yard had apparently been given over to the building of midget submarines and Kaitans, or human torpedoes. There must have been about 200 of them in various stages of completion. The indications, since practically all of the Japanese fleet had been sunk, were that they had decided to expend all of their efforts toward the sinking of the invasion fleet with these midget submarines.

In view of the fact that all of these midgets or Kaitans would have had to be carried on a larger ship to the launching area, it is doubtful if they would have been of much value even if they had been completed in time, except possibly for use against transports anchored near the landing beaches.

In going through the shops, one could not help being impressed with the primitive nature of their setup. All of their tools and everything in sight appeared to be of poor quality and more or less make-shift.

After leaving the dock yard we proceded to the former HIJMS Nagato. The Nagato, which was then at the navy yard, had been hit by two bombs during the Third Fleet raids on July 15 and 16. One bomb hit the bridge, killing the Captain, Executive Officer and a number of others; the other hit just forward of the main mast, knocking overboard the smoke stack and the top mast. I climbed up to the top of the foremast, which is constructed in a pagoda-like fashion and gave the ship a top heavy appearance. All of the anti aircraft guns had been removed in accordance with the terms of the surrender. I also took a look around below decks and visited the Admiral's cabin in which the Commander in Chief of the Japanese combined fleets entertained Admiral Bristol and the other visiting foreign admirals and me so royally in 1928 at the coronation naval review.

The table in the Admiral's cabin was covered with instruments and samples of clothing found among the ship's stores and it was very difficult to realize that this was the same place where the impressive dinner referred to above was held.

The ship was in charge of seven U.S. Naval Officers and about 60 men who were placed on board for security purposes. They had, however, gotten up steam and the ship's generators were furnishing electricity. Apparently no one knows so far what will ultimately be done with the ship or dock yard.

My first glimpse of Istanbul, then called Constantinople, was from the porthole of an Italian steamer at anchor near Leander's tower in the Bosphorous in the early morning of November 28, 1921. Nothing was visible except the tops of the minarets of the hundreds of mosques which dot the area as the surface of the city, the Bosphorous, and the Golden Horn were covered with a thick blanket of fog.

Little did I know at that time that I was to make my home in the American Embassy there for the next three years. Constantinople is fascinating at any time but it so happened that the next three years were to prove to be among the most interesting in its long and varied history.

My former shipmate, Glenn Howell, and I were returning from two year's tour of duty on the China Station and had planned a three day visit to the Turkish capital before boarding the Simplon Orient Express for Paris, thence aboard S.S. Leviathan to our respective homes in the U.S.A.

As soon as the fog lifted on that bright November morning the entire city, the Golden Horn, the Bosphorous, and Scutari on the Asiatic Mainland were revealed in all their glistening beauty. Our arrival being unheralded, we hired a caique from the many which surrounded the ships and, piloted by our red-fezzed caique-ji, were soon on our way to the landing at Galata near the bridge which spans the Golden Horn between Galata and Stamboul, (The old Turkish Quarter).

With the assistance of some Hamals (porters) we cleared the Customs, hired an arriba (victoria) and were soon on our way to the Pera Palace Hotel. In the usual manner of tourists, we spent the first day sightseeing but, recalling that my mother had asked me to call on a former schoolmate of hers. I found upon inquiring that she and her husband, Rear Admiral Mark L. Bristol U.S.N., our U.S. High Commissioner to Turkey, were living in the American Embassy, only a few blocks away from the Pera Palace Hotel where we were staying. Mrs. Bristol was an attractive and lovely lady whose charm superbly fitted her as a distinguished representative of the U.S. Both Mrs. Bristol and I were born in Mobile, Alabama, and her family and mine had known each other all their lives. My family has lived in Mobile for well over 100 years. Before World War I Mobile was very little different from the way it had been in the middle of the 19th Century. Having been under 5 flags it still savored of the flavor of Spanish and French Culture and its people favored the customs and traditions of the "Old South" with all of its beauty and grace.

I prevailed upon my travelling companion to go with me and together we presented ourselves at the door of the American Embassy. There we were greeted by a very ferocious looking Turk, called a Kavass (body-guard) resplendent in the most magnificent uniform I have ever seen before or since. Hassan, whose name I learned later, took our cards and returned soon after with an invitation from Admiral and Mrs. Bristol to join them at tea. They had just finished a game of bridge with some personal friends. After a very pleasant visit, which far exceeded the usual twenty minutes official call, we returned to the Pera Palace and were changing for dinner when a mutual friend, Lieutenant Hamilton Vose Bryant U.S.N., announced himself at the hotel desk and soon thereafter bounded into our room. "Ham" always "bounded" because he was always in a hurry, but the message he brought almost stopped us in our tracks. It happened that just about that time

Admiral Bristol was about to lose two of his aides, of whom Bryant was one, and Admiral Bristol wanted to find out if we would be interested in joining his staff.

We told "Ham" that we would think it over but that we had heard that there were a number of White Russian cabarets run by Czarist refugees in the town and we were planning to visit them that evening. "Ham" said that he knew them all and he would "show us the town" as soon as we were ready. We gleefully accepted and have never regretted an instant of it as the food, singing and dancing surpassed anything that I had seen. Ham's parting words were "Remember, the Admiral would like to see you both tomorrow morning at the Embassy at 10 o'clock."

Ten o'clock arrived all too soon "after a night on the town", but by that time my friend Glenn who was seriously interested in a very attractive and talented young lady in New York, decided it was not the time to delay his return to the States.

Being "footloose and fancy-free" however at 10 a.m. I duly presented myself to Admiral Bristol at his office in the Embassy who, after several searching questions invited me to join his Staff as Aide and Flag-Lieutenant. Having just left the U.S. Asiatic fleet where I had spent approximately two years, I was primarily interested in how long the new duty would last, but Admiral Bristol estimated not more than six months, which I thought would be just right. I stayed however three years and he was there almost three years more after I left. However, I don't regret a moment of my three years because they were interesting not only from a personal but an International point of view.

Having spent most of my time since World War I either in Guantanamo, Cuba, or the Orient, I was not aware of the intensely interesting situation which had developed in the Near East following World War I.

After the collapse of the Turkish Armies in October 1918, Talaat and Enver Pasha who were the titular heads of Government under Sultan Mohammed VI escaped and soon thereafter, the Allies (British, French, Italians and Greeks) took over the administration of Constantinople.

A new Turkish Cabinet, favorable to the Allies under the leadership of Damad Ferid Pasha was set up in March 1919.

Soon thereafter, the Italians landed at Adalia, their first step toward the taking over of Southwestern Anatolia (Asia Minor).

On May 14, 1919, with the approval of the Allies and supported by Allied Naval Forces, the Greeks landed in Smyrna.

Within a few days, May 19, 1919, Mustapha Kemal Pasha, the hero of the Dardanelles Campaign, took over at Samsun as Inspector of the Turkish 3rd. Army. Being an ardent nationalist, he began at once to organize resistance to the further dismemberment of Turkey for which he was officially dismissed from the army by the Sultan and outlawed.

It was about this time that Rear Admiral Mark L. Bristol U.S.N., who had been ordered to Constantinople earlier, took over as U.S. High Commissioner to Turkey. The United States had never been at war with Turkey but, at the instigation of their German allies, Turkey had broken diplomatic relations with the U.S. on April 20, 1917. Throughout World War I and until Admiral Bristol's appointment as High Commissioner, U.S. affairs had been handled by the Swedish Legation.

The original purpose of ordering Admiral Bristol to Constantinople, where he arrived on board the destroyer Schley in January 1919 was merely to investigate the situation there after

World War I. American interests there included the tobacco business, as large quantities of Turkish tobacco were grown along the shores of the Black Sea and exported to the U.S., two American colleges, Robert College and Constantinople College (otherwise known as the American School For Girls), plus the activities of the American Red Cross, and other relief organizations. There were also many American missionaries scattered throughout the Near East. Admiral Bristol's excellent reports and capable handling of the many sensitive situations existing there at the time were soon recognized in Washington. Other ships were ordered to his command and in a short time, as stated above, he was elevated from the station of Senior Naval Officer present, which in our government includes certain prerogatives which personal rank alone does not enjoy, to the status of High Commissioner. His long tenure in that position, as well as the friendly relations between the U.S. and modern Turkey, which exist even until today, are a tribute to his ability, understanding and farsightedness, as a diplomat as well as a flag officer in the U.S. Navy.

In addition to being High Commissioner, Admiral Bristol was also commander of the U.S. Naval Detachment in Turkish Waters (later changed to Eastern Mediterranean) which at one time consisted of as many as twenty destroyers, several tenders, the Naval yacht Scorpion, and a sizable Supply Base on shore. The Scorpion was our former stationnaire which under the capitulations, the United States, like other leading powers, had permitted to keep in Constantinople in order to safeguard the American Embassy personnel.

This dual assignment of Admiral Bristol's led to a most unusual situation whenever the Commander of U.S. Naval Forces in European Waters, a Vice Admiral Long arrived in Constantinople. Because as High Commissioner with the rank of Ambassador, Rear Admiral Bristol was senior to Admiral Long, but as Commander of the U.S. Naval Detachment, Rear Admiral Bristol was junior to Vice Admiral Long. Therefore, when Rear Admiral Bristol, as High Commissioner, returned Vice Admiral Long's call he received a 19 gun salute, but when he paid his first call as Detachment Commander he received 13 guns.

After Mustapha Kemal's dismissal from the Army he convened a Nationalist Congress at Erzerum and later at Sivas, after which, in the Declaration of Sivas, the Nationalists affirmed the Unity of Turkish territory and declared against Allied occupation and the formation of an Armenian State. Out of this grew the National Pact which, among others, enunciated the following principles: self-determination, the security of Constantinople, the opening the straits, the rights of minorities, and abolition of the Capitulations. The Capitulations were the name given to a group of extra-territorial privileges which had existed for many hundreds of years. They consisted of special rights which had been wrested from Turkey by foreign governments dating back to Venetian times. Among these was the right of maintaining armed yachts, called "stationaires", in Constantinople for the protection of Embassy personnel. This was, of course, regarded by the Turks as an infringement of their Sovereignty.

In October 1919, the Nationalists won the elections in Parliament and the new Cabinet of Ali Riza of the Sultan's Government attempted conciliation with the Nationalists, but this did not work because by this time the Nationalists had the "bit between their teeth" and were not about to be dominated by by the Sultan and his Government.

On January 28, 1920 the National Pact was adopted by the Parliament in Constantinople.

Many of the Nationalist members of the Parliament then, secretly and by night, crossed the Bosphorus to join the provisional government set up by the Nationalists at Angora (Ankara) with Mustapha Kemal as President and the Parliament of the Constantinople government was dissolved on April 11, 1920.

In the meantime, although protesting that they did not intend to deny the City to the Turks, an Allied Force under the British General Milne, occupied Constantinople.

The announced plan of the Allies was to keep the Straits open and protect the Armenians, but it is believed that their real object was to check the spread of Nationalism. Many Nationalists were denounced by the Sultan's Government and exiled.

One of the first acts of the new provisional government was to make an agreement with Russia by which they obtained much needed Military supplies.

On June 10, 1920 the Treaty of Sèvres, prepared by the Paris Peace Conference, was presented to the Sultan's Government at Constantinople. The Treaty would have practically obliterated the Turkish nation. It was vigorously protested by the Sultan and uncompromisingly opposed by the Nationalists.

Later in June the Greeks began their advance into the interior of Anatolia, reaching as far as the Sakkaria River, and even threatened Angora (Ankara). They also took Brusa and Adrianopolis.

On August 10, 1920, the Constantinople Government signed the Treaty of Sevres which, in effect, doomed the Sultan and his

Government.

Therefore, with the exception of the Greeks, Mustapha Kemal had suceeded in ridding the heartland of Turkey of his enemies.

In February 1921, the London Conference of Allied Powers with both the Constantinople and Nationalist Governments, as well as the Greeks, broke down with no agreement. Mustapha Kemal then took matters into his own hands. He made a separate agreement with the Italians in March 1921 which they undertook to evacuate Anatolia in return for economic concessions.

The Greeks reached the high point of their advance into Anatolia in August 1921 but, as stated above, failed to reach Angora.

The Franklin Bouillon Understanding between France and Mustapha Kemal was reached following months of hostility in Cilicia. At this time France, finally agreed to evacuate Cilicia, also in return for economic concessions.

It was about this time, November 28, 1921, that I arrived in Constantinople. Thus, as the personal Aide to the High Commissioner, living in the Embassy as a member of the Admiral and Mrs. Bristols official family, I had the extraordinary privilege of an eye-witness view of the transformation of the Ottoman Empire, which had been in existence over 600 years, into the Turkish Republic. The Sultan was still on his throne, Turkish men still wore fezzes, their women most becoming tcharchoffs, and the muezzins still called the faithful to prayer. The meetings of the religious sect of Whirling Dervishes were most exciting events to watch, and even the Howling Dervishes which by that time had more or less degenerated into a tourist attraction, were worth seeing.

The Constantinople Bazaar, a medieval edition of the modern shopping center, was always a fascinating spot to visit. It consisted of an enormous, old, rambling one story building, with a ceiling suggestive of the tops of many tents joined together, under which were congregated hundreds of stalls filled with every conceivable type of merchandise, from kitchen utensils to Oriental rugs, some of which was worth thousands of dollars. A favorite pass time on rainy days was for a group of friends to get together and spend the morning or afternoon in the Bazaar.

None of us who lived in the area would ever buy anything of value on the first visit. Sometimes it would take many visits, extending over a period of six months or so, to conclude the purchase of an article of great value like a Persian chest. This battle of wits was, of course, part of the fun, and we knew many of the merchants, whom we used to scold for bringing out their less valuable merchandise and selling it to unsuspecting tourists for outrageous prices which they would not have dared to ask us.

At that time, there wasn't a modern fire-engine in the whole City. The only fire fighting equipment consisted of water tanks and pumps carried separately by groups of men who made their living by selling their services to the owners of the buildings which were on fire. Unfortunately, serious delays would often occur while the owners and fire-fighters agreed on a price.

Any one of eight languages, English, French, Italian, Turkish, Greek, Armenian, Russian or German, could be heard in various parts of the city. Fortunately, among foreigners, English and French were the most generally accepted means of communication. So among my first duties was to brush up on my meagre knowledge of French. the nedd of which was recognized when a Secretary from the Sublime Porte (Foreign Office), in his impeccable French, called my office and invited Admiral Bristol to come and see the Grand Vizier. My duties included being Chief of Protocol of the Embassy, organizing the Embassy parties, making the High Commissioner's appointments, supervising his transportation, including his cars and the Admirals barges, his orchestra, the European chefs as well as accompanying him to all official functions.

In addition to a staff of nine U.S. Naval officers, our High Commissioner had a Counsellor of Embassy, First, Second and Third Secretaries, two Military Attaches, and two Commercial Attaches.

One of my most agreeable duties was to go out to the large merchant cruise ships like the Mauretania, Homeric, etc, which were taken off the North Atlantic run in the winter, in the Admirals Barge and meet the passengers who had letters of introduction to the High Commissioner and Mrs. Bristol. One of the most unusual of the the tourist attractions were the underground reservoirs called cisterns which had been built years ago to supply the city with water in case of siege. There were hundreds of others of course, like Santa Sophia, the Seraglio, the Blue Mosque and so on, and by the time I left Constantinople I could easily have obtained a license as an official guide.

The British, French and Italian Forces of Occupation, as well as the Greeks, had not only troops but naval detachments in Constantinople, and one of the unusual features of this occupation was that many of the officers of these forces also had their families with tehm. These, together with the diplomatic representatives, their staffs, and families, as well as the Turkish Imperial families and some members of the Russian Imperial Court, such as Prince Yresopoff and Baron and Baroness Wrangle made an absolutely glittering international society.

At that time, before the Kemalist Revolution had gathered momentum, political conditions in Constantinople were relatively quiet. The opportunity was thus afforded for study and enjoyment of this picturesque and fascinating area. Located on the European shore of the Bosphorus, Constantinople is about twenty miles from the Black Sea, and on the northern edge of the Sea of Marmora which connects at its South Western extremity with the Dardanelles. On the European side of the Bosphorus, between Constantinople and the Black Sea lies Therapia, the site of the summer embassies of many of the great powers before World War I, and the center of all summer social activities in that area. Behind Therapia, and extending almost to the Black Sea, was the Black Forest, a favorite picnic area for the whole region.

Across from Therapia on the Asiatic side, about ten miles inland, was located the Polish Village, an almost unbelievable area peopled entirely by Poles and their descendants, who had fought with the Turks against the Russians in the Crimean War. For this service, they and their families had been given this plot of land in perpetuity, tax free. Here, therefore had been built a village similar in all respects to a village in Poland, complete with polish style houses, thatched roofs, etc. I spent a day and a night in this village while on a hunting trip and throughly enjoyed the delicious Polish country style food.

Another most picturesque section was Ayoub at the head of the Golden Horn. A famous old Turkish cemetery there surrounds an area known as the "Sweet Waters of Europe" so called because, at this point, a stream of fresh water flows into the Golden Horn, an arm of the Bosphorus which is, of course, salt water. A similar area on the Asiatic shore of the Boshporous is also known as the "Sweet Waters of Asia". Also on the Asiatic side were large clearings where the British sometimes held "point to point" races or "trooping of the colors" ceremonies on the King's Birthday. These were staged by the mounted troops of the British Forces of Occupation. They were most colorful events and were always attended by the Diplomatic Corps, Naval and Military Forces and High Turkish officials.

The Sea of Marmora, between the Bosphorous and the Dardanelles was equally attractive for recreation area, and lastly those interested in the Gallipoli Campaign could within a few days explore the battle-fields and also see some of the remains of the allied ships wrecked on the shore at the Mediterranean entrance to the Dardanelles.

From an historical point of few this whole terrain is hallowed ground. For instance, on the Asiatic side of the Bosphorous, the remains of the Turkish fort Anatoli Hissar, from which the Turks launched their attack against Constantine in 1453 and the ruins of Roumeli Hissar, the Turkish Fort on the European side of the Bosphorous, are still standing. From the roof garden of the American Embassy it was easy to visualize the chain which the defenders of Constantinople stretched across the Golden Horn in 1453 in order to prevent the Turkish approach in boats from that direction. Lastly one can wander over the old walls at the Western end of the city through which the Turkish hordes finally entered and captured the city. Ruins of earlier civilizations abound here as it is a fertile field for continuing investigations by archeologists.

Life for the common people of Constantinople continued as it had been since the end of World War I. It was an era of Nationalism in which Turkish shops were closed Fridays, Jewish shops on Saturdays, and Sunday was, of course, a holiday for the Christian popoulation. The magnificent old church of Santa Sophia was still used as a Mosque and one of the most impressive religious rites that I can remember was to see that enormous nave on the "Night of Power" during Ramadan filled with thousands of Turks that were praising Allah according to their custom.

The Sultan of Turkey, Mehmed VI regularly attended prayer at one of the many mosques in Constantinople and this was an occasion which attracted thousands of onlookers along the route and at the mosque which he had selected. Privileged guests, including our parties, often were invited to have Turkish coffee in the Sultans palace after his return from prayer.

Thousands of Czarist refugees walked the streets looking for jobs, most of them unsuccessfully. Many of them were living in former Turkish Army barracks which had been evacuated when the Allied Forces of occupation took over. They were mostly supported by money supplied by the American Red Cross and the Near East Relief Societies. General Wrangle, his wife Baroness Wrangle and their children were there, as were many other Russian nobility, some of whom lived in the former Russian Imperial Embassy which had been re-arranged to accomodate more refugees by subdividing the ball-room into smaller living spaces using blankets as partitions. On stag parties it was a real treat to see General Wrangle, who always wore his Cossack uniform, perform his Cossack "sword dance".

One party, which will always stand out in my memory, was a dinner given in honor of Mrs. Bristol at the Czarist Russian Embassy (still under control of the White Russians) on the top of a hill at Bayonkdere overlooking the Bosphorous on a perfectly gorgeous moonlight night in summer. Mrs. Bristol had been the head of the Russian Relief Organization and won the appreciation and gratitude of the thousands of Russian refugees in Constantinople at that time. The dinner was given in the garden of the Embassy and the setting was really like a dream. For entertainment all through the dinner of about eight courses, there were talented Russian singers and dancers. The moonlight shinning down through the trees gave a sort of Elysian aspect to the whole evening. After the party was over and the glasses were thrown over our shoulders in accordance with the Russian custom after the last toast I started to escort the daughter of the General Commanding the Italian Forces of Occupation in Constantinople down to the Admiral's Barge at the dock at the foot of the hill. Mrs. Bristol came up to me and said, "No you don't, Juliane", and offered her arm to me instead. She explained later that my Mother would never forgive her if she let me become romatically involved with a foreigner.

In March of 1922, the Allied Powers agreed to a revision of the Treaty of Sevres, which had never been ratified by either Turkish government, and attempted to settle the Greco-Turkish conflict, but the Turks refused to grant an armistice until the Greeks had evacuated Anatolia.

The Greeks in July 1922, under the leadership of King Constantine advanced through Eastern Thrace toward Constantinople and threatened to capture the City. This would hardly have been possible from a military point of view because Constantinople was already occupied by British, French and Italian troops, but, since it was well known that the British Prime Minister, Lloyd George, was favorable to the Greeks there was speculation that the

British, who had the largest garrison in Constantinople, might not oppose the entry. Furthermore, there was an old saying among the Greeks that one day they would recapture Constantinople, when they had a King named Constantine, which was the case at that time.

Excitement in Constantinople ran quite high, therefore, and emergency plans were made to concentrate all American women and children at the American embassy and evacuate them on U.S. Naval ships. General Harrington, the British General commanding the Allied forces of Occupation left suddenly for London to confer with the British Prime Minister, but after a few days the tension relaxed as the Allied powers issued an ultimatum to Greece forbidding the occupation of Constantinople.

Soon thereafter, the Turks began a counter offensive against the Greeks. To those of us who were not directly involved but were, nevertheless, eyewitnesses there was a certain amount of humor connected with these manouevrings, because, not withstanding the fact that the British and French were technically allies and jointly occupying Constantinople, it was widely rumored that the British were furnishing arms to the Greeks and the French were likewise helping the Turks.

On August 30, 1922, the Turks recaptured Afium Karahissar, and Brusa on September 5th. The Greek armies were driven in confusion to the Coast. A few days later the Turks took Smyrna which was almost completely destroyed by fire. No one knows who started the fire but each side blamed the other. An American destroyer on the scene participated in the rescue of many refugees who were literally driven by the flames into the sea. Prime Minister Lloyd George appealed to the Allied Powers and British

Dominions to join in defense of the Straits (Dardanelles) against the Turks.

Both the French and Italians refused and only Australia and New Zealand, which had furnished the famed Anzacs (Australian and New Zealand Arms Corps), in World War I showed any interest, but on September 16 a British force under the overall command General Harrington occupied Chanak, a former British fort on the Dardanelles.

In October, a conference between the Allies and Ismet Pasha, representing the Turkish Nationalists, met at Moudania. The Allies agreed to the return of Adrianople and Eastern Thrace to the Turks, and the Turks agreed to the neutralization of the straits under international control.

By this time, from our embassy roof garden, the bayonets of the Turkish Nationalist soldiers could be seen glistening in the sun-light on the hills above Scutari on the Asiatic side of the Bosphorous opposite Constantinople. This was not a good omen for the Sultan, so, on November 17, 1922 he was evacuated on the British battleship Malaya and dropped out of sight.

Mustapha Kemal then proclaimed that his successor, Abdul Mejid, a cousin of the former Sultan, would become Caliph rather than Sultan thus ending in name, as well as in fact, the existence of the Ottoman Empire, which at one time included a large part of Eastern Europe as well as many countries bordering on the Mediterranean.

In view of subsequent events, this showed what a clever sense of timing Mustapha Kemal had, as there were meny that felt that the abolition of the Sultanate would create a great uproar throughout the Mohamedan World, inasmuch as the Sultan was the head of the Moslem religion in Turkey as well as Chief of State.

This change, however, was made without any sizeable opposition, because the Caliph was not deposed at that time.

The scene was now set for the Turks to cash in on their recent military successes so, on November 20, 1922, a peace conference between them and the Allies convened in Lausanne, Switzerland. Though not bona-fide members of the conference Ambassador Childs from Rome, Minister Grew from Berne and Rear Admiral Bristol attended as observers. Of course, I accompanied Admiral Bristol as his aide. Our delegation was quartered at the Beau Rivage Hotel and I had the unusual opportunity of sitting as U.S. representative on the Health and Sanitary Committee in the place of our regular observer who was frequently to ill to attend the sessions. Each of the leading nations of Europe, including Soviet Russia, had representatives at the Conference, most of whom lived at the Beau Rivage Hotel, where banquets were frequently held included some of the most distinguished personalities in Europe including their wives. Among them were Lord and Lady Curzon, Sir Horace and Lady Rumbolt, M. Bompard of France, Marquis Garroni of Italy, M. Venizelos of Greece, Ismet Pasha the Turkish representative, and M. Tchicherin, the Soviet delegate.

After heated disputes about the abolition of Capitulations and the Status of Mosul, the Conference broke up temporarily on February 4, 1923. It resumed its deliberations on April 23rd with Minister Joseph Grew as our observer and concluded its work on July 24th 1923.

After our return to Constantinople I had the unique experience of flying over Constantinople in a British fighter plane. In my opinion this flight of several squadrons of British fighter planes was "laid on", as the British phrase it, to impress the Turks and expedite the conclusion of the peace treaty, which it apparently did, but for me it was that time a rare opportunity to see the city of Constantinople from the air. It was an inspiring sight, studded with minarets and almost surrounded by the Bosphorous, sea of Marmora and Golden Horn.

Also in the spring of 1923 I visited Odessa in Soviet Russia in one of our destroyers which was participating in the American Relief Administration plan to relieve the famine-ridden sufferer of Russia. At that time one of Admiral Bristol's destroyers was acting as station ship in each of the larger Soviet Black Sea ports to facilitate the arrival and discharge of thousands of tons of wheat which were the gift of the American people to the starving Russians. As my visit only lasted a few days, it was not possible to acquire much information, but the city of Odessa looked quite forlorn with the heads knocked off all the Czarist monuments and the long bread-lines which were in evidence all over the city. One evening I was invited, in a group of officers, to the apartment of one of the Bolshevik liaison officers named Margolis who told us that the whole house had formerly belonged to his whole family but had been divided by the government into eight apartments. At that time the Bolsheviks were still trying to get along without money but our host told us that this did not really work as, more often that not, the bread supply would give out while large numbers of people with bread tickets would still be standing in line.

When the Lausanne Treaty, which replaced the Treaty of Sevres was finally concluded the Turks surrendered all claims to their conquered territories, but retained possessions of Eastern Thrace to the Maritza River. They also retained the Island of

Imbros and Tenedos, but lost the rest of the Aegean Isles to Greece. Great Britain got Cyprus, and Italy retained the Dodecanese. In return for Turkish promises of judicial reforms the Capitulations were abolished. The Turks also agreed to protect minorities and a separate Turkish-Greek agreement provided for a compulsory exchange of populations. The Straits were demilitarized. They were to be available to ships of all nations in time of peace and war as long as Turkey remained neutral. If Turkey were at war they would still be open to all neutral, but not enemey ships. Turkey was not required to pay any reparations.

After my return from Odessa, Captain Maurice Churcher, R.A. British army and I made a trip to the battlefield of the Dardannelles Campaign as the guests of the C.O. Squadron Leader Blount R.A.F. To the Anzacs (Australian, New Zealand Army Corps) who fought in World War I this is hallowed ground. The tragedy of this campaign was that the Allied navies and ground forces never co-operated together, so that they were each defeated separately. The Turkish stand at Galipoli was, of course, where Mustapha Kemal made his reputation. The Turks had the tactical advantage of holding the highlands as opposed to the Allies who had to fight their way up from the beaches through terrain that was at times almost impassable. The British finally gave up as their loss of life was too costly.

On August 23rd 1923, the Allied Forces of Occupation evacuated Constantinople. After all of the pomp and ceremony attendant upon the occupation, to those who remained behind this seemed like a great defeat for the Allies.

The Turks took possession of Constantinople on the 6th of October, but officially the status of Americans and American Naval Forces in Turkey was not changed except that the name of the U.S. Naval Detachment in Turkish Waters was changed to U.S. Naval Detachment in the Eastern Mediterranean.

On October 14, Angora was made the Capital of the Turkish State, and two weeks later the Turkish Republic was formally proclaimed with Mustapha Kemal as President and Ismet Pasha as Prime Minister.

On October 17, Consul E.L. Ives, brother-in-law of the later to become famous Adlai Stevenson, Consul General R.C. Treadwell, who was making an inspection trip of U.S. Consulates in the Near East, Lieut. Comdr. Thomas Kinkaid, later to become the hero fo the 2nd Battle of the Philippine Sea in World War II, and I embarked in the U.S.S. Mac Leash, a destroyer and visited the leading ports of the Eastern Mediterranean. Among these were Mitylene, Smyrna, Rhodes, Mersina, Alexandretta, Nicosia (Cyprus), Beirut, from which we went on a side trip to Damascus, Baalbek and Alexandria thence we visited Cairo, Memphis, Luxor, and the Valley of the Kings including the newly discovered Tutankamen's Tomb. Returning to Constantinople we touched at Pireus from which we visited, Athens and Salonika the birthplace of Mustapha Kemal.

Early on March 24th, again exibiting his fine sense of timing, President Kemal abolished the Caliphate and ordered the members of the Imperial family to leave Turkey within three weeks. Poor Abdul Mejid, the Caliph was allowed only two hours in which to collect such of his possessions as he could take with him in a car, and one of his four wives before being hustled to the Bulgarian

Border during the night of March 2-3, 1924. Other members of the Imperial family, whose possessions they could not take with them became the property of the Turkish Government. Most of these emigrés settled eventually in Switzerland, Portugal, or France. I was at the railway station the night that most of the members of the Imperial Family, many of whom were our personal friends, left and it was one of the most touching occasions in my memory because they were leaving their homeland and most of their possessions. We were especially sorry for Prince Usman Fuad and his beautiful Egyptian wife. They had been close friends of ours in the Embassy and he had been fifth in line to the Sultanate.

On July 10, 1924, the U.S. Army Air Force planes making the first around the world airplane flight stopped at Constantinople for rest and fuel. Among the pilots was the then Lieutenant "Hap" Arnold who was later to become a five star general and Chief of the Army Air Corps in World War II.

Later in the month Admiral Bristol, his wife, Second Secretary J. Pierrepont Moffet, Lieut. Comdr. Kinkaid, his wife and I went by private railway car to Ankara, the new capital of Turkey, where our High Commissioner called on Mustapha Kemal and his Prime Minister, Ismet Pasha. At that time very little had been done to change the appearance of Ankara from that of a primitive Turkish village and the American High Commissioner's delegation was housed in one of the new, three bedroom residences, as was his Delegate to the Nationalist Government in Ankara.

After leaving Ankara our party continued on what was to have been the Berlin to Bagdam railway, stopping at Afium Kara(Kara) Hissar, one of the high points of the Greek invasion, Konia where we all bought some beautiful rugs, thence through the Taurus mountains to Adana and Tarsus, where we saw the tombs of

Jonah, Sardanopoulos, and the Arch of St. Paul.

Embarking on the destroyer Edsall we visited Cyprus and Rhodes as the guest of Italian Governor Largo. Among other things we were shown the spot where it is believed the Collosus of Rhodes was located, although it fell into the sea long ago. Our next port of call was Patmos, where to our great surprise we found a native who had lived for many years in Mobile, Alabama, where both Mrs. Bristol and I as well as another officer on board the Edsall had been born and raised. Our Greek friend who was on the dock when I went ashore to make arrangements to visit the Monastery where St. John is recorded to have seen the Revelation, astounded me by asking if the beautiful "Helen Moore Bristol was on board." I don't know how he knew that but he had run a fruit stand in Mobile for many years and had heard of both of our families.

On August 12, 1924, Mrs. Bristol, Admiral Bristol, his entourage and I embarked on board the Naval yacht Scorpion for a six weeks cruise in the Mediterranean and a motor-trip. The High Commissioner's official car was carried on board and later unloaded in Venice.

Our first stop was at Mt. Athos in Greece. This is the site of many monasteries and churches of the Greek Orthodox Church. Ladies are forbidden in this area, which was a great sorrow to Mrs. Bristol and the other ladies in our party.

After stopping in Brindisi for refuelling, we continued on to Venice where we were met by our Naval Attache to the American Embassy in Rome and his wife, Mrs. Castleman, and the American Consul in Venice and his wife, Mrs. Young. After enjoying the sights of Venice and bathing at the Lido, we had the car unloaded and proceeded on our way through the Italian Alps, across the Brenner Pass, and the Southeastern part of Germany to Vienna. There we were entertained by the American Minister to Austria and his wife and did some extensive sightseeing.

This was the period of rampant inflation and, being banker for the Admiral's party, I recall that the latter's dinner for the American Minister cost six million kronen. In fact I noticed in some towns in Southern Germany that articles displayed in the shop windows had numbers attached to them which enabled you to find their price after multiplying it by a large placard in the center of the window which was changed several times a day accordance with the rate of exchange. You can imagine from this how complicated my function was as banker for five people! In seven different currencies! In Budapest Admiral Bristol called on Admiral Horthy who was then Regent of Hungary while the remainder of the party went shopping.

We ended our motor-trip at Trieste where the official car was again loaded on the Scorpion. Thence we had a leisurely trip down the Dalmatian Coast stopping at Spalato (Split), Ragusa (Dibrovnik) and Cattaro. From Cattaro we motored to Cettinge the Capitol of Montenegro over the most winding road I have ever seen which climbed right up the face of the cliff. Centinje looked exactly like a musical comedy scene of the period of the "Prince of Graustark".

Our next port of call was Corfu, now belonging to Greece, a feature of which was the Kaiser's Winter Palace.

Returning via the Corinth Canal we visited the ruins of the Oracle of Delphi, a monument to ancient superstition. Our next stop was at Athens, where we were entertained by the

American Minister and also revisited the sights which most of the members of our party had seen before.

While we were away from Constantinople the Turkish Constitution was adopted on August 20th. This in effect completed the formation of the new government. It also marked the end of the revolution begun by Mustapha Pasha five years earlier. One of the most remarkable features of this revolution was the virtual absence of blood-shed among political enemies, such as occurred in the French and Russian revolutions, notwithstanding the fact that many people have for years looked upon the Turks as a bloodthirsty people. As an observer during the greater part of this revolution, I should like to say that I have always found the Turkish people to be peace-loving, honest, fair and friendly.

Although many abortive attempts had been made previously to overthrow the authority of the Sultan, it is believed that the success of this one was largely due to the imagination, tenacity, and determination of one man i.e. Mustapha Kemal. He was born as said before, in Salonika, Macedonia, of lower-middle-class parents in 1881, with very poor prospects for the future. His education tended to be a compromise between his mother's choice with a Moslem religious background, and his father's more liberal tendencies.

At an early age Mustapha exhibited very strong tendencies toward the liberal side, and became deeply influenced by foreign customs, to which he exposed in the cosmopolitan city of Salonika.

In addition to his military genius, he had a fixed determination to free his people from the despotism of the Sultan and the intrigue connected with the Ottoman Empire with its Capital at Constantinople. With that object in mind, he decided early in his revolutionary campaign not only to dethrone the Sultan, but to move the capital to Ankara where foreign influence would be at a minimum. By the summer of 1924 he had accomplished his principal objectives.

As stated in the beginning, it was my privilege to serve as Aide to the High Commissioner at the American Embassy in Constantinople while many of these history making events were taking place and it was with a deep feeling of nastalgia that, in obedience to orders, on October 12, 1924, I embarked in the U.S.Scorpion and began my voyage home.

www.ingramcontent.com/pod-product-compliance
Lightning Source LLC
Chambersburg PA
CBHW080622170426
43209CB00007B/1498